LIVING *Water*
A DAILY EXPERIENCE

DR. STEPHEN TRAMMELL

Auxano
PRESS

Tigerville, South Carolina
www.AuxanoPress.com

LIVING Water

A DAILY EXPERIENCE

DR. STEPHEN TRAMMELL

Published by Auxano Press
Tigerville, South Carolina
www.AuxanoPress.com

Book design by Jacque Sellers

Cataloging-in-Publication Data

Trammell, Stephen.

　　　　Living Water : a daily experience/by Stephen Trammell.

　　　　　　　　384 p. 22 cm.

　　　　Summary: 365-day devotional designed to enhance the reader's daily walk with God.

　　　　Includes index.

　　　　ISBN 978-0-982-6630-2-8 (pbk.)

　　　　1. Devotional Calendars.　2. Devotions, Daily.
　　　　3. Devotional Literature. 4. Spiritual Growth.　5. Meditations.
　　　　6. God-Meditations. 7. Discipleship.　8. Prayer Books and Devotions.
　　　　I. Title.

242.2 –dc22

DEDICATION

In loving memory of Louis Boyd,
he lived to benefit others.

FOREWORD

Pastor's churches become very much like themselves - as do their books. Stephen Trammell is a special man, and that always translates to a special book. Warm, gentle, genuine, filled with grace, and very, very much like his dear Savior, Stephen and Stephen's book are a living devotion that will touch your life with blessing and make each day special.

As the Israelites eagerly awaited God's fresh manna each new morning, these daily pages will nourish your soul with each new dawning day.

The best part of my life has been the blessed early mornings with the Master - in the garden – alone. With Living Water, this year will be the best year of all.

Dr. John R. Bisagno
Pastor Emeritus
Houston's First Baptist Church

ACKNOWLEDGMENTS

Ministry is truly a portrait of teamwork. To publish a book requires countless hours of investing time and energy and maximizing resources. I am so fortunate to serve in one of the most amazing churches on the planet with the most engaging and creative staff. My best friend and our Senior Pastor, Dr. David Fleming, sets the pace for ministry excellence. I am thankful to God for his leadership and for his commitment to draw out the best in each of us. I am also indebted to my administrative assistant, Mary Shemroske, for keeping my schedule and office environment extremely organized and conducive to ministry efficiency and effectiveness.

To the entire staff, deacons, and members of Champion Forest Baptist Church, thank you for loving my family and me and for modeling Christ so faithfully. You are the epitome of servitude and authentic Christianity.

God has assembled a dream team who has made this project a reality: Chris Todd, Lee Harn, Joey Mouton, and Jacque Sellers. Jacque designed the cover and the interior layout. She is truly gifted by God and touches the members of Champion Forest Baptist Church on a daily basis. I also want to thank Heather Garza for honoring God by investing so much time in proofreading and editing the final draft. Heather's journalistic touch is exhibited on each page.

It has been an honor to partner with Dr. Ken Hemphill of Auxano Press in this project. He has been a tremendous friend, mentor, and godly example of Kingdom focused living. I also appreciate Kenneth Priest for adding such value to this project. Thank you for making this journey so pleasant.

I am always grateful to God for allowing me to be reared by a godly mother, Judy Trammell. Thank you Mother for modeling the value of serving God through the local church.

I want to express my appreciation to the love of my life for over twenty years now, Tonya. Thank you for believing in me and for keeping your "yes" on the altar as we respond to the echo of God's whisper. You have made tremendous sacrifices to be on mission with God. To my children, Tori and Austin, thank you for bringing me such joy and allowing me to be the most blessed daddy in the whole world. You are the apple of my eye.

LIVING WATER
INTRODUCTION

What will be different in eternity because of your life on earth today? That question challenges me to invest my energy and influence wisely each day to make an impact that will outlive me. In light of eternity, life on earth is so brief. I don't want to waste one moment. Therefore, to make every moment count, I must treasure every moment.

God has created us for His global glory. We matter to God and He has demonstrated His love for us by sacrificing that which is closest to His heart, His one and only Son, Jesus. God provided for the forgiveness of our sins through the atoning work of Jesus on the cross so that we could enjoy unbroken fellowship with Him. In Christ, our sin is removed and our unrighteousness is replaced with the righteousness of Christ. We become a new creation whereby God inhabits us by the Holy Spirit and empowers us to be on mission with Him. Our purpose is to bring glory to God by continuing the ministry of Jesus on the earth.

Do you have a growing relationship with Christ? The key to a vibrant love relationship with Christ can be found in the word, daily. God has orchestrated your life on the earth in increments of twenty-four hours per day. You can fulfill God's plan for your life within the daily allotments given to you by God. In other words, God's will can be accomplished in the twenty-four hours you are given each day.

Let me invite you into the journey of treasuring your moments alone with the Lord each day. You make room for what you value. Join me in making room for a daily quiet time. Secure a place where you can spend some meaningful moments with the Master each day. I am a morning person, so I prefer to wake up early in the morning and go straight to my place of solitude in the den of our home. In my rhythm of life, I usually do best that which I do first. It is important for me to give my best to the most important activity of the day, namely, spending time alone with Jesus. If mornings are not effective for you, maybe carve out some time around lunch or in the evening. Find a time and place that is most beneficial in allowing you connect with God.

Once you have secured a place for your daily quiet time, choose a plan to implement each day. For example, have this devotional book, your Bible, and something to capture your thoughts such as a pen and notepad or an electronic device. First, read the devotional written for that particular date. Jot down a few nuggets that God brings to your mind. Then, spend some time reading God's Word. You may want to read a chapter each day and increase the number of chapters as you embrace the discipline of a daily quiet time. I enjoy reading through books of the Bible.

As you read God's Word, write down or type insights God gives you. Don't be in a hurry. Meditate on the verses God draws you to and record what you sense God is saying to you.

Invest time in prayer. One of the most powerful ways to enhance your prayer life is to pray Scripture. Personalize the verses you read by praying them to God. I have included many daily devotionals that will help you grow in your prayer life.

Jesus will give you Living Water as you commune with Him each day. It is truly a daily experience that will change your life. No one will ever satisfy your thirst like Jesus.

> *"Jesus answered her, 'If you knew the gift of God and who it is that asks you for a drink, you would have asked him and he would have given you living water.'" John 4:10 (NIV)*

My prayer is that your walk with God will be enhanced as you experience the Living Water Jesus provides. I am on the journey with you and look forward to what God does in us and through us as we experience Him daily.

RECAPTURE YOUR DEVOTION

"And the people said to Joshua, 'We will serve the LORD our God and obey him.'" Joshua 24:24 (NIV)

Joshua exhorted the children of Israel to review their spiritual markers and to remove their idols. God had spoken through Joshua to bring the children of Israel into alignment with God's best. God's Word demands a response. They responded with a commitment to serve the Lord and to obey Him.

As you review the past 365 days and anticipate the fresh start of the New Year, recapture your devotion to God. Don't neglect your love relationship with God. Assess your devotion by looking at your time allocation. How much time do your carve out to read the Bible and to pray? How much time to do you spend in the spiritual disciplines of solitude and meditating on God's Word? Do you live with a continual heightened awareness of God's Presence?

> • *"And now, dear children, continue in him, so that when he appears we may be confident and unashamed before him at his coming." 1 John 2:28 (NIV)*
> • *"Dear children, keep yourselves from idols." 1 John 5:21 (NIV)*

You have a clean slate and a new beginning. What will you do with this New Year that God has given you? Will you serve the Lord and obey Him? Recapture your devotion to God.

January 2
RETURN TO YOUR FIRST LOVE

"Yet I hold this against you: You have forsaken your first love."
Revelation 2:4 (NIV)

Jesus affirmed the church at Ephesus for their good deeds, hard work, perseverance, and discernment. They had endured hardships for His name. The church at Ephesus appeared to be healthy from an external point of view. However, Jesus confronted the reality of their spiritual condition. They had forsaken their first love.

One of Satan's primary tools to oppose the work of God is to get God's children to do ministry in the flesh. It is possible to perform good deeds and to help others while neglecting your love relationship with Jesus. When you bypass your love relationship with Jesus, you bypass the spiritual energy He provides.

God wants you to do His work His way. God's work is motivated by love. The most important relationship in your life is your love relationship with Jesus. He is to be your first love. When you forsake your first love, your life drifts into imbalance, your motives become tainted, and your fruit becomes tarnished.

Make Jesus your top priority. He not only demands first place, He deserves first place.

REMEMBER WHERE YOU WERE

"Remember the height from which you have fallen!" Revelation 2:5a (NIV)

Think back to the time when your relationship with Jesus exhibited true intimacy. Do you remember how sweet your daily time alone with Him was? Do you recall how you could not wait to read the Bible and to practice His Presence? Do you remember how you would hunger and thirst for Jesus? Can you remember the height of your relationship with Jesus?

So where are you now in your love relationship with Jesus? What is your current level of intimacy? If your commitment has become cluttered and your devotion to the Lord has become diluted, it is time to remember the height from which you have fallen. It is time to identify what has caused you to drift from your intimacy with Jesus.

- *"Love the Lord your God with all your heart and with all your soul and with all your mind and with all your strength."* Mark 12:30 (NIV)
- *"This is love for God: to obey his commands. And his commands are not burdensome, for everyone born of God overcomes the world. This is the victory that has overcome the world, even our faith."* 1 John 5:3-4 (NIV)

God has provided the way for you to know Him personally and intimately through your saving relationship with Jesus. Now that you have a right relationship with God based on the atoning work of Jesus on the cross, you can draw near to God and He will draw near to you (James 4:8).

RESTORE YOUR PRIORITIES

"Remember the height from which you have fallen! Repent and do the things you did at first. If you do not repent, I will come to you and remove your lampstand from its place." Revelation 2:5 (NIV)

Jesus exposed the true spiritual condition of the church in Ephesus. He graciously gave them the opportunity to repent and return to their first love. Their gospel influence was at stake. The kingdom impact they could make for the Lord in Ephesus was limited to their level of devotion in their love relationship with Christ.

God is not a God of disorder (1 Cor 12:33). God has established priorities for your life. Your top priority is your love relationship with Jesus. If your devotion to the Lord has become diluted, then repent and return. Change your mind about your current reality and your changed behavior will follow. Repent of those things that are causing you to drift in your love relationship with Jesus and return to your first love.

- *"But seek first his kingdom and his righteousness, and all these things will be given to you as well." Matt 6:33 (NIV)*
- *"Not that I have already obtained all this, or have already been made perfect, but I press on to take hold of that for which Christ Jesus took hold of me." Phil 3:12 (NIV)*

Your influence in this generation is directly linked to your love relationship with Jesus. Is He number one in your life? Is Jesus the object of your devotion and affection?

"The kingdom of heaven is like treasure hidden in a field. When a man found it, he hid it again, and then in his joy went and sold all he had and bought that field." Matthew 13:44 (NIV)

When I stood behind the pulpit to speak at the funeral of the surgeon who saved my life, it was as though time stood still. He had been our family doctor during my childhood and teenage years. He was a devoted husband, father, and deacon at my home church. Every scar on my body bears his workmanship from stitching up deeps cuts to performing emergency surgery following my jet ski accident during my junior year in high school. He was a godly man my family treasured.

There's something about death that makes us measure the value of life. When someone dear to us dies, we experience the agony of their loss and the joy of their gain. Knowing that we will see them again in Heaven brings such comfort. Knowing that they are in the Presence of God beholding the face of Jesus and walking on streets of gold generates the affirmation of our faith.

Jesus shared a parable that helps us understand what the kingdom of Heaven is like. When a man found treasure hidden in the field, he hid it again, and then in his joy went and sold all that he had and bought that field. The kingdom of Heaven is to be treasured. The kingdom of Heaven is worth being treasured.

Your most valued possession is the gift of eternal life that you received at the moment of your conversion. When Jesus became the Lord of your life, you became secure for eternity. You became a kingdom citizen. Death is not a wall to climb, but a bridge to cross. Jesus has made a way for you to face death with certainty and clarity.

January 6
FINDING LIFE

"And this is the testimony: God has given us eternal life, and this life is in his Son. He who has the Son has life; he who does not have the Son of God does not have life." 1 John 5:11-12 (NIV)

Where do you go to find life? Are you waiting for life to come sometime in the future? Are you putting life off until you have paid off your car, paid off your home, or entered into retirement? What are you waiting for?

Life is not around the corner. Life is found in one person. Life is a gift given by God. The life that is eternal is in God's Son. If you have the Son you have life. If you do not have the Son you do not have life. Until you receive God's gift of eternal life found in His Son, you will not know life.

Until you are ready to die, you are not ready to live. Finding life involves preparing for death. When you accept the reality of your mortality and choose to accept God's gift of eternal life, then you find life. Life is in God's Son. Jesus is the answer. Jesus affirmed that He is the way and the truth and the life (John 14:6). Do you know Him?

Now that you know Jesus, you have the privilege and responsibility to make Jesus known. Just as you have found life, you can help others find life by sharing Jesus with them. If they have the Son they have life. If they do not have the Son they do not have life. Give them the opportunity to have life.

RECAPTURE YOUR PASSION

"Now there was a man in Jerusalem called Simeon, who was righteous and devout. He was waiting for the consolation of Israel, and the Holy Spirit was upon him." Luke 2:25 (NIV)

Simeon was a religious man. He was righteous and devoted to God. The Holy Spirit was upon him. He lived with a strong sense of anticipation of the consolation of Israel. Simeon believed that the Messiah would come to restore Israel. He believed firmly in the promises of God.

Do you live each day expecting God to do what He said He would do? Is your life marked by the anticipation of God accomplishing His plans? You do not exist to just take up space on this planet. God wants to do a great work in your life so that He can do a great work through your life. Anticipate His activity. God is working to bring people into a growing relationship with Jesus. Anticipate God's invitation for you to join Him in His redemptive activity. There is a place for you on God's team.

Simeon lived with such a passion to see the Christ. He anticipated the fulfillment of God's promise. He was waiting with expectancy for the consolation of Israel.

What moves you? What makes you come alive to the things of God? Recapture your passion to join God in His redemptive activity.

January 8
HOLY SPIRIT AND REVELATION

"It had been revealed to him by the Holy Spirit that he would not die before he had seen the Lord's Christ." Luke 2:26 (NIV)

The Holy Spirit is not an object, but rather the third Person of the Trinity. God the Father created us. God the Son redeemed us. God the Holy Spirit sealed us. As one of my pastor friends likes to say in reference to salvation, "God thought it, Jesus bought it, and the Holy Spirit wrought it."

Simeon received revelation from God by the Holy Spirit that he would not die before he had personally seen the Lord's Christ. God the Holy Spirit communicated this truth to Simeon.

- *"The man without the Spirit does not accept the things that come from the Spirit of God, for they are foolishness to him, and he cannot understand them, because they are spiritually discerned."* 1 Cor 2:14 (NIV)
- *"But you, dear friends, build yourselves up in your most holy faith and pray in the Holy Spirit." Jude 1:20 (NIV)*

The Holy Spirit points us to Christ. As followers of Jesus, we are indwelt by the Holy Spirit and enabled to discern the things that come from the Spirit of God. Our role, as Simeon demonstrated, is to be sensitive to the prompting of the Holy Spirit.

PROCLAIM HIS NAME

"Moved by the Spirit, he went into the temple courts. When the parents brought in the child Jesus to do for him what the custom of the Law required, Simeon took him in his arms and praised God, saying: 'Sovereign Lord, as you have promised, you now dismiss your servant in peace. For my eyes have seen your salvation, which you have prepared in the sight of all people, a light for revelation to the Gentiles and for glory to your people Israel.'" Luke 2:27-32 (NIV)

Simeon had positioned his life to encounter Christ. Once he encountered the Messiah, Simeon proclaimed that Jesus was a light for revelation to the Gentiles and for glory to His people Israel. This proclamation was made in front of Joseph and Mary who were simply obeying the requirements of the custom of the Law.

Once Jesus comes into your life and transforms you, it is negligent to be silent. You have been graciously given the cure to the cancer of sin through the shed blood of Christ. Proclaim that reality! You have been rescued from the flames of hell and positioned in Christ for eternity. Proclaim that reality! You were sinking deep in sin, but Christ paid the penalty for your sin and purchased your salvation. Proclaim that reality!

What if you became contagious in your Christianity? Share the wonderful life-changing message of Jesus and help populate the Kingdom of Heaven. Souls are worth saving!

One way to get a pulse on someone's spiritual destiny is to simply transition your conversation to life after death. Be willing to ask people where they plan to spend eternity. Ask them to share their spiritual story with you. If they have one, they will be quick to share it with you. If they don't have a spiritual story, then you can help them establish one by sharing with them how they can know Jesus personally.

January 10
MIND OF CHRIST

"But we have the mind of Christ." 1 Corinthians 2:16 (NIV)

When you became of follower of Jesus Christ, you received the mind of Christ. Your mind is your seat of understanding. Your mind allows you to perceive feelings, to discern right from wrong, and to determine the best response to situations. Having the mind of Christ means that you perceive, discern, and do life like Christ.

The mind of Christ becomes the compass for your decision-making. He informs and enlightens what you see and how you view life. Having the mind of Christ forms your perspective on circumstances and opportunities.

Your daily intimacy with Jesus allows the mind of Christ to form in you. As you feed on God's Word and infuse your life with an abiding relationship with Jesus, the mind of Christ becomes more and more evident in your life.

Take note of the vital link between understanding and relationship. Jesus communicates with you by His Spirit. The Spirit, who is from God, will help you understand what God has freely given you. The Spirit lives in you and forms the mind of Christ in you.

Are you obeying what has already been revealed to you? Do you need more revelation or more obedience? Obey what you know! As you obey, the Spirit will reveal more of what Jesus wants you to know from our Heavenly Father.

"Yet a time is coming and has now come when the true worshipers will worship the Father in spirit and truth, for they are the kind of worshipers the Father seeks." John 4:23 (NIV)

Have you ever encountered God's Presence in a personal and powerful way in corporate worship with other believers? Then, as you exit the worship environment someone comments to you that he or she just didn't get anything out of that worship service. How can that be? You had a personal encounter with the Living God in corporate worship, and another person in the same environment was totally oblivious to the Presence of God.

You find what you look for. When you attend a worship service to critique the environment, the music, or the preaching, you totally miss the purpose of worship. Worship is not about you. Worship is about God. God is seeking true worshipers. God is the Seeker!

God is looking for people who will worship Him in spirit and in truth. What if worship became a lifestyle for you and you became the kind of worshiper the Father seeks? Maybe this Sunday you could enter the corporate worship environment with a clear focus to be the kind of worshiper the Father seeks. During your worship experience, ask yourself, "Am I currently being the kind of worshiper the Father seeks?"

Let's pray about this. Father, help us to be sensitive to You as the Seeker. Enable us to embrace worship as a lifestyle and to recognize that You are seeking true worshipers. Elevate our Seeker sensitivity. May our focus be on You and may our passion be to become the kind of worshipers that move Your heart. We love You, Lord, and desire that You become the object of our affection and devotion. We pray this in Jesus' Name, Amen.

January 12
EXIT STRATEGY

"There was also a prophetess, Anna, the daughter of Phanuel, of the tribe of Asher. She was very old; she had lived with her husband seven years after her marriage, and then was a widow until she was eighty-four. She never left the temple but worshiped night and day, fasting and praying. Coming up to them at that very moment, she gave thanks to God and spoke about the child to all who were looking forward to the redemption of Jerusalem." Luke 2:36-38 (NIV)

Anna embraced worship as a lifestyle. Night and day she fasted and prayed and worshiped in the temple. When Anna came up to Mary and Joseph, she gave thanks to God for Jesus. She brought glory to God and allowed her encounter with Jesus to affect her vocal chords. In response to her encounter, she spoke about Jesus to all who were looking forward to the redemption of Israel. She had something worth sharing with others.

What if you left the corporate worship experience speaking to others about Jesus and the redemption He provides? What if worship became a lifestyle for you and you embraced an exit strategy? Whether you are exiting a private worship experience or a corporate worship environment, your strategy can be to activate your vocal chords to express the amazing life-changing message of Jesus.

Not only is our worship a witness to others, but our worship should result in witnessing to others through verbal interaction. Our speech should be intentional and eternal in response to encountering the Living God. When we worship God as He deserves and allow Him to form us and fashion us for His glory, we will not be able to resist telling His story. In Christ, we have a story worth sharing and a life worth living.

What's your exit strategy?

YOUR UPBRINGING

"Every year his parents went to Jerusalem for the Feast of the Passover."
Luke 2:41 (NIV)

Growing up in a single-parent family after my parents divorced had its challenges. As I reflect on my upbringing, the one constant in my life was weekly church participation. My mom brought my brother and me to church consistently with her each week. It was very evident that her walk with God was valuable to her and that her service to God through our local church was important. She faithfully modeled Christ before us and imparted the value of serving God. In the midst of adverse circumstances related to divorce, my mom demonstrated that serving God through the ministry of the local church was worth giving your life to.

Joseph and Mary exhibited religious devotion to God and to parenting their children. Each year they went to Jerusalem to participate in the Feast of the Passover. They annually celebrated what God did, as recorded in the Old Testament, when He allowed the destroyer to pass over the children of Israel because they had placed blood on the sides and tops of the doorframes of their houses (Ex 12:7, 13, 23). Joseph and Mary were faithful to travel to Jerusalem each year to participate in this Jewish festival celebrating the Passover.

As you reflect on your upbringing, identify the spiritual heritage you received. What did your parents value? What did your parents model? Perhaps you have memories of a healthy spiritual upbringing that have added value to your life. Maybe you cannot recall favorable memories of a healthy spiritual upbringing. In God's abundant provision of mercy and grace, you can begin establishing a healthy spiritual heritage to pass down to others.

January 14
INTENTIONAL PARENTING

"These commandments that I give you today are to be upon your hearts. Impress them on your children. Talk about them when you sit at home and when you walk along the road, when you lie down and when you get up. Tie them as symbols on your hands and bind them on your foreheads. Write them on the doorframes of your houses and on your gates." Deuteronomy 6:6-9 (NIV)

The people of God embraced this confession of faith, known as the Shema, to acknowledge their commitment to the One true God and their obedience to His commandments. Loving God and obeying His commands were the marching orders for the people of God to employ. This way of life was to be personal and familial. It was not enough to love God and obey His commands personally. This lifestyle of obedience to God was to be modeled faithfully and handed down intentionally.

With the privilege of parenting comes the awesome responsibility of modeling Christ in the home. God wants our homes to be a place of intentional parenting. As parents, we have been given the assignment to lead our children into a growing relationship with Christ. We are to model what God wants us to multiply through our children. The lifestyle of loving God and keeping His commandments is to be visible in our homes. Our children should not receive mixed signals from us as to what our God-given priorities are. We are to impress upon our children the commandments we have received from God that are upon our hearts.

God wants us to intentionally model Christ before our children. God wants us to intentionally live lives of moral purity before our children. What are you impressing upon your children?

PARENTING THE MESSIAH

"When he was twelve years old, they went up to the Feast, according to the custom. After the Feast was over, while his parents were returning home, the boy Jesus stayed behind in Jerusalem, but they were unaware of it."
Luke 2:42-43 (NIV)

Can you imagine what it would have been like to parent the Messiah? How would you embrace the responsibility of parenting the Son of God? Joseph and Mary were devoted to God and faithful to the task. Jesus was unique in that He was the Son of God and was born of a virgin. It is important also to remember that Joseph and Mary had other children (Matt 13:55-56).

If you have ever been separated from your children by accident, you know the terror of the experience. Your heart drops to your feet and your mind begins racing. You frantically search for your child until he or she is found. Your terror cascades into refreshing comfort. The restoration of your valued possession brings instant relief.

Jesus was left behind. As the massive caravan moved a day's journey away from Jerusalem, Joseph and Mary realized that Jesus was not in their company. Luke tells us, "After three days they found him in the temple courts, sitting among the teachers, listening to them and asking them questions" (Luke 2:46 NIV). That must have been the longest three days of their lives up to that point.

Your parenting is not always going to be flawless. You will make mistakes along the way. You may experience some delays and detours along the way. However, you must position your parenting for impact. Ask God for wisdom to make decisions that will benefit your children and add value to their upbringing. Depend on God's provision of grace to fill in the gaps where you may fall short. Only God can provide the way for you to parent your children His way!

January 16
CLARITY AND MATURITY

"Now get up and stand on your feet. I have appeared to you to appoint you as a servant and as a witness of what you have seen of me and what I will show you." Acts 26:16 (NIV)

Paul stood before King Agrippa to give witness to his personal salvation story. Paul was converted from a persecutor of the church to a preacher of the Gospel. He recalled his Damascus road experience in the hearing of King Agrippa and other bystanders. Bringing clarity to his life purpose, Paul identified his appointment by Christ as a servant and as a witness. Paul was investing his life in the process of knowing Jesus and making Jesus known.

Jesus affirmed that Paul was a servant and a witness of what Paul had seen of Jesus. Paul encountered Christ personally on the road to Damascus. This personal encounter was a defining moment for Paul that radically changed his forever. Not only was Paul's eternal destiny changed, but his life mission was changed. The focus of Paul's life became that of proclaiming Christ. In his letter to Timothy, Paul said, "And of this gospel I was appointed a herald and an apostle and a teacher" (2 Tim 1:11 NIV).

What have you seen of Christ? Since your conversion experience, what have you seen of Christ? Is Jesus a living reality in your life? As Dr. Johnny Hunt says, "If you are going to reign in this life, Jesus must reign in your life."

You have been appointed as a servant. In God's display of mercy and grace, you have been appointed a witness of what you have seen of Christ. Jesus has more to show you! Are you ready for His revelation?

YOUR REAL BOSS

"Slaves, obey your earthly masters with respect and fear, and with sincerity of heart, just as you would obey Christ. Obey them not only to win their favor when their eye is on you, but like slaves of Christ, doing the will of God from your heart. Serve wholeheartedly, as if you were serving the Lord, not men, because you know that the Lord will reward everyone for whatever good he does, whether he is slave or free." Ephesians 6:5-8 (NIV)

Where do you work? Now think about your workplace and rediscover your ultimate boss, Jesus. Therefore, you are working for Jesus. When you are working, in the workplace, for the Lord, what does that look like?

Snapshot #1: You willingly do what you are asked to do.

When your passion is to please Jesus, you will obey your earthly boss. Your obedience is not based on how your boss treats you; your obedience is based on pleasing your ultimate boss, Jesus.

Snapshot #2: Your attitude will be consistent with your actions.

Your beliefs determine your behavior. If you believe that Jesus is your ultimate boss and if you believe that you are truly working for him, then your actions at work will be consistent with your beliefs. Your actions will reflect the authenticity of your attitude.

Snapshot #3: Your actions are consistent when no one is watching.

Do you give your best when no one is looking? You know that Jesus, your ultimate boss, is all-knowing and all-seeing. He is watching even when your earthly boss is not in visual contact. What you do when no one is watching is a clear indicator of your caliber of character.

LOVE IN ACTION

"If I speak in the tongues of men and of angels, but have not love, I am only a resounding gong or a clanging cymbal. If I have the gift of prophecy and can fathom all mysteries and all knowledge, and if I have a faith that can move mountains, but have not love, I am nothing. If I give all I possess to the poor and surrender my body to the flames, but have not love, I gain nothing."
1 Corinthians 13:1-3 (NIV)

The "Love Chapter" has been read most often in weddings. Marriage is a portrait of love in that one spouse is to seek to meet the needs of the other spouse. Love is putting others first. Love flows from God because God is love (1 John 4:8). As the Source of love, God demonstrated His love to us by allowing Christ to die in our place (Rom 5:8). As you read the Bible, you will see a common thread of God's love in action to restore fallen humanity. Love takes the initiative just as God took the initiative to bring us into a right relationship with Himself.

- *"Love is patient, love is kind. It does not envy, it does not boast, it is not proud. It is not rude, it is not self-seeking, it is not easily angered, it keeps no record of wrongs. Love does not delight in evil but rejoices with the truth. It always protects, always trusts, always hopes, always perseveres."* 1 Cor 13:4-7 (NIV)
- *"And now these three remain: faith, hope and love. But the greatest of these is love."* 1 Cor 13:13 (NIV)

Is there anyone you find difficult to love? Choose to love that person not based on what they can do for you or based on what they have done for you or to you. Choose to love that person based on what God has done for you. Love is a choice. God chose to love you long before you chose to love Him. Now seek to love those Christ died for.

PROPER RESPONSE

"'Then Jesus came from Galilee to the Jordan to be baptized by John. But John tried to deter him, saying, 'I need to be baptized by you, and do you come to me?'" "Jesus replied, 'Let it be so now; it is proper for us to do this to fulfill all righteousness.' Then John consented." Matthew 3:13-15 (NIV)

John had been preaching a baptism of repentance to prepare the way for Jesus. People came from Jerusalem and all Judea in order to be baptized by John in the Jordan (Matt 3:5). When Jesus came to Galilee to be baptized, John was hesitant in that he did not feel worthy. Jesus acknowledged that the proper response to fulfill all righteousness was for John to baptize Him. John consented and Jesus brought honor to God.

God gives us the freedom to choose Christ or to reject Him. "Yet to all who received him, to those who believed in his name, he gave the right to become children of God--children born not of natural descent, nor of human decision or a husband's will, but born of God" (John 1:12-13 NIV). As we choose to receive God's gift of eternal life through our faith in the completed work of Jesus on the cross, our next proper response is to follow Jesus in believer's baptism.

Have you made the proper response to God's invitation for salvation? Have you made the proper response of obedience to follow the example of Jesus in believer's baptism? If not, why not? What is keeping you from making the proper response?

January 20
IDENTIFY WITH CHRIST

"When all the people were being baptized, Jesus was baptized too".
Luke 3:21 (NIV)

Jesus was baptized too? Why was it necessary for Jesus to be baptized? I thought He was sinless. What would Jesus need to repent of? The Bible affirms His sinlessness.

- *"For we do not have a high priest who is unable to sympathize with our weaknesses, but we have one who has been tempted in every way, just as we are--yet was without sin." Heb 4:15 (NIV)*
- *"For you know that it was not with perishable things such as silver or gold that you were redeemed from the empty way of life handed down to you from your forefathers, but with the precious blood of Christ, a lamb without blemish or defect." 1 Peter 1:18-19 (NIV)*

Jesus did not allow John to baptize Him as an act of repentance. Jesus had no sin to repent of. So why did Jesus participate in this public baptism? Jesus set an example for us to follow. Jesus modeled the value of honoring God. The baptism of Jesus established the clear portrait of turning from sin and turning to Christ alone for salvation.

Just as my wedding ring does not make me married, it lets others know that I am married. So it is with baptism in that baptism does not save you; it lets others know that you have been saved. Your baptism by immersion is a public display of the internal reality of your salvation experience. The reality of your covenant relationship with Christ is demonstrated through your act of obedience in following Jesus in believer's baptism. Your baptism is the public profession of your faith in Jesus.

Have you been baptized, too?

The Testimony of Baptism

"When all the people were being baptized, Jesus was baptized too. And as he was praying, heaven was opened and the Holy Spirit descended on him in bodily form like a dove. And a voice came from heaven: 'You are my Son, whom I love; with you I am well pleased.'" Luke 3:21-22 (NIV)

Did you notice the activity of the Trinity in this passage? Read it again and see if you can locate God the Father, God the Son, and God the Holy Spirit. The word "Trinity" is not found in the Bible, but the doctrine of the Trinity can be easily located. At Jesus' baptism, we read about the Holy Spirit descending on Jesus like a dove. We read about the voice of God from Heaven affirming Jesus at His baptism.

- *"One witness is not enough to convict a man accused of any crime or offense he may have committed. A matter must be established by the testimony of two or three witnesses." Deut 19:15 (NIV)*
- *"Anyone who rejected the law of Moses died without mercy on the testimony of two or three witnesses." Heb 10:28 (NIV)*

The testimony of God and the testimony of the Holy Spirit gave witness to the Lordship of Christ at the inauguration of His public ministry. Jesus was baptized to identify with those He came to seek and to save (Luke 19:10). Jesus brought glory to His Father by His obedience in baptism.

God created you for His glory. Jesus lived a sinless life and died a sacrificial death to provide you with life abundant (John 10:10) and life eternal (1 John 5:11,13). You have been given the Holy Spirit as a deposit. You are saved, sealed, and secure.

January 22
RECEIVE GOD'S AFFIRMATION

"When all the people were being baptized, Jesus was baptized too. And as he was praying, heaven was opened and the Holy Spirit descended on him in bodily form like a dove. And a voice came from heaven: 'You are my Son, whom I love; with you I am well pleased.'" Luke 3:21-22 (NIV)

Jesus was about thirty years old when He began his ministry (Luke 3:23). The inauguration of Jesus' public ministry featured affirmation from His Heavenly Father. God affirmed that Jesus was His Son. It would be similar to an earthly father saying to his son, "Son, I'm proud of you!"

God provided Jesus with an affirmation of His love. Jesus would draw on the love of His Heavenly Father as He navigated the path of suffering. In the Garden of Gethsemane, Jesus affirmed His love and loyalty to His Heavenly Father by praying, "Not my will, but Your will be done" (Matt 26:39-44).

Jesus heard the precious words of affirmation, "With you I am well pleased." Jesus brought pleasure to His Heavenly Father through His obedience and willingness to finish His work (John 4:34). God affirmed Jesus with these words at the inauguration of His public ministry.

You are loved by God. In fact, you are the apple of His eye (Psalm 17:8). Walk in the light of God's redemptive work in your life. God came to your rescue so that you could join Him in rescuing others. You are His workmanship (Eph 2:10). Be affirmed by God!

Not Ashamed

"If anyone is ashamed of me and my words, the Son of Man will be ashamed of him when he comes in his glory and in the glory of the Father and of the holy angels." Luke 9:26 (NIV)

Believer's baptism by immersion is a public proclamation of your faith in Jesus. Jesus identified with you through baptism so that you could identify with Him through baptism. Your identification with Christ is a bold and courageous act of obedience. If you have not identified with Christ through baptism, what is keeping you from taking that clear step of obedience? What would you be ashamed of? There's nothing to fear!

- *"I am not ashamed of the gospel, because it is the power of God for the salvation of everyone who believes: first for the Jew, then for the Gentile." Rom 1:16 (NIV)*
- *"Do your best to present yourself to God as one approved, a workman who does not need to be ashamed and who correctly handles the word of truth." 2 Tim 2:15 (NIV)*

There's no need to be ashamed. When you identify with Christ through baptism, you demonstrate your faith in the atoning work of Jesus on the cross. In baptism, you testify of His resurrection power that brought you out of darkness into the kingdom of light. You can bear the name of Christ with honor. He has given His all for you so that you can have an abiding love relationship with Him that is personal and eternal.

Don't be ashamed of Christ. If you have not been baptized by immersion since your conversion experience, then make things right with the Lord by obeying His command.

January 24
JOINING GOD

"Now those who had been scattered by the persecution in connection with Stephen traveled as far as Phoenicia, Cyprus and Antioch, telling the message only to Jews. Some of them, however, men from Cyprus and Cyrene, went to Antioch and began to speak to Greeks also, telling them the good news about the Lord Jesus." Acts 11:19-20 (NIV)

Antioch was the third largest city in the Roman Empire next to Rome and Alexandria. It was located three hundred miles north of Jerusalem. The city was a pagan metropolis with a population of about 500,000 people. Those who had been scattered by the persecution in Jerusalem in connection with Stephen were sharing the message of Christ with Jews in Phoenicia, Cypress, and Antioch. Some men from Cyprus and Cyrene began to share the message of Christ with the Greeks in Antioch.

- *"On that day a great persecution broke out against the church at Jerusalem, and all except the apostles were scattered throughout Judea and Samaria."* Acts 8:1 (NIV)
- *"Those who had been scattered preached the word wherever they went."* Acts 8:4 (NIV)

The believers were willing to bloom where God planted them. Even though relocated as a result of persecution, they chose to share the good news of Jesus wherever they went.

To join God in His redemptive activity, you must be willing to bloom where God plants you. Think about your current life situation. Think about those in your sphere of influence. God has you right where you are so that you can share Christ with those He has brought into your path.

EVIDENCE OF GRACE

"News of this reached the ears of the church at Jerusalem, and they sent Barnabas to Antioch. When he arrived and saw the evidence of the grace of God, he was glad and encouraged them all to remain true to the Lord with all their hearts."
Acts 11:22-23 (NIV)

What did the evidence of the grace of God look like when Barnabas arrived in Antioch? What did he see about the church in Antioch that made him think of the grace of God? He noticed that the Lord's hand was with them and that great numbers of people were brought to the Lord (Acts 11:21,24). He witnessed sacrificial and spontaneous giving (Acts 11:27-30). The church in Antioch was serious about prayer, fasting, Christ-exalting worship, and missions (Acts 13:1-3).

Had Barnabas not been willing to leave his comfort zone in Jerusalem and travel 300 miles north to Antioch, he would have missed seeing the evidence of the grace of God in the church in Antioch. Barnabas would have missed joining God in His redemptive activity in Antioch. Barnabas would have missed personally seeing the free expression of the loving kindness of God at work in the midst of Jews and Greeks worshiping together.

What is keeping you from joining God in His redemptive activity? As Henry Blackaby says, "You cannot stay where you are and go with God." For you, it may not mean a physical relocation. Joining God always produces a spiritual change in you so that you surrender fully and completely to His agenda. Be willing to leave your comfort zone in order to join God in His redemptive activity.

THE JOURNEY

"Then Barnabas went to Tarsus to look for Saul, and when he found him, he brought him to Antioch. So for a whole year Barnabas and Saul met with the church and taught great numbers of people. The disciples were called Christians first at Antioch." Acts 11:25-26 (NIV)

Why did Barnabas need Saul? It would have made more sense for Barnabas to go back to Jerusalem and get Nicolas, one of the early deacons who happened to be from Antioch. Instead, Barnabas searched with intensity to locate Saul in order to bring Saul into the journey of what God was doing in the church in Antioch. Barnabas was very familiar with the calling God placed on Saul's life.

> • *"When he came to Jerusalem, he tried to join the disciples, but they were all afraid of him, not believing that he really was a disciple. But Barnabas took him and brought him to the apostles. He told them how Saul on his journey had seen the Lord and that the Lord had spoken to him, and how in Damascus he had preached fearlessly in the name of Jesus." Acts 9:26-27 (NIV)*

Barnabas included Saul in God's activity in the church in Antioch. Partnering in ministry, Barnabas and Saul met with the church and taught great numbers for a whole year (Acts 11:26). Can you imagine sitting under the teaching of Barnabas and Saul for a year?

The Christian life is not a solo flight. God wants you to bring others into the journey. Right now there are people in your sphere of influence who would benefit greatly by joining God in His redemptive activity as a result of your invitation. Be willing to search for them just as Barnabas searched for Saul.

SENSITIVITY TO GOD'S ACTIVITY

"The disciples were called Christians first at Antioch." Acts 11:26 (NIV)

As you join God in His redemptive activity, your sensitivity to His agenda will heighten. You will begin to see people the way God views them. Your heart for the lost will increase as you embrace the true meaning of being a Christian. In the language of the New Testament, the word Christian means to be of the party of Christ. It means to be identified as a little Christ. This word is used three times in the New Testament: Acts 11:26, Acts 26:28, and I Peter 4:16.

- *"Then Agrippa said to Paul, 'Do you think that in such a short time you can persuade me to be a Christian?'" Acts 26:28 (NIV)*
- *"However, if you suffer as a Christian, do not be ashamed, but praise God that you bear that name." 1 Pet 4:16 (NIV)*

God was doing a redemptive work in the city of Antioch and the disciples joined God in His activity. Their irresistible influence in the pagan metropolis of Antioch caused the pagans to tag the disciples as Christians. It was considered a term of derision. The disciples in Antioch were deemed from the party of Christ.

If you were to ever be identified with anyone, there's no greater person to be identified than Jesus Christ. In fact, the Bible says, "Salvation is found in no one else, for there is no other name under heaven given to men by which we must be saved" (Acts 4:12 NIV). As you join God in His redemptive activity, be willing to be identified by others as a Christian. Your life should draw people to Christ, not repel them from Christ. Let others see Christ in you!

January 28
UNLEASH GENEROSITY

"The disciples, each according to his ability, decided to provide help for the brothers living in Judea. This they did, sending their gift to the elders by Barnabas and Saul." Acts 11:29-30 (NIV)

God blesses generosity. You cannot join God in His redemptive activity and employ a stingy mindset. You cannot be selfish and effectively join God in His redemptive activity. Joining God involves being generous with your resources just as God has been generous toward you.

The church at Jerusalem was instrumental in birthing the church in Antioch. Now the mother church in Jerusalem is in financial need and the daughter church in Antioch responds by generously meeting the need. The grace of God was evidenced by the sacrificial and spontaneous generosity exhibited by the church in Antioch.

Sir Winston Churchill is noted for saying, "We make a living by what we get, but we make a life by what we give." What are you currently giving to fund the Lord's work? Are you sacrificial in your giving?

Let's make a life by bringing the life of Christ to a dark and decaying world through our generosity. Placing the needs of others before our own is the first step!

MAKE ROOM FOR WORSHIP

"He went to Nazareth, where he had been brought up, and on the Sabbath day he went into the synagogue, as was his custom. And he stood up to read."
Luke 4:16 (NIV)

You make room for what you value. When you value participating in the ministry of your local church, you will make room in your life for that ministry. If you value short-term mission trips, then you will make room in your annual calendar of events to go on a short-term mission trip. Whatever you value will receive your time, energy, and attention. Whatever you value will be a guarded priority in your life.

Jesus valued the weekly worship experience in the synagogue on the Sabbath (Saturday). The synagogue had been a consistent part of His life for thirty years at this particular point. After His baptism and 40 days of temptation in the desert, Jesus returned to Galilee and went to His hometown of Nazareth. As was His custom, He went into the synagogue.

Much of Jesus' identity was connected to the synagogue. He had grown up being exposed to the reading of Scripture each Sabbath in the local synagogue. On this day, He stood to read. He participated in the flow of the service and contributed to the experience.

You are the sum total of your habits. In other words, you will become what you habitually invest your life in. You are in the process of becoming who you are in Christ. Value weekly participation in the local church. Value connecting with God in worship with other believers. Value weekly interaction with other believers in a small group Bible study. Make it your custom to grow in your love relationship with Jesus. Your identity is found in Christ.

January 30
BRING OTHERS TO CHRIST

"The scroll of the prophet Isaiah was handed to him. Unrolling it, he found the place where it is written: 'The Spirit of the Lord is on me, because he has anointed me to preach good news to the poor. He has sent me to proclaim freedom for the prisoners and recovery of sight for the blind, to release the oppressed, to proclaim the year of the Lord's favor.'" Luke 4:17-19 (NIV)

As Jesus stood up in the synagogue to read, He was given the scroll of the prophet Isaiah and then He found the place from which He wanted to read. The passage Jesus read was what we now know as Isaiah 61:1-2. Jesus identified the ministry that He was anointed to employ. He identified the focus of His ministry as preaching the good news to the poor, proclaiming freedom for the prisoners, proclaiming recovery of sight to the blind, releasing the oppressed, and proclaiming the year of the Lord's favor.

> • *"Then he rolled up the scroll, gave it back to the attendant and sat down. The eyes of everyone in the synagogue were fastened on him, and he began by saying to them, 'Today this scripture is fulfilled in your hearing.'" Luke 4:20-21 (NIV)*

Isaiah prophesied some 700 years before Christ was born that the Messiah would be anointed for this particular ministry. Jesus affirmed that He is the fulfillment of that prophecy.

Have you been the recipient of the ministry of Christ? Has your character and conduct been transformed? Now that you know Jesus personally, you are commissioned to embrace His ministry to bring others into His family. The ministry of Christ on earth is now your ministry. You may be the only Jesus others see!

CLARIFY YOUR IDENTITY

"All spoke well of him and were amazed at the gracious words that came from his lips. 'Isn't this Joseph's son?' they asked." Luke 4:22 (NIV)

Jesus shared from Isaiah 61:1-2 in the hearing of those in the synagogue and identified Himself as the fulfillment of that prophecy. The people spoke well of Him. Amazed at Jesus' gracious words, they tried to reconcile His professed identity by asking, "Isn't this Joseph's son?"

The people were confused. Their understanding of the coming Messiah did not position them to anticipate a carpenter's son from Nazareth as the Messiah. The humanity and humility of Jesus did not line up with their view of the Messiah. They were expecting a mighty military leader with position and prominence who would restore Israel.

As followers of Christ, we can identify with His dual identity. Though virgin born, Jesus had an earthly father and a Heavenly Father. We too have an earthly father and our Heavenly Father.

- *"Our fathers disciplined us for a little while as they thought best; but God disciplines us for our good, that we may share in his holiness." Heb 12:10 (NIV)*
- *"How great is the love the Father has lavished on us, that we should be called children of God! And that is what we are! The reason the world does not know us is that it did not know him." 1 John 3:1 (NIV)*

Your identity in Christ is formed and fashioned by your Heavenly Father. God has created you for His glory. You are God's workmanship (Eph 2:10) and you belong to God (1 Pet 2:9). If you ever forget who you are in Christ, look up! You are a child of the King!

February 1
Affirm Your New Identity

"All the people in the synagogue were furious when they heard this. They got up, drove him out of the town, and took him to the brow of the hill on which the town was built, in order to throw him down the cliff. But he walked right through the crowd and went on his way." Luke 4:28-30 (NIV)

Jesus communicated to His hearers in the synagogue that a prophet is not accepted in his hometown. He was implying that many would miss the fact that He was the Messiah and forfeit the benefits just as many in Israel did not enjoy the benefits of the ministry of Elijah. The people were so furious with Jesus that they tried to throw him down the cliff. Jesus' popularity in His hometown was not very positive!

Your identity is not based on what people say about you. Your identity in Christ is based on what God says about you. Your destiny is determined by the loving provision of your Heavenly Father. In the midst of opposition and being misunderstood, you can stand firm in the security of your identity in Christ.

- *"You did not choose me, but I chose you and appointed you to go and bear fruit--fruit that will last. Then the Father will give you whatever you ask in my name." John 15:16 (NIV)*
- *"If the world hates you, keep in mind that it hated me first." John 15:18 (NIV)*

Find a place of solitude and begin to eliminate the voices of falsehood and tune in to the voice of Truth! Speaker and author Beth Moore likes to say, "God is who He says He is. God can do what He says He can do. I am who God says I am. I can do all things through Christ. God's Word is alive and active in me. I'm believing God!"

"The harvest is past, the summer has ended, and we are not saved."
Jeremiah 8:20 (NIV)

How much time do you have left on earth? How many people will die without a saving relationship with Jesus Christ within the next twenty-four hours? What difference will your life make in light of eternity?

Jesus modeled a deep abiding passion for souls. The Bible says, "For the Son of Man came to seek and to save what was lost" (Luke 19:10 NIV). Jesus never lost His focus of redeeming the lost. He did not neglect His mission to save the lost at any cost.

How many lost people are in your sphere of influence? What kind of relational bridge are you building to them? What are you willing to do to introduce them to a saving relationship with Jesus?

Pray this prayer with me. Father, forgive me for my passive neglect. Forgive me for being so self-absorbed that I have minimized the urgency of soul-winning. Elevate my soul consciousness. Give me eyes to see lost people in their desperation. Anoint me with the courage of Jesus. Empower me to be Your witness and to be Your laborer in the harvest field. In Jesus' Name, Amen.

February 3
CRISIS OF BELIEF

"When he had finished speaking, he said to Simon, 'Put out into deep water, and let down the nets for a catch.'" Luke 5:4 (NIV)

Jesus had been teaching the crowd from Simon's boat. The water's surface propelled the teachings of Jesus with clarity to the hearers. Simon was in the boat with Jesus and overheard His teachings. The lesson was going to be directed Simon's way. Jesus challenged Simon's faith by asking him to transition the boat to deeper waters. The request escalated as Jesus exhorted Simon to let down the nets for a catch.

What is a carpenter doing telling a fisherman how to fish? Fishermen in that region knew that fishing the shallow waters at night was the protocol for success. Yet, Jesus issues a seemingly impractical call to fish the deeper waters during the daylight. Simon experienced a crisis of belief. He had to wrestle the words of this carpenter up against his own personal experience as a commercial fisherman. Simon knew the waters and the industry. Would he consider obeying the words of Jesus?

Sometimes life doesn't make sense. Sometimes the way of Jesus is counter to the way of logic. Jesus invites us to join Him in the journey of faith. Faith is not a blind leap in the dark. Faith is trusting that Jesus knows what is best for us. We come to the place of experiencing the crisis of believing our own way or the way Jesus illuminates.

Simon was willing to take Jesus at His Word and to trust Him with the results. Simon silenced the voice of doubt and amplified the voice of Truth.

What are you currently wrestling with? Are you willing to take God at His Word and trust His prompting?

"Simon answered, 'Master, we've worked hard all night and haven't caught anything. But because you say so, I will let down the nets.'" Luke 5:5 (NIV)

Do you remember those words you frequently heard as a child? You may have challenged something your parent said and then they responded emphatically with, "Because I said so!"

Simon had one of those moments in his own boat with Jesus. After a long night of fishing and coming up "empty-netted," Simon and his partners were in the process of completing the task of washing their nets. Jesus borrows Simon and his boat in order to teach the crowd aligning the shore. Jesus then asks Simon to maneuver the boat into the deep waters and to let down his nets for a catch.

Addressing Jesus as Master, Simon recounted his all-night fishing experience and the fact of catching no fish. Then Simon says to Jesus, "But because you say so, I will let down the nets."

Simon demonstrated loyalty to Jesus. By his actions, Simon was in essence saying, "Jesus, I trust you and whatever is mine is yours and whatever you ask of me I will obey." Embracing Jesus as Captain of his boat, Simon exemplified surrender and submission. He was willing to make Jesus the Lord of his boat and his life.

Have you given Jesus dominion over every area of your life? Is Jesus truly Lord in your life? Have you given Him full authority in your private life? Does Jesus have full reign in the public and visible areas of your life? Your loyalty to Christ is proportionate to your willingness to surrender to the Lordship of Christ. Make Jesus the Captain of your boat! Give Him full access and full authority over every environment of your life!

February 5
God's Way

"When they had done so, they caught such a large number of fish that their nets began to break. So they signaled their partners in the other boat to come and help them, and they came and filled both boats so full that they began to sink." Luke 5:6-7 (NIV)

God's way is always best! You will never go wrong obeying God. He knows you and He knows what is best for you. Everything God invites you to do allows you to participate in His Kingdom activity.

Simon and his fishing partners experienced a miraculous catch of fish because Simon was willing to obey Jesus. Blessing follows obedience. Simon responded to Jesus' invitation to let down his nets for a catch in the deeper waters in the daytime. The fishermen normally fished in the shallow waters at night in that region of the Lake of Gennesaret (also known as the Sea of Galilee). However, Simon was willing to fish Jesus' way and reap the tremendous benefits.

Both boats were filled so full that they began to sink. Doing life God's way is always the right choice. Even when God's directive doesn't add up in your logical thinking, you can count on God's way to be the best option.

Can God speak through a donkey (Num 22:30), cause an axhead to float (2 Kings. 6:5-6), and provide water from a rock (Num 20:8)? Yes, God can! Can God handle your situation? Yes, God can!

Will you trust God and submit to His way? Will you seek the Lord (Isaiah 55:6) and draw near to Him (James 4:8)? Will you trust in the Lord (Prov 3:5-6)? Now, walk in the light God gives you!

AWE OF SERVING JESUS

"When Simon Peter saw this, he fell at Jesus' knees and said, 'Go away from me, Lord; I am a sinful man!' For he and all his companions were astonished at the catch of fish they had taken, and so were James and John, the sons of Zebedee, Simon's partners." Luke 5:8-10 (NIV)

What produced such awe in Simon's heart to cause him to respond to Jesus the way he did? Simon recognized that he was in the presence of the Divine. Jesus was more than a carpenter from Nazareth. Jesus was the Master of the wind, the waves, and the fish. Jesus demonstrated His omnipotence.

Simon and his fishing partners were astonished at the catch of fish they had taken. Yet, Simon was gripped more by Jesus than the catch of fish. Simon recognized his own personal sinfulness in light of the holiness of Jesus. We see similar responses from Isaiah and John when they encountered the Lord.

- *"'Woe to me!' I cried. 'I am ruined! For I am a man of unclean lips, and I live among a people of unclean lips, and my eyes have seen the King, the LORD Almighty.'"* Isaiah 6:5 (NIV)
- *"When I saw him, I fell at his feet as though dead. Then he placed his right hand on me and said: 'Do not be afraid. I am the First and the Last. I am the Living One; I was dead, and behold I am alive for ever and ever! And I hold the keys of death and Hades.'"* Rev 1:17-18 (NIV)

Don't lose the awe of serving your Master, Jesus Christ. He is worthy of your wonder and awe. Jesus is holy and deserves reverence and honor. As you engage in activities throughout the day, whether menial or magnificent, remember the awe of serving Jesus!

February 7
FOCUS YOUR LIFE

"Then Jesus said to Simon, 'Don't be afraid; from now on you will catch men.'"
Luke 5:10 (NIV)

If you're not fishing, you're not following. Following Christ will result in faithfully and intentionally fishing for souls. When you follow your Rabbi, Jesus, you go where He goes and you do what He does.

Jesus alleviated Simon's fear by clarifying his life-focus. Instead of fishing for fish, Simon was being invited to a life of fishing for souls.

- *"The fruit of the righteous is a tree of life, and he who wins souls is wise."* Prov 11:30 (NIV)
- *"I pray that you may be active in sharing your faith, so that you will have a full understanding of every good thing we have in Christ."* Philem 1:6 (NIV)
- *"Be merciful to those who doubt; snatch others from the fire and save them; to others show mercy, mixed with fear--hating even the clothing stained by corrupted flesh."* Jude 1:22-23 (NIV)

Focus your life on that which is closest to the heart of Jesus. Souls! Focus your life on fishing for souls. Join God in His redemptive activity by bringing others into a saving relationship with Jesus. Share your personal salvation story (1 Pet 3:15-16) and invite others to become followers of Jesus Christ. Focus your life on souls! Eternity is at stake!

LEAVE YOUR BOAT

"So they pulled their boats up on shore, left everything and followed him."
Luke 5:11 (NIV)

Salvation is an event followed by a process of maturation. Once you become a follower of Christ, your eternal destiny is radically altered and your daily activity should be intentionally allocated. The daily spiritual disciplines of prayer, Bible intake, solitude, journaling, worshiping, witnessing, serving, and persevering become growing attributes of your walk with God.

What do you need to leave in order to follow? What is keeping you from full devotion to Christ? What boat do you need to pull up on shore in order to follow Christ? Your boat may be preoccupation with hobbies. Your boat may be infatuation with your career or intoxication by excessive media consumption. Perhaps your boat is fixation on security, stability, and predictability. Everyone has a boat that needs to be beached!

- *"Jesus replied, 'No one who puts his hand to the plow and looks back is fit for service in the kingdom of God.'" Luke 9:62 (NIV)*

What do you need to "stop doing" in order to be fully devoted to Jesus? What do you need to "start doing" in order to give your undivided loyalty to Christ? Take a few moments to develop a "stop doing" list and then a "start doing" list! Identify the boat that is hindering your love relationship with Christ and pull it up on shore and leave it. If you want to cleave to Christ, be willing to leave the boat on the shore!

February 9
DE-CLUTTER YOUR MIND

"Test me, O LORD, and try me, examine my heart and my mind; for your love is ever before me, and I walk continually in your truth." Psalm 26:2-3 (NIV)

What's going on in your mind? What have you been thinking about lately? God has given you the ability to think, reason, and make decisions. God has given you the ability to know and understand. You have the wonderful ability to contemplate, consider, and calculate. You are blessed with the capacity to ponder, prepare, and produce. How are you harnessing the potential God has placed within you?

- *"You will keep in perfect peace him whose mind is steadfast, because he trusts in you." Isaiah 26:3 (NIV)*

Is your mind at peace? Write down the specific items that are bothering you. Think through the issues that are pressing up against you. Now place those items before the Lord in prayer. Give each issue to the Lord. Release them! Now receive the Lord's provision of grace to be single-minded. Focus your thoughts on Jesus and His Lordship. Allow Him to be your source of strength and your anchor of stability.

De-clutter your mind by unloading the hurtful thoughts and the anxious thoughts that perplex you. Write them down! Speak them aloud! Release them to the Lord!

Replace those toxic thoughts with healthy reminders of who you are in Christ. You belong to God. You are His treasure and His masterpiece (Eph 2:10). You have everything you need for life and godliness (2 Pet 1:3). You are more than a conqueror (Rom 8:37). You are complete in Christ.

DE-CLUTTER YOUR LIFE

"Moses' father-in-law replied, 'What you are doing is not good. You and these people who come to you will only wear yourselves out. The work is too heavy for you; you cannot handle it alone.'" Exodus 18:17-18 (NIV)

Living in a fallen world has immediate and progressive challenges. Sinfulness and selfishness dominate our culture. We live with an immense amount of pressure to perform at home, at school, at work, and at play. Our lives are bombarded with information and endless opportunities to expend our energy.

Do you have margin in your life? Margin is the space between your load and your limit. God has given you all the time you need to accomplish His plan.

Moses reached a breaking point due to being overextended and overwhelmed. The masses of people each wanted a piece of him. They wanted his time, his attention, and his decision making prowess. Though serving as judge over Israel, Moses failed to exercise proper judgment over his own life.

God came to the rescue by bringing Jethro into Moses' life. Jethro lovingly spoke into Moses' life to declare, "What you are doing is not good." Moses couldn't see the unhealthy path that he was on. Jethro saw it clearly and succinctly. Jethro was willing to help Moses de-clutter his life.

What is overwhelming you right now? Has your load exceeded your limit? You may want to ask someone you know and love and trust to help you examine your life. Allow that person to give you feedback on what they see going on in your world. Their perspective could help you see what you are not seeing.

February 11
WHATEVER IT TAKES

"Some men came carrying a paralytic on a mat and tried to take him into the house to lay him before Jesus. When they could not find a way to do this because of the crowd, they went up on the roof and lowered him on his mat through the tiles into the middle of the crowd, right in front of Jesus." Luke 5:18-19 (NIV)

Who was instrumental in bringing you to faith in Christ? Can you recall the investment they made in your life to influence you toward Christ? Your salvation experience may be connected to the influence of a godly parent or grandparent. Perhaps you can trace the impact made by a teacher or a coach that God placed in your life.

These men were willing to embrace a whatever it takes attitude to get their friend to Jesus. They did not allow obstacles to deter their mission. They were committed to getting their friend to Jesus at any cost. They were fully convinced that Jesus was the answer to their friend's life. As a result, the men lowered their friend down through the roof to get him to Jesus.

What if you decided to do whatever it takes to bring others to Jesus? What if your life was that focused and that concentrated on the mission of bringing people to Jesus? Are you convinced that Jesus is the hope of the world?

Today, God wants to use you in shining His light and sharing His love. Today, God wants to use you to build intentional relationships with others so that they can know Jesus personally and eternally.

INTENTIONAL RELATIONSHIPS

"After this, Jesus went out and saw a tax collector by the name of Levi sitting at his tax booth. 'Follow me,' Jesus said to him, and Levi got up, left everything and followed him." Luke 5:27-28 (NIV)

Tax collectors in Jesus' day were despised. Levi was a Jew who collected taxes for the Roman government. In order to increase his personal income, Levi required more from his countrymen than the government demanded. Levi's fellow Jews despised him and deemed him as a traitor.

Jesus calls the least likely candidates to join His team. Levi was chosen by Jesus and willingly left everything to follow Jesus. Levi was willing to leave his career and forfeit his income in order to be on mission with Jesus. Following Jesus involved trusting Jesus with his life and his future.

There's not a person on earth Jesus can't use. There's not a person alive that Jesus cannot transform. Jesus calls us to Himself in salvation and transforms us for His service. Jesus factors in our past and our sin when He saves us and sets us apart for His mission of seeking and saving the lost (Luke 19:10).

Is there anyone in your sphere of influence who reminds you of Levi? Do you know of someone whom you would consider despised and unfit for the kingdom of God? God has created that person for a divine purpose. Will you allow God to use you to bring that person into an abiding relationship with Jesus?

You can build intentional relationships with people so that the salvation story can be shared and received. The people you think are unreachable are actually prime candidates for the personal experience of receiving the gift of eternal life. There's no one beyond the reach of God's grace.

February 13
THE REAL PARTY

"Then Levi held a great banquet for Jesus at his house, and a large crowd of tax collectors and others were eating with them." Luke 5:29 (NIV)

Jesus changed Levi's life. Shifting from being a tax collector to being a follower of Jesus, Levi wanted to honor Jesus by hosting a banquet at his house. Levi invited a large crowd of tax collectors along with others. The sinner chose to invite his fellow sinners to hear the Savior. Levi wanted his friends to experience the life transformation that comes through a personal relationship with Jesus. Levi provided them with the opportunity to be with Jesus.

At that point in Levi's life, his sphere of influence included those who were despised by their fellow Jews. Tax collectors were not esteemed, but rather considered traitors. Yet, Levi reached out to them because he was one of them. Levi was willing to create an environment in his home to honor Jesus and to invite others to receive the salvation Jesus provides.

Think about the people God has placed in your life. Do you have a Levi in your sphere of influence? Is there anyone you have written off as unreachable? Remember that Jesus came to seek and to save the lost (Luke 19:10).

Begin to pray for the Levi God has placed in your life. Watch for opportunities to build an intentional relationship with that person in order to share the plan of salvation with that person.

How would you define love? Is love a verbal expression, an act of kindness, or a gift extended to another? Is love being willing to do what you do not enjoy in order to benefit someone else? Is love a natural flow from a heart that is full?

- *"'A new command I give you: Love one another. As I have loved you, so you must love one another.'" John 13:34 (NIV)*
- *"'By this all men will know that you are my disciples, if you love one another.'" John 13:35 (NIV)*
- *"But God demonstrates his own love for us in this: While we were still sinners, Christ died for us." Rom 5:8 (NIV)*
- *"Whoever does not love does not know God, because God is love." 1 John 4:8 (NIV)*
- *"This is love: not that we loved God, but that he loved us and sent his Son as an atoning sacrifice for our sins." 1 John 4:10 (NIV)*
- *"We love because he first loved us." 1 John 4:19 (NIV)*

Jesus is the model to follow. Jesus defined love by His willingness to die for the church and to rise again for the church. He gave His life so that we could live with Him eternally and love others intentionally. Jesus is the ultimate portrait of unconditional love.

How are your primary relationships? Do those closest to you feel loved the most by you? Think about the adjustments that you need to make in order to better communicate love to them.

February 15
GRACE FOR THE RACE

"For it is by grace you have been saved, through faith--and this not from yourselves, it is the gift of God--not by works, so that no one can boast."
Ephesians 2:8-9 (NIV)

We need grace for the race called life. Outside of God's grace, we would have never discovered the salvation we now have in Christ. God graced us with the gift of eternal life in response to our faith in the completed work of Jesus on the cross. It is not from ourselves. Salvation was initiated by God and extended to us by His grace. We do not work for salvation. But, once we are saved, we will want to work so that others can receive the gift of eternal life. Our work is sharing the grace found in Christ with others who have not come into a saving relationship with Christ.

- *"The Word became flesh and made his dwelling among us. We have seen his glory, the glory of the One and Only, who came from the Father, full of grace and truth." John 1:14 (NIV)*
- *"Let us then approach the throne of grace with confidence, so that we may receive mercy and find grace to help us in our time of need." Heb 4:16 (NIV)*

There's no room for boasting about the salvation we have graciously received from God. The gift of eternal life has been made possible through the sacrificial death of Jesus upon the cross. Jesus died and rose from the dead so that we could be recipients of His grace and live in union with Him for eternity.

Grace enables you to pray. Grace gives you access to our Holy God. You need God's grace for every step of the race. And remember, the grace that saves you is the same grace that keeps you. God's grace will bring you safely home.

SIMPLIFY AND FOCUS

"Jesus answered them, 'It is not the healthy who need a doctor, but the sick. I have not come to call the righteous, but sinners to repentance.'" Luke 5:31-32 (NIV)

The Pharisees missed their reason for existence. They thought the purpose of life was to be religious and to strictly observe their legalistic religious customs. They thought too highly of themselves and critically judged others through the grid of their own rigid religious system. Jesus ministered among the Pharisees and often spoke directly to them, yet they missed the Messiah.

Jesus clarified His purpose as that of calling sinners to repentance. Jesus came to build the kingdom of God with those who need His mercy, His grace, and His forgiveness the most. The self-righteous behavior of the Pharisees blinded them from the truth. The Truth was standing right in front of them and they missed Him!

Jesus came to call people just like you and me to repentance. We were bankrupt spiritually and morally before Jesus came to our rescue. We were enemies of God and saturated in our sinfulness and selfishness. We were unfit and unclean for entry into the kingdom of God. Our greatest need was for the Great Physician to remedy us from our spiritual disease and to restore us to a right relationship with Himself. Jesus provided the opportunity for us to turn from our sin and to trust Him alone for salvation.

His mission is our mission. Now, simplify and focus your life on bringing others into a growing relationship with Jesus. Your assignment from the Lord is to be actively populating Heaven.

Why are you here? You are here to do what Jesus did!

February 17
SPIRITUAL BANKRUPTCY

"Looking at his disciples, he said: 'Blessed are you who are poor, for yours is the kingdom of God.'" Luke 6:20 (NIV)

Our condition before we came to Christ was that of spiritual bankruptcy. We had nothing to offer God due to our sin nature. Our fallen state disqualified us from the kingdom of God. Our righteousness just did not come close to measuring up to God's holiness and perfection.

In the Sermon on the Mount, Jesus shared what we call the Beatitudes. Matthew provides the expanded version, and Luke gives us the key ingredients of the message Jesus shared. Jesus identified the inner life of a person who is happy. This happiness is a result of recognizing your personal sin and separation from our holy God. The spiritual bankruptcy causes you to look to the One who redeems you from your sin and reconciles you to a right relationship with God. The kingdom of God becomes a reality to you when you acknowledge your sin and turn to Jesus alone for salvation.

- *"As it is written: 'There is no one righteous, not even one; there is no one who understands, no one who seeks God.'"*
  Rom 3:10-11 (NIV)
- *"God made him who had no sin to be sin for us, so that in him we might become the righteousness of God." 2 Cor 5:21 (NIV)*

Are you happy? Are you rightly related to God through a personal relationship with Jesus? His happiness is not connected to circumstances, but to your position in Christ. If you are in Christ, His life flows through you and delivers you from your spiritual bankruptcy. You become His treasured possession! Now that you possess Christ, you can profess Christ and be blessed!

LOVING DIFFICULT PEOPLE

*"'But I tell you who hear me: Love your enemies, do good to those who hate you, bless those who curse you, pray for those who mistreat you.'"*Luke 6:27-28 (NIV)

Have you ever been mistreated or hated? Did it make you want to retaliate? That is a natural reaction. Jesus modeled how every believer should respond to difficult people. We are to love our enemies. We are to benefit difficult people by doing good to them, blessing them, and praying for them. The reality is that we cannot always control how others treat us, but we can control how we respond to them.

- *"When they hurled their insults at him, he did not retaliate; when he suffered, he made no threats. Instead, he entrusted himself to him who judges justly."* 1 Pet 2:23 (NIV)
- *"Jesus said, 'Father, forgive them, for they do not know what they are doing.' And they divided up his clothes by casting lots."* Luke 23:34 (NIV)

Jesus set the example for us to follow. Jesus also gives us the power to treat others based on Jesus' treatment of us. We do not deserve His love, yet He loves us unconditionally. We do not deserve His goodness, yet He is so good to us. We do not deserve His blessings, yet He showers us with one blessing after another. Jesus even intercedes for us. That is so much more than we deserve. The word "grace" comes to mind, doesn't it?

February 19
JUDGING OTHERS

"How can you say to your brother, 'Brother, let me take the speck out of your eye,' when you yourself fail to see the plank in your own eye? You hypocrite, first take the plank out of your eye, and then you will see clearly to remove the speck from your brother's eye." Luke 6:42 (NIV)

Cynicism and criticism are alive and well. Take in a few moments of a reality television show and you will quickly discover that our culture thrives on judging others. The standard we use for others is usually vastly different than the standard we use on ourselves.

Jesus confronted the error of judging others without first examining our own lives. We have a way of making ourselves feel good about our own condition by fixating on the worst in others. We tend to use a microscope to view others and then an out-of-focus pair of binoculars to examine ourselves. Our view of others and our view of ourselves become skewed.

Hypocrisy is the act of appearing to be something you are not. Jesus says that once you address the plank in your own eye, then you will be able to see others clearly.

> • *"Search me, O God, and know my heart; test me and know my anxious thoughts. See if there is any offensive way in me, and lead me in the way everlasting." Psalm 139:23-24 (NIV)*

Once you have prayed and asked God to reveal sin in your life, confess your sin and receive God's provision of forgiveness. Now it is time to yank the plank!

When Your Heart Speaks

"The good man brings good things out of the good stored up in his heart, and the evil man brings evil things out of the evil stored up in his heart. For out of the overflow of his heart his mouth speaks." Luke 6:45 (NIV)

Did you know that your mouth will tell on your heart? Whatever is in your heart will eventually come through your mouth. The words you speak reveal what's in your heart. If your heart is impure, then your words will give evidence of that impurity. If your heart is gentle and compassionate, then your words will unveil that reality.

How's your heart? Evaluate the words you speak and you will get a clear indication of the condition of your heart. Jesus identified the heart connection to the words we speak. Jesus explained that whatever we store in our heart will come out.

The writer of Proverbs reminds us to guard our heart, for it is the wellspring of life (Prov 4:23). The condition of your heart determines how you treat others, how you speak to others, and how you think of others. If your heart is cold and indifferent, then your compassion for others will be minimal. If your heart is warm and tender, then your interaction with others will be saturated with the love and kindness of Christ.

Do your words build others up or tear them down? Do your words build bridges or erect walls? Does your speech draw others to Christ or repel them from Christ? It's a matter of the heart!

February 21
STABILITY

"I will show you what he is like who comes to me and hears my words and puts them into practice. He is like a man building a house, who dug down deep and laid the foundation on rock. When a flood came, the torrent struck that house but could not shake it, because it was well built." Luke 6:47-48 (NIV)

Obedience to God's Word leads to stability. It is not enough to be a hearer only. Putting God's Word into practice is essential to building your life on a solid foundation and being blessed (James 1:25). Adversity will come. Seasons of uncertainty will come. Storms will arise. However, you will not be shaken and you will not be shifted because of the stability resulting from obeying God's Word.

Disobedience to God's Word leads to instability. Can you imagine building a house without a foundation? When the storms come, your house will not stand. Failing to hear God's Word and to put it into practice is like building your life on shifting sand. Disobedience produces unhealthy and unwanted consequences.

You are a spiritual house in which the Holy Spirit lives. You are the walking tabernacle of the Presence of God (1 Cor 6:19-20). God has a specific plan for your life that includes hearing His Word and putting it into practice. God's will is for you to obey His Word.

Are you obeying what God has already revealed to you through His Word? Are you loving God and loving others? "Why do you call me, 'Lord, Lord,' and do not do what I say?" (Luke 6:46 NIV).

LOVE AND FORGIVENESS

"Therefore, I tell you, her many sins have been forgiven--for she loved much. But he who has been forgiven little loves little." Luke 7:47 (NIV)

What's the relationship between forgiveness and love? God loves us so much that He sacrificed His only Son to atone for our sins (John 3:16). Jesus loves us so much that He was obedient to death, even death on a cross (Phil 2:8). God demonstrated His love for us by taking the initiative to provide for the forgiveness of our sins (Rom 5:8).

The level of forgiveness we have received from God affects the level of our love for others. A person who has experienced a large measure of compassion from others will in turn be more compassionate toward others. Jesus says that he who has been forgiven little loves little. The capacity to love others is fashioned by the level of forgiveness that we have received. Our desperation to be forgiven for our sins cascades us with an appreciation for the love God has lavished on us (1 John 3:1).

Is there anyone in your life whom you are having a difficult time loving? If so, begin to measure the forgiveness God has extended to you over your lifetime. Search the depths of your heart to recover the love God has faithfully demonstrated to you. Now choose to treat this person with the same level of love and forgiveness that you have graciously received from God. God is not asking you to do anything He has not already done for you.

February 23
A NOBLE HEART

"But the seed on good soil stands for those with a noble and good heart, who hear the word, retain it, and by persevering produce a crop.'" Luke 8:15 (NIV)

How well do you receive God's Word? Your level of receptivity is a direct reflection of the condition of your heart. Your heart is the soil upon which the seed, God's Word, is sown. As you hear, read, and feed on God's Word, the seed is sown in your heart. If you have a noble and good heart, then the seed will take root in your life and produce a harvest.

It starts with your heart. Ask God to search your heart (Psalm 139:23). The light of His holiness will reveal the true condition of your heart. Does your heart resemble the hard path, or the rocky ground, or the thorn infused ground? You can become calloused toward the things of God. You can become distracted by the magnetic pull of worldliness and materialism. It is possible to choke out the Word of God by the worries of this life.

Purify your heart before the Lord. Remove the impurities that constrict the flow of the Holy Spirit in your life (Eph 4:30). Take the initiative to purify your body, the Temple of the Holy Spirit (1 Cor 6:19).

- *"Since we have these promises, dear friends, let us purify ourselves from everything that contaminates body and spirit, perfecting holiness out of reverence for God." 2 Cor 7:1 (NIV)*

Keep your heart noble and good. Consistently take in God's Word through hearing, reading, and feeding on God's Word each day. Your level of receptivity will be evidenced through the level of productivity in the harvest.

"One day Jesus said to his disciples, 'Let's go over to the other side of the lake.' So they got into a boat and set out." Luke 8:22 (NIV)

God will get you to the other side. His plan for you is personal. God designed you with His purpose in mind. You are not an accident. Before you were born, God knew you (Jer 1:5). You are here at this very moment because God ordained your existence. God has a special plan for your life that includes your past, present, and future. God's plan factors in your choices. You are not an impersonal robotic creature. You are a personal relational being with the purpose of God in your heart. God knows you by name, and even the hairs upon your head are numbered (Luke 12:7).

God's plan for you is eternal. There's more in store than what you see in the here and now. God has placed eternity in your heart to position you for eternal life (Eccl 3:11). Your life goes beyond the grave. God's plan for you extends beyond the immediate and includes eternal life. As you receive the gift of eternal life by faith, your forever is changed. Heaven becomes the place where you will live with God forever.

The disciples responded to Jesus by getting into a boat and setting out. Jesus said, "Let's go over to the other side." Jesus did not say, "Let's see if we can make it to the other side." When Jesus is in your boat, there's nothing to fear. Jesus will get you to the destination safely and right on time. Enjoy the journey!

February 25
STORMS IN LIFE

"As they sailed, he fell asleep. A squall came down on the lake, so that the boat was being swamped, and they were in great danger." Luke 8:23 (NIV)

Why does God allow storms to come into our path? God is more concerned about our character than our comfort. His passion is for us to become like Christ. If God allows a storm, He will use that storm to reveal Himself and to refine our character. There are some things you learn in a storm that you cannot learn on the calm sea. The storm provides the environment in which we learn to trust God by taking Him at His Word. We learn to view our circumstances from God's perspective.

The disciples were in great danger from their personal perspective. While the storm was raging, Jesus was sleeping. Jesus knew the outcome before they even set sail. Jesus oriented His life according to the Father's agenda. God's will supersedes any storm and any distraction. God will accomplish His plan in the midst of life's storms.

Your character development matters to God. The friction of each storm in your life will be guided by the hand of God to sand the rough edges from your life in order to perfect Christ in you. If God allows a storm to come into your life, He will orchestrate the movement of that storm to conform you into the image of Christ (Rom 8:28-29). God works in all situations to bring you into perfect union with Christ and to effectively portray Christ through your life.

Every storm has a season and is used of God for a divine reason. What storm are you in? Have you detected the loving hand of God at work in the midst of the storm to produce Christ-likeness in you? Maintain God's perspective while you trust His provision to see you through.

FORTIFYING YOUR FAITH

"The disciples went and woke him, saying, 'Master, Master, we're going to drown!' He got up and rebuked the wind and the raging waters; the storm subsided, and all was calm. 'Where is your faith?' he asked his disciples. In fear and amazement they asked one another, 'Who is this? He commands even the winds and the water, and they obey him.'" Luke 8:24-25 (NIV)

Without a test, there is no testimony. Jesus provided the disciples with an opportunity to fortify their faith and to solidify their testimony. Fearing for their lives, the disciples woke Jesus and alerted Him of their plight. Jesus got up and changed their circumstances by rebuking the wind and the waters. The storm subsided and all was calm.

Their life lesson was delivered in the form of a question, "Where is your faith?" Jesus wanted the disciples to think about where they were placing their confidence. Did the disciples place their confidence in the boat or in the Master of the wind and the waves?

- *"We live by faith, not by sight." 2 Cor 5:7 (NIV)*
- *"And without faith it is impossible to please God, because anyone who comes to him must believe that he exists and that he rewards those who earnestly seek him." Heb 11:6 (NIV)*

The disciples asked one another, "Who is this?" Your answer to that question is vital. Is Jesus just a good man who performed good deeds while upon the earth? Or, is Jesus the Master of your life and your forever? Place your confidence in Jesus alone for salvation and trust Him to see you through the storms of life. Jesus can save you from your sin and from eternal damnation. The same Jesus who has provided for your eternal security can provide for your immediate stability in the midst of your storm. Entrust your life to Jesus completely. Jesus is in the boat!

February 27
SHARE YOUR STORY

"The man from whom the demons had gone out begged to go with him, but Jesus sent him away, saying, 'Return home and tell how much God has done for you.' So the man went away and told all over town how much Jesus had done for him."
Luke 8:38-39 (NIV)

This demon-possessed man had not lived in a house, but lived in the tombs for a long time. When the demons came out of the man, Jesus gave them permission to go into a herd of pigs. The herd rushed down the bank into the lake and drowned. When the people of that region came to Jesus, they saw this man sitting at Jesus' feet. The man was dressed and in his right mind. Jesus instructed the man to "return home and tell how much God has done for you."

What is your story? How did Jesus reveal Himself and His salvation plan to you? Revisit the circumstances leading up to your salvation event. Consider the people God brought into your path to introduce you to Jesus. Begin to pray and thank God for each person specifically.

Review the changes that have taken place in your life since receiving God's gift of eternal life. Calculate the progression of your faith and the levels of maturity gained over the years. Remember, salvation is an event followed by a process of maturation. What is different about your life now?

Share your story! Let others know what the Lord has done for you. Proclaim the Good News of Jesus with those who do not have a personal relationship with Him. Testify of the atoning work of Jesus on the cross and the victory over sin, death, and hell. Share with others how Jesus came to your rescue and delivered you from the kingdom of darkness and placed you in the kingdom of light.

"As Jesus was on his way, the crowds almost crushed him. And a woman was there who had been subject to bleeding for twelve years, but no one could heal her. She came up behind him and touched the edge of his cloak, and immediately her bleeding stopped." Luke 8:42-44 (NIV)

Has your life been interrupted recently? Has your schedule, routine, or plan been shifted as a result of an unexpected interruption? Jesus had that experience as He was on His way to heal the twelve-year-old daughter of Jairus. Jesus was on his way to their home to perform a miraculous healing touch when His plans were interrupted.

In the midst of the crowds pressing in on Jesus, there was a woman who had been subject to bleeding for twelve years. No one could heal her. She was desperate and determined that Jesus could heal her. She came up behind Jesus and touched the edge of His cloak and her bleeding stopped immediately. Jesus noticed that power had gone out from Him and so He asked His disciples, "Who touched me?"

The woman came trembling at Jesus' feet and told Him why she had touched Him and then affirmed her healing. Jesus responded to her by saying, "Daughter, your faith has healed you. Go in peace."

Jesus turned this interruption into an opportunity to be a blessing to someone in need. Of course, this interruption delayed His arrival at the home of Jairus. Someone from the house of Jairus announced that his daughter was dead. Did she die because of the delay? Jesus went into their home and took her by the hand and said, "My child, get up!"

The interruption Jesus encountered became a pronounced opportunity to heal the woman and the child. Will you turn your interruptions into opportunities for God to do something special through you?

March 1
HEALING TOUCH

"They laughed at him, knowing that she was dead. But he took her by the hand and said, 'My child, get up!' Her spirit returned, and at once she stood up. Then Jesus told them to give her something to eat." Luke 8:53-55 (NIV)

Jairus, the synagogue ruler, only had one daughter. She was twelve. Upon hearing of her death, Jesus said to Jairus, "Don't be afraid; just believe, and she will be healed" (Luke 8:50 NIV). Jesus honored His word and provided complete healing. The emphasis is not on the faith healing, but on the faith Healer. Jesus is the Great Physician.

Sometimes healing does not come in our preferred timeframe. Whether it is your personal healing that is needed or praying for someone else to be healed, God does not always provide the healing we desire. God will choose to heal some people and choose not to heal others. We tend to struggle trying to understand why God would allow good people to suffer and allow bad people to be healed. Let's be reminded of the sovereignty of God and His omniscience. Our finite minds cannot comprehend the mind of our infinite God.

We can trust in God's timing. God will accomplish His purpose and plan in His perfect timing according to His will. God will provide us with His sufficient grace to enable us to endure the seasons of uncertainty (2 Cor 12:9). We may not know what tomorrow holds, but we know who holds tomorrow.

Every believer will experience the ultimate healing in Heaven. There will be no sin, sickness, or suffering in Heaven. Until then, let's operate in the grace God provides to see us through the storms of life. Until then, let's continue to pray for healing and rejoice when the healing comes. Take God at His Word and walk in the nourishment He provides.

MEETING NEEDS

"They all ate and were satisfied, and the disciples picked up twelve basketfuls of broken pieces that were left over." Luke 9:17 (NIV)

God wants to use you to meet needs. In order to meet needs, you must be sensitive to the needs of others. Living a life of "other-centeredness" is essential to joining God in His personal touch ministry. Selfishness will blind you to the needs around you. Selfishness will steer your focus inward every time.

Jesus told the disciples to feed the multitudes. The number of men was five thousand not including the women and children. Jesus was asking the disciples to feed over fifteen thousand people. All they could find was a little boy with a sack lunch with five loaves of bread and two fish. "Taking the five loaves and the two fish and looking up to heaven, he gave thanks and broke them. Then he gave them to the disciples to set before the people" (Luke 9:16 NIV). Jesus multiplied what He had been given in order to meet the physical needs of the masses. They all ate and were satisfied!

Where did the twelve basketfuls of leftovers come from? There is a valuable lesson to learn here. Just bring Jesus what you have. Jesus will take what you have and multiply it to meet needs. God will never ask you to do anything without providing everything you need to accomplish His will. Perhaps you know the saying, "Where God guides, He always provides."

Will you make yourself available for God's use this week? Will you look for opportunities to meet the needs that God brings into your path? Be sensitive. Be selfless. Be willing to seize the opportunities God gives you.

March 3
WHO DO YOU SAY I AM?

"No one who denies the Son has the Father; whoever acknowledges the Son has the Father also." 1 John 2:23 (NIV)

Do you believe that Jesus is who He says He is? Do you believe that Jesus is the Son of God and lived a sinless life and died a sacrificial death to atone for the sins of the world? What you believe about Jesus affects your eternal destination. What you believe about Jesus affects your level of living in the immediate.

After asking the crowd their understanding of who He was, Jesus asked Peter, "Who do you say I am?" As revealed to him by God, Peter pronounced that Jesus was the Christ, the Son of the living God (Matt 16:16). That confession of faith was paramount to Peter's salvation and to Peter's maturation in the faith. Peter later affirmed, "Praise be to the God and Father of our Lord Jesus Christ! In his great mercy he has given us new birth into a living hope through the resurrection of Jesus Christ from the dead" (1 Peter 1:3 NIV).

Who do you say Jesus is? Your understanding of the life and Lordship of Jesus is vital to your union with Christ and your usefulness in the kingdom of God. As Dr. David Fleming says, "You cannot be wrong about Jesus and right with God." Your understanding of the Person and work of Jesus is crucial. To be right with God, you must be right about Jesus.

It is not enough to know proper facts about Jesus. You must know Jesus personally through an abiding relationship with Him that is real and personal because eternal life is found in Jesus alone (1 Jn. 5:11-12).

THE POWER OF DAILY

"Then he said to them all: 'If anyone would come after me, he must deny himself and take up his cross daily and follow me.'" Luke 9:23 (NIV)

Every day is a new beginning. Each day provides you with new opportunities to experience God's Presence and to join Him in His activity. The new day is a launching pad for your daily decision to fully surrender to the Lordship of Christ. To live in moment-by-moment union with Christ demands a daily decision to deny self, take up His cross, and follow Him. To be a follower of Jesus is more than just believing that Jesus died and rose again. Following Jesus is a daily experience of walking in His steps and doing what Jesus did.

Being a follower of Jesus Christ is a conscious decision to know Him personally and intimately. Your love relationship with Christ is to be vibrant and growing. What needs to change in your daily routine in order to grow in your walk with Christ? As John Maxwell wrote, "You will never change your life until you change something you do daily." The power of daily is evidenced by your devotion to make decisions that will benefit your relationship with Christ.

What adjustments do you need to make in order to become more like Christ? Is your life Christ-centered or self-focused? Are you choosing to follow the way of Jesus or drifting into the current of the world?

What do you need to stop doing? What do you need to start doing? Each day matters and each decision you make will enhance or inhibit your walk with Christ.

No Room for Shame

"If anyone is ashamed of me and my words, the Son of Man will be ashamed of him when he comes in his glory and in the glory of the Father and of the holy angels." Luke 9:26 (NIV)

Do you conceal your Christianity? Can you be accused of being a closet Christian? Do those in your sphere of influence know that you are a follower of Jesus Christ? There's nothing to be ashamed of. In Christ, you have been adopted into God's family and sealed by the Holy Spirit (Eph 1:5,13). You have been rescued from darkness and placed in the kingdom of light (Col 1:5). God has placed you in the display window of life to portray His grace to a dark and decaying world (1 Tim 1:16).

Embrace the attitude of Paul who affirmed, "I am not ashamed of the gospel, because it is the power of God for the salvation of everyone who believes: first for the Jew, then for the Gentile" (Rom 1:16 NIV). The gospel that brought you hope and eternal life is the same gospel that you represent in this life. Don't be ashamed of the Good News that transformed your life. Don't withhold the cure to the cancer of sin that will set others free just as you have been set free.

Jesus was not ashamed to identify with the lost by becoming flesh (John 1:14). For a person to be ashamed of Christ and His words is to deny the One who gave His all to provide for the forgiveness of sin. There's no room for shame when it comes to identifying with Christ. To align with Christ is an honor to behold.

"The LORD had said to Abram, 'Leave your country, your people and your father's household and go to the land I will show you. I will make you into a great nation and I will bless you; I will make your name great, and you will be a blessing. I will bless those who bless you, and whoever curses you I will curse; and all peoples on earth will be blessed through you.'" Genesis 12:1-3 (NIV)

Has God ever asked you to do something that was uncomfortable? Have you ever sensed that God wanted you to make a decision that would alter your current reality?

Abram was confronted with a word from God that would drastically change his path. God's instructions were not specific. In fact, God just told Abram to leave and go to a land He would show him. Abram was not on a mission, but on mission with God.

Being on mission with God is relational. If you want to obey God and trust Him to reveal His plan for your life, then you must be willing to walk with Him and get to know His voice. God does not need you to be on a mission. God wants you to make a choice to be on mission with Him. He is in charge. He has an agenda for you to fulfill.

Abram had to trust God to show Him the way. As Abram obeyed, God would reveal his next step. Does that connect with you? Are you coming to the place where you realize that God wants you to simply choose to be on mission with Him and trust Him with the details? As you obey, God will reveal the way.

March 7
TAKING THE NEXT STEP

"So Abram left, as the LORD had told him; and Lot went with him. Abram was seventy-five years old when he set out from Haran." Genesis 12:4 (NIV)

What is keeping you from obeying God? Do you fear the unknown? Are you uncomfortable making a move without having more information? Maybe God has chosen to limit His revelation to match your obedience. Once you obey what He has already said, then He will show you the next step.

Abram took God at His word! He simply obeyed God. God told Abram to leave and go to a land that He would show him. Guess what? Abram left, as the Lord told him. He obeyed.

You can never go wrong obeying God. His way is always the best way. Even when it doesn't make sense or seem remotely logical, God's way is the right way. If you are confused about your next step, just obey what He has already said. Start there!

Identify what you are wrestling with right now? What is keeping you from taking the next step? Place that fear or frustration before the Lord in prayer and see how He helps you take the next step.

WAIT FOR GOD'S TIMING

"God also said to Abraham, 'As for Sarai your wife, you are no longer to call her Sarai; her name will be Sarah. I will bless her and will surely give you a son by her. I will bless her so that she will be the mother of nations; kings of peoples will come from her.'" Genesis 17:15-16 (NIV)

Can you imagine becoming a parent at age ninety or one hundred? That's difficult to fathom. However, the greater challenge would be to desire parenthood and have to wait until you were almost a century old to realize the dream.

Abraham and Sarah had to learn to live with delays. God had promised to bless them and to make them into a great nation. However, they had to walk in obedience to God and wait for His timing.

Have you noticed how our personal timetable doesn't always line up with God's timetable? We tend to want our blessing now. We don't usually "wait" very well.

God has a divine purpose in our delays. Sometimes delays are a result of poor choices we have made and sometimes a consequence of poor choices those around us have made. Either way, God can use delays to portray His grace. God has the final say, doesn't He? Nothing happens without God's permission. If God allows a delay in your life, He will utilize the delay. Now rest in God's timing. Entrust your life to Him.

March 9
GUARDING YOUR TOP PRIORITY

"When they reached the place God had told him about, Abraham built an altar there and arranged the wood on it. He bound his son Isaac and laid him on the altar, on top of the wood. Then he reached out his hand and took the knife to slay his son." Genesis 22:9-10 (NIV)

Is there anything in your life that takes priority over your relationship with Jesus? Are there any allurements sifting your affection away from your devotion to Christ? Do you have an Isaac in your life that you are unwilling to sacrifice?

Abraham demonstrated absolute loyalty and devotion to God by his willingness to sacrifice his promised son. Abraham and Sarah were beyond child bearing years. Yet, God provided the miracle of Isaac's conception. Now God is asking Abraham to sacrifice that which was promised to him. What is standing in the way of your realization of unbroken fellowship with God? What is taking the number one place of prominence in your life which is reserved for God? Whatever that item, ambition, or person is may be your Isaac.

Could it be that God wants you to sacrifice that Isaac in your life to enable God to have top priority in your life? God wants first place in your daily walk. God wants to be the supreme object of your energy and affection. He not only deserves it, but He demands it.

Spend a few moments taking inventory of your current priorities and identify what is preventing God from being your top priority.

GOD'S PROVISION

"Abraham looked up and there in a thicket he saw a ram caught by its horns. He went over and took the ram and sacrificed it as a burnt offering instead of his son. So Abraham called that place The LORD Will Provide. And to this day it is said, 'On the mountain of the LORD it will be provided.'"
Genesis 22:13-14 (NIV)

God's provision always exceeds our sacrifice. Just when you think you have given God your all, He surpasses your sacrifice with His provision. God will never ask you to do anything that exceeds His provision. God's timing is not limited by our schedule. His provision always comes through at the perfect moment. God is never late. We serve an on-time God. Sometimes it may seem as though God waits until you are in the fourth quarter with only a few seconds left on the clock. Yet, God's provision appears right on time.

Abraham obeyed God and demonstrated his reverence for God. In response, God provided a substitute for Isaac at the exact moment of greatest need.

What did Abraham learn about God through his willingness to trust and obey God in every situation? He learned that God was dependable and trustworthy. In response to the encounter of God's provision, Abraham acknowledged God as Jehovah Jireh, the Lord Will Provide.

What is keeping you from obeying God and trusting Him to provide?

March 11
STAYING VERTICAL

"For this reason, ever since I heard about your faith in the Lord Jesus and your love for all the saints, I have not stopped giving thanks for you, remembering you in my prayers." Ephesians 1:15-16 (NIV)

The most incredible relationship you can ever have is vertical. Having a right relationship with God through Jesus Christ is the ultimate relationship. Think about the vertical beam of the cross. Allow it to represent your relationship with God. What does that relationship look like currently in your life?

Paul identified the evidence of one's right relationship with God as faith expressing itself through love. When you are living in harmony with God, your faith will be apparent. The Ephesians embraced their vertical relationship with God to the extent that Paul heard about their faith from his prison cell.

What is your faith relationship with God saying to those in your sphere of influence? In what environment is your faith in God most tested? How's your vertical relationship with God expressed in your home, at work, at church, and in your neighborhood?

Spend some time assessing your vertical relationship. Let God have His way in your life so that your faith will be evident to all.

COVERED IN PRAYER

"I have not stopped giving thanks for you, remembering you in my prayers."
Ephesians 1:16 (NIV)

Is somebody praying for you? I want you to begin to calculate where you would be had it not been for the people who have prayed for you. Your name, your circumstances, and your future have been placed before the throne of God by those people who have prayed for you.

God has a unique way of prompting people to pray for you. He will nudge them with a gentle reminder of your life. They may respond by praying for you to realize God's will. Maybe they pray for you to have a heightened awareness of God's Presence and activity.

Paul exhibited a deep love for the saints in Ephesus. He constantly thanked God for them and for their obvious faith in the Lord and their love for their fellow believers. Paul consistently remembered them in his prayers. They were as natural to his prayer life as water to a fish.

Carve out a few moments right now to thank God for the people who have prayed for you. This could get emotional! It's okay. You matter to God and He deeply loves you and cares for you.

March 13
KNOWING GOD

"I keep asking that the God of our Lord Jesus Christ, the glorious Father, may give you the Spirit of wisdom and revelation, so that you may know him better."
Ephesians 1:17 (NIV)

God wants you to know Him intimately. God invites you into the process. You must participate with God in developing and maintaining intimacy with Him. He makes the relationship possible through the atoning work of Jesus on the cross. You get the privilege of knowing God and growing in your knowledge of God.

Paul had a loving desire to see the saints at Ephesus grow in their relationship with God. From prison, he prayed for their sanctification. Meditate on his prayer.

Why would Paul pray that God would give the saints at Ephesus the Spirit of wisdom and revelation? He prayed that specifically so that they would know God better. In other words, there is room to grow. Yes, there's more to explore.

We are finite. God is infinite. There's so much more to know about God and more to explore in knowing God. The beauty of a love relationship with God is that it is progressive. You can continually grow to know God more. What a privilege! What an honor! What a responsibility!

THE EYES OF YOUR HEART

"I pray also that the eyes of your heart may be enlightened in order that you may know the hope to which he has called you, the riches of his glorious inheritance in the saints." Ephesians 1:18 (NIV)

Do you remember the Polaroid cameras that produced the photo for you within a minute of you taking the picture? Now we have digital cameras that provide a picture instantly. The old Polaroid cameras were considered innovative back then. You would take a picture and then watch it develop right before your eyes.

That process of development is similar to the Greek word, photizo, which Paul uses in his letter to the saints in Ephesus. This particular Greek word is translated as "enlightened."

Your heart, which represents your capacity to understand and comprehend God's truth, has room to grow. Your ability to know, grasp, and understand has the potential to develop. You can grow in your knowing.

God wants you to be enlightened. God desires for you to develop in your knowledge of Him.

Personalize Ephesians 1:18 and pray through it by asking God to open the eyes of your heart. God will unveil His Word to you in a personal and powerful way.

March 15
ENDURING REJECTION

"He then began to teach them that the Son of Man must suffer many things and be rejected by the elders, chief priests and teachers of the law, and that he must be killed and after three days rise again." Mark 8:31 (NIV)

Rejection hurts. Have you been there? When you don't feel that you measure up to a standard that has been established or an expectation that has been articulated, rejection seeps in. You begin to experience pain, discontentment, and insecurity. During those times when you are misunderstood, rejection begins to shadow your vision and stifle your optimism.

Jesus lived in the midst of steep legalism in His day. The elders, chief priests, and teachers of the law sought to shackle others by their self imposed rules and regulations. They promoted religion by works which embodied excessive "do's and don'ts" that totally bypassed intimacy with our Heavenly Father.

The suffering of Jesus included rejection. He was not accepted by those who claimed to be religious. Rejection was perpetual during His three and a half year public ministry. His being rejected ultimately led to His being crucified. When you compare your current bouts with rejection to that of Jesus, it seems as though your encounters with rejection are light. Yet, they are real and they are painful. Rejection hits us hard and tends to knock the wind out of us.

What kind of rejection are you currently facing? How long has the rejection lingered? There is good news on the way that will give you a whole new perspective on how to respond to rejection. Spend some time sharing your hurt with Jesus in prayer. Let Him hear you express your pain as you call out His Name.

LEGALISM

"Indignant because Jesus had healed on the Sabbath, the synagogue ruler said to the people, 'There are six days for work. So come and be healed on those days, not on the Sabbath.'" Luke 13:14 (NIV)

Legalism bypasses relationship. Instead of operating out of an abiding relationship with Christ, it is possible to embrace an external religion. You can gravitate toward measuring your level of spiritual maturity with the standard of outward appearance. You can be so steeped in legalism that you totally neglect the internal component that God values.

Jesus had miraculously healed a woman crippled by an evil spirit for eighteen years. She immediately exhibited a straight posture and praised God. This woman had been set free. However, the synagogue ruler was indignant because Jesus healed on the Sabbath. The synagogue ruler was so steeped in legalism that he missed the wonderful life-changing work of the Lord of the Sabbath.

> • *"The Lord answered him, 'You hypocrites! Doesn't each of you on the Sabbath untie his ox or donkey from the stall and lead it out to give it water? Then should not this woman, a daughter of Abraham, whom Satan has kept bound for eighteen long years, be set free on the Sabbath day from what bound her?'" Luke 13:15-16 (NIV).*

Have you allowed legalism to rob your love relationship with Christ? God looks at your heart and wants you to operate your life from the abiding relationship that He has established for you in Christ. Walk in the freedom of God's grace and seek to grow in the daily expression of your faith. Let others see Jesus in you. Be a conduit of grace just as God has lavished His grace on you.

March 17
ENJOY REST FOR YOUR SOUL

"Come to me, all you who are weary and burdened, and I will give you rest. Take my yoke upon you and learn from me, for I am gentle and humble in heart, and you will find rest for your souls. For my yoke is easy and my burden is light."
Matthew 11:28-30 (NIV)

Jesus is always on time. He knows just what we need right when we need it. His invitation to join Him and to find rest in Him is the antidote to our fast paced lifestyle. As one person said, "If we don't learn to come apart, we will come apart!"

Why do we feel guilty when we slow down? Why do we gravitate toward the performance trap and end up equating productivity with spirituality? Sometimes the most spiritual move we can make is to slow down and experience the rest Jesus offers.

Be sure to notice in our verse for today that there is a prerequisite to encountering His rest. We must be willing to come to Him. We must be willing to take the initiative to respond to His invitation. That just doesn't fit our adrenaline addicted society. We tend to long for the next high or the next rush. Maybe we can just capture a few more sips of caffeinated coffee. Will that deliver what we need most?

Perhaps the invitation is to come to the place of total reliance upon God. If I yoke up with Him, then I will have to be willing to go where He goes and embrace the pace He sets. Remember, His yoke is easy and His burden is light. Sounds refreshing!

STAYING ON MISSION

"Then Jesus went through the towns and villages, teaching as he made his way to Jerusalem." Luke 13:22 (NIV)

In the final six months of His earthly ministry, Jesus stayed on mission with God. Embracing the reality of His impending sacrifice for the sins of the world and enduring the agony of the cross, Jesus continued to travel and teach. Jesus extended personal touch ministry as He remained focused on the mission of seeking and saving the lost. As Jesus did life on the dusty roads, He made room for others.

We spend so much of our time on our way to the next activity or event. Think about how many times each day you find yourself on your way to fulfill a commitment or to meet a deadline. There are so many tugs on your time and attention. As you are on your way, God wants you to make the most of that transition time. Maybe you are on your way to work or on your way to school and you decide to maximize the travel time by praying for others. You could use your daily commute to quote Bible verses or to sing songs of worship and praise to God.

Be creative in how you use your time when you are on your way. Instead of viewing time sitting in a doctor's office as a waste of time, capture those moments to read God's Word or to text message notes of encouragement to others. Allow God to use you to be a blessing even during times of transitioning from one event to another or from one meeting to another.

Keep the main thing the main thing. Staying on mission with God is a perpetual discipline that requires sensitivity to God's activity. God wants to do a work in you so that He can do a work through you. Give God room to work!

March 19
A LOADED QUESTION

"Someone asked him, 'Lord, are only a few people going to be saved?'"
Luke 13:23 (NIV)

Have you ever wondered how many people will be in Heaven? As Jesus was on his way to Jerusalem, someone asked him if only a few people were going to be saved. That is a very important question. The answer to that question has eternal implications.

What made this person ask such a question? Maybe he embraced a false sense of security as a Jew assuming that he was safely in the fold of the people of God. It could be that this individual noticed how the number of followers of Christ had dwindled as Jesus' popularity reduced while persecution had elevated. Maybe the person asking the question had a genuine concern for the salvation of humanity.

God has provided the way for everyone who turns to Christ to be rescued from eternal damnation. Are you willing to participate with God in the redemptive process? Are you willing to be used of God to shine His light and share His love with a dark and decaying world?

Consider those who do not have a saving relationship with Jesus. Will the saved be few? You can make a difference in the population in Heaven. Your life is a witness. Will you intentionally build relationships with those who do not know Christ in order to bring the Good News to them? Allow others to experience the salvation that you have received. Let others enjoy the wonderful peace of having the assurance of Heaven and eternal life.

A Redemptive Answer

"He said to them, Make every effort to enter through the narrow door, because many, I tell you, will try to enter and will not be able to." Luke 13:23-24 (NIV)

Can you visualize the front door to the home you grew up in? You can probably describe the color, texture, and specific features of that door. Access to your home was granted through that door.

Jesus said that we must enter through the narrow door to gain access into eternal life and Heaven. In order to access salvation, we are to strive to enter through the narrow door. The door to salvation is Jesus.

- *"I am the gate; whoever enters through me will be saved. He will come in and go out, and find pasture." John 10:9 (NIV)*
- *"'Salvation is found in no one else, for there is no other name under heaven given to men by which we must be saved.'" Acts 4:12 (NIV)*

You cannot work your way to Heaven and you cannot get to Heaven on your own. Even on your best day, your righteousness is not sufficient to gain salvation. There is no other way to get to Heaven outside of the redemptive plan of God. God provided for the forgiveness of your sin through the atoning work of Jesus on the cross. You access this salvation by placing your faith in Jesus alone.

The gift of eternal life has been made available. Your response to God's offer of salvation will determine where you spend eternity. Enter through the narrow door. The door is Jesus!

March 21
TIMELY DECISION

"But he will reply, 'I don't know you or where you come from. Away from me, all you evildoers!'" Luke 13:27 (NIV)

The clock is ticking. There is a limited amount of time to respond to God's offer of salvation. Why would anyone gamble with his or her eternal destination? Why would anyone delay his or her response to God's offer of Heaven and eternal life? No person knows how much time he or she has left on the earth. Sadly, there are some who delay their decision to follow Christ until it is too late.

The window of opportunity closes at death or the Rapture, depending which comes first in a person's lifetime. When you die, it is too late to receive the gift of eternal life if you have not already done so. Once Jesus raptures the church, it will be too late for those who failed to place their faith in Jesus alone for salvation.

In witnessing to people over the years, I have heard many people remark that they were planning to have fun, experience everything this world has to offer, and then get right with God right before they die. Now that is presuming upon the grace of God. How dangerous to assume that you can flirt with the things of this world and then right at the end, get right with God!

Be a bridge builder to those who do not have a saving relationship with Jesus. Live each day with a sense of urgency. Live expectantly knowing that Jesus could rapture the church at any moment. Live in light of His return.

COMPASSION IN ACTION

"At one time we too were foolish, disobedient, deceived and enslaved by all kinds of passions and pleasures. We lived in malice and envy, being hated and hating one another. But when the kindness and love of God our Savior appeared, he saved us, not because of righteous things we had done, but because of his mercy. He saved us through the washing of rebirth and renewal by the Holy Spirit, whom he poured out on us generously through Jesus Christ our Savior, so that, having been justified by his grace, we might become heirs having the hope of eternal life." Titus 3:3-7 (NIV)

Don't hide what is on the inside. God made the first move to come to your rescue. His initiative to reconcile you to Himself was birthed out of His unconditional love for you. God has such a wonderful plan for your life that includes your past, your pain, and your present situation. Be careful not to lose sight of where you were when God made Jesus known to you. Don't detach from the reality of your former condition. Allow your past to be a reminder of how gracious God is and how His mercy endures forever.

When you consider the love God has demonstrated in your own life, it will motivate you to love others with the measure of love you have received. When you calculate the depth of the forgiveness God has granted to you, it will stir you to extend forgiveness to others in the same measure. God saved you not in response to your righteousness, but out of His abundant mercy. Choose to be merciful toward others as God has been toward you.

God has generously poured out His Holy Spirit on you and allowed you to experience the new birth in Christ. You have been justified by His grace. Having the hope of eternal life, you have become an heir with Christ. This is the time to celebrate God's compassion in action.

March 23
VALUE PEOPLE

"Then Jesus told them this parable: 'Suppose one of you has a hundred sheep and loses one of them. Does he not leave the ninety-nine in the open country and go after the lost sheep until he finds it? And when he finds it, he joyfully puts it on his shoulders and goes home. Then he calls his friends and neighbors together and says, "Rejoice with me; I have found my lost sheep." I tell you that in the same way there will be more rejoicing in heaven over one sinner who repents than over ninety-nine righteous persons who do not need to repent.'" Luke 15:3-7 (NIV)

People matter to God. Until you value what God values, you won't see what God sees. God sees people where they are and where they could be in Christ. God values people so much that while we were still sinners, Christ died for us (Rom 5:8). Why would the Creator of the universe value the rebellious and fallen people He created? Why would God be so compassionate toward those who are disconnected and defiant?

Jesus portrayed the willingness to leave the ninety-nine sheep in order to go after the one lost sheep. The one lost sheep is just as valuable to the owner as the ninety-nine that are safe in the open country. The shepherd is willing to risk his own life in order to go after the one sheep. Once the sheep is found, the shepherd returns and invites his friends and neighbors together to rejoice in the rescued runaway.

When one sinner repents, there is more rejoicing in Heaven over that one sinner than over ninety-nine righteous persons who have no need to repent. One sinner reconciled to God produces a celebration in Heaven that earth cannot compete with. God values people.

What if you began to view people the way God does? How would the next person you meet benefit from your new perspective? People matter to God! Do they matter to you?

KNEEL IN PRAYER

"For this reason I kneel before the Father." Ephesians 3:14 (NIV)

Kneeling keeps you standing. Why would Paul assume the posture of kneeling in prayer on behalf of the saints in Ephesus? Paul had already surrendered his life and agenda to God. Kneeling was simply an outward expression of his inward position in Christ.

The Father is worthy of your humility and dependence. He alone is worthy of your passionate adoration and worship. Your Heavenly Father is the source of life. He rescued you from the hell bound path you were on. The Father willingly gave His best to take your place upon the cross. Your sin debt has been paid in full.

Now, what are you in need of? What do you need that your Heavenly Father has not provided? God is more than enough. His resources are unlimited. His generosity is immeasurable.

Has anything driven you to your knees lately? Have you been kneeling before the Father on behalf of someone in your sphere of influence? When you come to the place of desperation, you will find that your Heavenly Father has already been working. He is not surprised by your surprises. Nothing ever occurs to God. He already knows.

Find a place to kneel before God in prayer. Share the depths of your heart with the Lord and call out to Him as you pray. Be specific with everything that is draining you and discouraging you. Entrust every detail of your life and your uncertainties to the Lord's care.

RENEW YOUR STRENGTH

"But those who hope in the LORD will renew their strength. They will soar on wings like eagles; they will run and not grow weary, they will walk and not be faint." Isaiah 40:31 (NIV)

God never intended for you to live the Christian life in your own strength. Joining God in His activity requires His divine energy and strength. Navigating the storms of life demands strength you do not have outside of God's enabling. The Christian life is not a solo flight. God invites you to participate in the divine nature (2 Pet 1:4).

The Lord will renew your strength as you place your total dependency and confidence in Him. Acknowledge the Lord as the source of your strength. Live expectantly with your eyes focused on the Lord and His mission. Operate with complete assurance that God is who He says He is and that God will do what He says He will do.

As you hope in the Lord, He will renew your strength. As you hope in the Lord, He will cause you to soar like an eagle. As you rely upon the Lord's provision, He will enable you to run and not grow weary, to walk and not be faint.

Living the Christian life in a fallen world will include seasons of soaring, running, and walking. Your pace will fluctuate and your terrain will vary. The circumstances of life will change from moment to moment. The one constant feature in your life is the Person and Presence of your abiding Savior, Jesus. Anchor your life to the Rock of Ages.

FOCUSED DETERMINATION

"Jesus entered Jericho and was passing through. A man was there by the name of Zacchaeus; he was a chief tax collector and was wealthy. He wanted to see who Jesus was, but being a short man he could not, because of the crowd. So he ran ahead and climbed a sycamore-fig tree to see him, since Jesus was coming that way." Luke 19:1-4 (NIV)

On His way to Jerusalem, Jesus passed through Jericho. This city was one of the greatest taxation centers in Palestine and featured world-famous balsam groves, which perfumed the air for miles. On this particular day, something else was in the air. We meet a chief tax collector named Zacchaeus. He was at the top of the financial pyramid and had many tax collectors under him. Though Zacchaeus was big in wealth, he was little in stature.

Jesus was coming through town and Zacchaeus wanted to see Him. Unable to see over the crowd, Zacchaeus decided to climb a "seek-Him-more" tree, that is, a sycamore tree. Now he was up in the air at a level where he could see Jesus clearly. Zacchaeus was determined to see Jesus, even if it meant climbing a tree.

What motivated Zacchaeus to go to such an extreme to see Jesus? Had he already heard about Jesus healing the blind beggar on the edge of town (Luke 18:35-43)? Maybe Zacchaeus was searching for the true meaning of life and had not found it. Perhaps his income was not sufficient to meet the deepest need of his heart.

It is possible to lose your focus in this world filled with so many voices and allurements. There are countless distractions that dilute our devotion to the One who has given us life. Would you be willing to climb a tree if that is what it took to encounter the Lord? Are you making room for a daily, unhurried connect time with Jesus? Do you truly seek Him daily?

March 27
INFLUENCE YOUR WORLD

"When Jesus reached the spot, he looked up and said to him, 'Zacchaeus, come down immediately. I must stay at your house today.' So he came down at once and welcomed him gladly. All the people saw this and began to mutter, 'He has gone to be the guest of a "sinner."'" Luke 19:5-7 (NIV)

You have a choice. You can be a thermostat and set the environment or you can be a thermometer and reflect the environment. Jesus chose to be a thermostat. Jesus leveraged His influence to transform Zacchaeus and his family. Jesus was intentional about bringing life-change to this chief tax collector and his family.

The people criticized Jesus for His actions. We are introduced to this concept of muttering and grumbling in the Old Testament as the children of Israel grumbled against God, Moses, and Aaron (Ex 16:6-8). Jesus was willing to be misunderstood and criticized in order to bring eternal life to Zacchaeus and his family. Jesus was willing to endure opposition to present this family with the opportunity to be transformed by His love.

Will you influence your environment or be influenced by your environment? Will you become like those around you or will they become like you? It depends upon your decision to be a thermostat or a thermometer. God has placed you here to be salt and light to influence this decaying and dark world with the purity and the light of His love (Matt 5:13-16). God has planted you right where you are so that you can bloom for His glory and bring others into the kingdom of light.

Are you willing to be criticized for loving the unlovable? Are you willing to be misunderstood for extending grace to the despised and forgotten? Be a thermostat for the glory of God!

"But Zacchaeus stood up and said to the Lord, 'Look, Lord! Here and now I give half of my possessions to the poor, and if I have cheated anybody out of anything, I will pay back four times the amount.'" Luke 19:8 (NIV)

The fruit of conversion is a life of obedience. When you are genuinely converted from being a slave to sin to being a slave to righteousness, the evidence of that transformation shows up in your daily talk and walk (Rom 6:17-18). Salvation transforms your conversation and your conduct. From the moment of conversion, you embrace a lifestyle of working out what God has worked in (Phil 2:12).

Zacchaeus experienced authentic conversion. Upon placing his faith in Jesus alone for salvation, Zacchaeus had an immediate desire to make things right with those he wronged. His saving faith in Jesus was producing in him the appetite for living righteously. Convicted of his personal sin, Zacchaeus chose to give half of his possessions to the poor and to pay back four times the amount to those he cheated.

It is possible to profess Christ and not possess Christ. Is Christ in you? Do you have the Spirit of Christ (Rom 8:9)? In order to claim to live in Christ you must walk as Jesus did (I John 2:6). Possessing Christ is demonstrated through instant and perpetual obedience. To know Christ is to obey Christ.

Are you giving clear evidence of your salvation to those in your sphere of influence? Is there anyone you need to forgive? Is there anyone you need to extend an apology to? Are your horizontal relationships right and unbroken? Let others see Jesus in you!

March 29
IN THE WRONG PLACE

"Jesus said to him, 'Today salvation has come to this house, because this man, too, is a son of Abraham. For the Son of Man came to seek and to save what was lost.'" Luke 19:9-10 (NIV)

Zacchaeus demonstrated the same kind of faith that Abraham evidenced in the Old Testament when he was willing to sacrifice his only son. In response to Abraham's obedience, God provided a ram as a substitute (Gen 22:12-13). God provided salvation to Zacchaeus in response to his saving faith in Jesus. The divine appointment impacted his entire house. When Jesus shows up, everything changes.

After pronouncing that salvation had come to the home of Zacchaeus, Jesus clarified His life mission. Jesus came to seek and to save what was lost. In the language of the New Testament, the Greek word for lost literally means in the wrong place. The lost sheep was in the wrong place (Luke 15:4-7). The lost coin was in the wrong place (Luke 15:8-10). The prodigal son was in the wrong place (Luke 15:11-25). In our text here, Zacchaeus was in the wrong place.

Jesus came to seek and to save that which is in the wrong place. I remember when I was in the wrong place and Jesus came to my rescue. Perhaps you remember being in the wrong place and you remember how Jesus came to your rescue.

His mission is our mission. The reason Jesus came is the same reason you are alive. Jesus wants you to be on mission with Him to seek and to save those who are in the wrong place. You have the key to the right place. You know the One who gave His life so that you can know eternal life and be able to share that gift with others.

"Ascribe to the LORD the glory due his name; worship the LORD in the splendor of his holiness." Psalm 29:2 (NIV)

Don't worship your work! Let your work be an act of worship. You have a choice. You can treat worship as a noun or a verb. As a noun, worship becomes something you go to on Sunday mornings in a building incorrectly referred to as the church.

As a verb, worship becomes something you do twenty-four-seven-three-sixty-five. Worship becomes a lifestyle. Instead of going to church to worship, you become the church worshiping.

What would be different about your workplace if you embraced worship as a verb? What would be different about your attitude and actions related to work if you began to turn your work into an act of worship? The heart of God is moved by how you work just as much as how you express your worship to Him on Sunday mornings in the corporate worship setting.

Your work matters to God. Your workplace matters to God. Turning your work into an act of worship will be one of the most important decisions you will make on this side of eternity.

Allow your worship to be a witness at work. There are individuals who need to know the One you worship. Until they have a personal relationship with Jesus, they will not have the hope of Heaven and eternal life. Bring your worship with you to work.

March 31
AUTHENTICATE YOUR FAITH

"Was not our ancestor Abraham considered righteous for what he did when he offered his son Isaac on the altar? You see that his faith and his actions were working together, and his faith was made complete by what he did."
James 2:21-22 (NIV)

Doing life requires faith. As a follower of Jesus Christ, you are in the minority on this planet. You are doing life on the narrow path in the midst of a fallen world. Your beliefs will be challenged. Living the Christian life will be marked by opposition and resistance. However, your faith in Christ and His provision will be authenticated by your actions.

Are you putting feet to your faith? Are you allowing your faith to hit the pavement of real life in the real world? Abraham serves as a wonderful example of trusting in God's provision no matter the cost. He was willing to sacrifice his only son in order to be obedient to God. As you know, God came to the rescue in the fourth quarter with a few seconds left on the clock. God provided the substitute. Why did God allow Abraham to go through such a trying experience? God was testing Abraham's faith.

Do you fully trust God to do what He says He will do? Do you fully trust God to empower you to do life His way during your short stay upon the earth? God wants to reveal His glory in you and through you as you live out your faith. Allow your faith to be expressed to a watching world by your actions. As you are doing life, your faith will either attract others to Christ or distract them from Christ. Will your actions give evidence to your vibrant faith in God?

QUENCH YOUR THIRST

"Jesus answered her, 'If you knew the gift of God and who it is that asks you for a drink, you would have asked him and he would have given you living water.'"
John 4:10 (NIV)

A man was on the side of the road with the hood of his car propped open. Another man drove up, stopped behind the car, and stepped out to approach the scene. The stranger asked permission to take a look and then requested for the stranded driver to try the ignition. The car started and the driver shouted in relief. Then he asked the gracious man, "What is your name?"

The reply came gently, "My name is Henry Ford."

Can you imagine the creator of the Ford Model T being the very one who showed up at just the right time to repair the car he invented? Little did the woman at the well know, but the Creator of the universe was sitting right in front of her. Had she known what we know by reading the account, the woman at the well would have been asking Jesus for a drink of living water.

As a child of God, you have direct access to the Creator and Sustainer of life. You have access to the living water that Jesus made available to the woman at the well. Pray through the following Scripture:

> • *"We know also that the Son of God has come and has given us understanding, so that we may know him who is true. And we are in him who is true--even in his Son Jesus Christ. He is the true God and eternal life." 1 John 5:20 (NIV)*

Jesus is near. Now choose to draw near to Him. Allow His living water to quench your thirst.

April 2
SATISFACTION GUARANTEED

"Jesus answered, 'Everyone who drinks this water will be thirsty again, but whoever drinks the water I give him will never thirst. Indeed, the water I give him will become in him a spring of water welling up to eternal life.'"
John 4:13-14 (NIV)

Nothing in this life will satisfy like the water Jesus provides.

Water is essential for survival on planet earth. Our body needs water to function properly. Water quenches our physical thirst. However, there is a thirst that water cannot satisfy. There is a thirst that only Jesus can quench.

- *"He has made everything beautiful in its time. He has also set eternity in the hearts of men; yet they cannot fathom what God has done from beginning to end." Eccl 3:11 (NIV)*
- *"They will neither hunger nor thirst, nor will the desert heat or the sun beat upon them. He who has compassion on them will guide them and lead them beside springs of water." Isaiah 49:10 (NIV)*

God has placed eternity in our hearts. There is a longing that can only be satisfied by the living water that Jesus provides. In His compassion, God draws us to Himself.

God has made the gift of eternal life available to us. There is frustration in trying to share with others something you haven't received personally. Make certain that you have personally received God's gift of eternal life. Now seize opportunities that God gives you to share the gift of eternal life with others.

TRUE WORSHIP

"'Yet a time is coming and has now come when the true worshipers will worship the Father in spirit and truth, for they are the kind of worshipers the Father seeks. God is spirit, and his worshipers must worship in spirit and in truth.'"
John 4:23-24 (NIV)

In His interaction with the woman at the well, Jesus confronted the reality of her relational choices. She shifted the focus of their conversation from her personal life to the subject of religion. She expressed her views on worship. Her theology of worship centered on the place of worship rather than the purpose of worship.

Jesus defined true worshipers as those who worship the Father in spirit and truth. Religion is not sufficient to develop a person into a true worshiper. In fact, just as a flu shot will give you just enough of the flu to keep you from getting the real thing, religion can inoculate you from developing a vibrant love relationship with God. Religion, ritual, and routine are not adequate. Without a personal relationship with Jesus Christ, a person cannot become a true worshiper of the living God.

Are you the kind of worshiper the Father seeks? Do you worship in spirit and in truth? Do you go to church to worship or do you go to church worshiping?

April 4
RECOGNIZE GOD'S ACTIVITY

"Then Jesus declared, 'I who speak to you am he.'" John 4:26 (NIV)

You will find what you are looking for.

If you begin to look for the activity of God, you will find Him at work. God is always at work around us. His activity is constant. God's redemptive activity is immediate and global. God is working right now and God is working around the world.

Jesus had been in close proximity to the woman at the well and was willing to put His Jewish lips to her Samaritan cup. Jesus had uncovered her past and informed her religious understanding.

Sometimes we miss the redemptive activity of God because we are distracted by our personal preferences and prejudices. Often we try to conform God into our image instead of allowing Him to conform us to the image of Christ.

In prayer, ask God to heighten your sensitivity to His activity. You may want to begin each day by reading a few chapters from the Gospel of John. Spend time walking with Jesus in the pages of Scripture. Look to see how Jesus joined God in His activity.

SHARE YOUR TESTIMONY

"Many of the Samaritans from that town believed in him because of the woman's testimony, 'He told me everything I ever did.' So when the Samaritans came to him, they urged him to stay with them, and he stayed two days. And because of his words many more became believers." John 4:39-41 (NIV)

God uses human instrumentality in the redemptive process. There is nothing like the power of a changed life. When someone turns from sin and to Jesus for salvation, that transformed life touches other people. The Samaritans knew the shadowy past of the woman at the well. They were familiar with her lifestyle and most impacted by her transformation.

The woman at the well was willing to go back into her city to share her salvation story. She was willing to go back to her fellow Samaritans to share her testimony. The Lord Jesus had transformed her life and she was compelled to let her new life in Christ be an instrument to bring others to salvation.

> • *"They said to the woman, 'We no longer believe just because of what you said; now we have heard for ourselves, and we know that this man really is the Savior of the world.'" John 4:42 (NIV)*

Are you helping people come to know Christ? Are you sharing your personal testimony? Do your family members know your salvation story? Look for opportunities this week to share your testimony and watch how God uses your life to draw others to Christ.

April 6
IN CHRIST ALONE

"I can do everything through him who gives me strength." Philippians 4:13 (NIV)

Jesus has saved us to represent Him on the earth. He has instructed us to love our enemies, to pray for those who persecute us, to forgive our debtors, to judge not, to go the extra mile, and to fulfill the Great Commandment and the Great Commission.

- *"Love the Lord your God with all your heart and with all your soul and with all your mind and with all your strength.' The second is this: 'Love your neighbor as yourself.' There is no commandment greater than these."* Mark 12:30-31 (NIV)
- *"Therefore go and make disciples of all nations, baptizing them in the name of the Father and of the Son and of the Holy Spirit, and teaching them to obey everything I have commanded you. And surely I am with you always, to the very end of the age."* Matt 28:19-20 (NIV)

It is impossible to obey Christ's instructions without His power. Jesus does not expect us to obey Him without His enablement. The Christian life is a life of total dependency upon Jesus and His provision.

How did Paul accomplish so much in the Lord's service? Paul lived in full surrender to Christ and in total dependency upon Christ's strength.

Are you relying on Christ's strength? You can do everything Christ calls you to do in the strength He provides. God can accomplish more through your life in six minutes than you can accomplish on your own in sixty years. Will you be found faithful? Rely on the strength Christ provides.

Know God's Will

"For this reason, since the day we heard about you, we have not stopped praying for you and asking God to fill you with the knowledge of his will through all spiritual wisdom and understanding." Colossians 1:9 (NIV)

One of the most profound prayers you can pray for others is for them to know God and to do His will. Knowing and doing God's will is the purpose of life. God has provided the way in Jesus for us to know God personally and to obey His will completely.

The knowledge of God's will comes through spiritual wisdom and understanding. In his letter to the church at Corinth, Paul affirmed, "The man without the Spirit does not accept the things that come from the Spirit of God, for they are foolishness to him, and he cannot understand them, because they are spiritually discerned" (1 Cor 2:14 NIV). Spiritual discernment comes from the Spirit of God living inside of you. At the moment of conversion, you were filled with the Holy Spirit. He lives in you to teach you and to remind you of the things Jesus did and said (John 14:26).

Pray that others might be saturated with the knowledge of God's will. When you pray for others, ask God to give them spiritual wisdom and understanding. As they come to know God's will they will have the opportunity to choose to obey God's will. You will be involved in the process through the avenue of intercessory prayer. What a wise investment of your time!

Are you in the center of God's will? Have you asked God to fill you with the knowledge of His will? Are you willing to ask God for spiritual wisdom and understanding to know His will? Bring honor to God by obeying His will.

April 8
SHARE YOUR FAITH

"I pray that you may be active in sharing your faith, so that you will have a full understanding of every good thing we have in Christ." Philemon 1:6 (NIV)

Our participation in God's redemptive activity includes actively sharing our faith. We are commissioned by God and for God to share His redemptive love to all 12,500 people groups on this planet. God has saved us and set us free so that we can shine His light and share His love with every individual. God wants us to share our faith with those He brings into our path. God also wants us to build bridges to people we have never met in order to share our faith with them.

Are you willing to seize the opportunities that God gives you? Are you willing to go on a short term mission trip in order to share your faith in other cultures? Your home is your mission field. Your neighborhood is your mission field. Your school is your mission field. Your work place is your mission field. Everywhere you go is terrain that God wants you to claim for His glory.

How many people will be in Heaven because of you? Will your life impact the population of hell? Will your testimony impact the population of Heaven?

God has given you the gift of eternal life so that you can personally share that gift with others. Don't mute your testimony. Don't conceal your testimony. Instead, reveal to others what God has done in your life to bring you to the point of salvation and abundant life.

"So do not be ashamed to testify about our Lord, or ashamed of me his prisoner. But join with me in suffering for the gospel, by the power of God, who has saved us and called us to a holy life--not because of anything we have done but because of his own purpose and grace. This grace was given us in Christ Jesus before the beginning of time, but it has now been revealed through the appearing of our Savior, Christ Jesus, who has destroyed death and has brought life and immortality to light through the gospel." 2 Timothy 1:8-10 (NIV)

Paul modeled his testimony before his son in the ministry, Timothy. Paul was consumed by the gospel. The Good News of Jesus Christ had radically transformed Paul's life and he unashamedly bore witness to the saving grace of Jesus to a lost and dying world.

- *"I am not ashamed of the gospel, because it is the power of God for the salvation of everyone who believes: first for the Jew, then for the Gentile." Rom 1:16 (NIV)*
- *"And even if our gospel is veiled, it is veiled to those who are perishing." 2 Cor 4:3 (NIV)*

What is there to be ashamed about? Jesus has saved you and called you to a holy life by His own purpose and grace. Jesus has destroyed death and has brought forth life through His gospel. You are armed with the most powerful message on planet earth. The gospel impacts life in the now and the hereafter. God has given you an eternal message empowered by His eternal Spirit that brings forth eternal life to everyone who believes. You have been given the keys to unlock hell and open Heaven for every person who turns from their sin and to Jesus alone for salvation. Hallelujah! Praise the Lamb of God!

April 10
MOVE BEYOND COMPLACENCY

"One who was there had been an invalid for thirty-eight years. When Jesus saw him lying there and learned that he had been in this condition for a long time, he asked him, 'Do you want to get well?'" John 5:5-6 (NIV)

We know more than we are doing. We know that we are to eat right, exercise, and get plenty of rest in order to be healthy. We know that we are to give, save, pay bills, and pay taxes. We know that we are to make the most of every moment that God gives us. We know that we are to forgive others, to love others, to pray for others, to be considerate of others, and to serve others. Yet, we don't always do the things we know we are supposed to do.

Jesus asked a thirty-eight year old invalid if he wanted to get well. That question seems out of place. Why wouldn't a lame man want to walk? What would keep a person from wanting to experience healing? It is a matter of want. If you had the "want to" then you would find a "way to" be healed.

Sometimes we can become comfortable with our misery. The question is, "Do you want to get well?" Do you want to continue living like you are living? Do you want to continue to operate in your current reality?

Jesus is the answer to your situation. Are you obeying what you know? Have you responded to what He has already revealed to you?

INSTANT HEALING

"Then Jesus said to him, 'Get up! Pick up your mat and walk.' At once the man was cured; he picked up his mat and walked. The day on which this took place was a Sabbath, and so the Jews said to the man who had been healed, 'It is the Sabbath; the law forbids you to carry your mat.'" John 5:8-10 (NIV)

What brings you personal comfort? What do you long for each day? Maybe you desire to be rid of relational tension. Maybe your idea of comfort is being nestled behind a good book. Perhaps you long for the mornings when you are winding up or you long for the evenings when you are winding down. The environment that brings you comfort may be that of peace and quiet or laughter and passionate verbal interaction.

The invalid of 38 years received the comfort of instant healing when Jesus said to him, "Get up! Pick up your mat and walk." And "at once" that man was healed. There was no delay. After 38 years, the lame man's healing came instantly.

The comfort of his instant healing was strained by the poison of legalism. The Jews were unable to celebrate the miracle of this man's healing because they were so transfixed by the fact that Jesus healed this man on the Sabbath. Their legalism kept them from recognizing the Lord.

Legalism bypasses relationship. God has not saved you from your sin and sealed you by His Holy Spirit so that you will live in the bondage of legalism. In Christ, God has saved you so that you can walk in the freedom of your new identity in Christ.

April 12
RACE TO PLACE

"Do you not know that in a race all the runners run, but only one gets the prize? Run in such a way as to get the prize. Everyone who competes in the games goes into strict training. They do it to get a crown that will not last; but we do it to get a crown that will last forever. Therefore I do not run like a man running aimlessly; I do not fight like a man beating the air. No, I beat my body and make it my slave so that after I have preached to others, I myself will not be disqualified for the prize." 1 Corinthians 9:24-27 (NIV)

When I read this passage it reminds me of my experience of training for a 5k race. You may think that I meant that I was training for a marathon, but I was training for my first ever 5 kilometer race. I grew up racing motocross, bmx, and jet skis. But it wasn't until I was in my mid-thirties that I embraced the challenge of a running race. I discovered that the intensity level in the training phase has proportionate benefits to the racing phase. Training matters!

The Christian life is very similar to that of a race. Jesus calls us to run with purpose, focus, and intensity. We are to run in such a way as to get the prize. The focus of the Christian life is not comfort but change. As we diligently run the race set before us, Jesus transforms us into His image. Knowing that we are going to receive a crown that will last forever, we are to run this race with passion and laser focus. Our lives are to be marked by discipline and self-control.

There's more to this life than preparing for and running in a 5k. God has an assignment tailor made for you to fulfill. God will comfort you as you comfort others and as He changes you. Allow God to empower you for the race. Be committed to finish strong!

EYES ON THE PRIZE

"Not that I have already obtained all this, or have already been made perfect, but I press on to take hold of that for which Christ Jesus took hold of me. Brothers, I do not consider myself yet to have taken hold of it. But one thing I do: Forgetting what is behind and straining toward what is ahead, I press on toward the goal to win the prize for which God has called me heavenward in Christ Jesus."
Philippians 3:12-14 (NIV)

Don't get too comfortable with your level of intimacy with God and your level of spiritual maturity. There's more to explore! Don't get too comfortable with your current understanding of the Bible. There's more to explore!

One indication of Paul's spiritual maturity was his recognition of lack of spiritual maturity. Paul was not satisfied to coast down lazy river. Instead, he embraced the posture of leaning forward to become everything God had purposed for Paul to become. Paul never lost sight of the past God delivered him from, but he focused on the future in order to press on toward the goal to win the prize.

Remember who you are in Christ and where God has brought you from. Remember why Jesus died for you and why God raised Him from the dead. Remember that you have been adopted into God's family and filled by His Holy Spirit. Now forget what is behind. Strain toward what is ahead and press on! Keep your eyes on the prize! Keep your eyes on the prize! Keep your eyes on the prize!

April 14
PLEASING GOD

"And we pray this in order that you may live a life worthy of the Lord and may please him in every way: bearing fruit in every good work, growing in the knowledge of God, being strengthened with all power according to his glorious might so that you may have great endurance and patience, and joyfully giving thanks to the Father, who has qualified you to share in the inheritance of the saints in the kingdom of light." Colossians 1:10-12 (NIV)

As you invest your time, energy, and resources, consider what matters most. Does it matter how much you acquire during your brief stay on the earth? Does it matter how many trips you make to distant lands? Does it matter how many accolades you receive from others? If not, then what really matters?

The answer is: living a life worthy of the Lord and pleasing to Him. That's what matters most! Now you can give your life to that. You can wisely invest your time, resources, and energy to that ultimate pursuit. What does that look like? That kind of life involves bearing fruit, growing spiritually, operating in His power, enduring patiently, and giving thanks joyfully.

Take a personal inventory. What are you giving your life to? Are you living a life worthy of the Lord? Is your life laser focused on pleasing God? If not, why not?

Begin making adjustments in your time allocation, your energy allocation, and your allocation of resources to bring your life into alignment with God's priorities. It's not about comfort; it's all about life change!

"Josiah was eight years old when he became king, and he reigned in Jerusalem thirty-one years. He did what was right in the eyes of the LORD and walked in the ways of his father David, not turning aside to the right or to the left."
2 Chronicles 34:1-2 (NIV)

Be Teachable.

Can you imagine an eight year old child becoming the President of the United States of America? That's hard to fathom. Yet, in the sovereignty of God, Josiah became the king of Judah when he was the tender age of eight. God enabled Josiah to reign for thirty-one years.

How does an eight year old rule his kingdom? He doesn't by himself. Josiah surrounds himself with people who can help. Josiah becomes an effective king by being teachable. Josiah allows others to speak into his life.

You need four people in your life to help you reach your God-given potential. You need a "Paul" who will mentor you. You need a "Timothy" to invest your life in. You need a "Barnabas" to encourage you and to bring out the best in you. And you need a "Nathan" to speak the truth in love to you.

Are you teachable? Do you allow God to stretch you and mold you and grow you? Are you willing to allow others to get close enough to you in order to learn from them?

Ask God to bring a Paul, a Timothy, a Barnabas, and a Nathan into your life. Be willing to be a Paul, to be a Timothy, to be a Barnabas, and to be a Nathan in someone's life. Seek to add value to others.

April 16
BE THIRSTY

"In the eighth year of his reign, while he was still young, he began to seek the God of his father David." 2 Chronicles 34:3 (NIV)

Be thirsty.

What caused Josiah, at the age of sixteen, to begin to seek God? When you look at his family tree, you find that both his father, Amon, and his grandfather, Manasseh, did evil in the eyes of the Lord. It is obvious that Josiah did not receive his spiritual heritage from them. When you look into the life of his great-grandfather, Hezekiah, you find a much different portrait.

> • *"Hezekiah was twenty-five years old when he became king, and he reigned in Jerusalem twenty-nine years. His mother's name was Abijah daughter of Zechariah. He did what was right in the eyes of the LORD, just as his father David had done."*
> *2 Chron 29:1-2 (NIV)*

I wonder if Josiah was influenced by the godly life that his great-grandfather, Hezekiah, lived. Another possibility is that Josiah began to seek God when he became a daddy, at the age of sixteen, to Jehoahaz. For me personally, when I became a daddy, my understanding of God's love and my pursuit of God intensified.

Regardless of your age or life stage, assess your level of thirst for God? Are you passionately seeking God daily and allowing Him to have full access to your mind, emotions, and will? Is there anything or anyone you desire more than you desire God?

Make Jesus your top priority. Draw near to Him and He will draw near to you. Let Jesus quench your thirst!

BE TENDER

"Tell the king of Judah, who sent you to inquire of the LORD, 'This is what the LORD, the God of Israel, says concerning the words you heard: Because your heart was responsive and you humbled yourself before the LORD when you heard what I have spoken against this place and its people, that they would become accursed and laid waste, and because you tore your robes and wept in my presence, I have heard you, declares the LORD." 2 Kings 22:18-19 (NIV)

Be tender.

At the age of twenty-six, Josiah encountered the reading of the Book of the Law. Though he was a king, Josiah allowed the Word of the Lord to impact his life. Instead of seeking to get God's Word to conform to his life, Josiah conformed his life to the Word of God.

- *"But the one who received the seed that fell on good soil is the man who hears the word and understands it. He produces a crop, yielding a hundred, sixty, or thirty times what was sown."*
  Matt 13:23 (NIV)

Do you read the Bible? When you read the Bible, are you allowing God's Word to take root in your life? Are you tender towards God and sensitive to what He speaks into your life? Jesus wants us to move from being hearers of the Word only, to being doers of the Word.

Is your heart responsive to God's Word? How do you respond? Have you allowed God's Word to affect you emotionally and intellectually? Strive to have a consistent daily intake of God's Word. A healthy daily discipline is to read four chapters of the Bible each day. In one year, you will have read through the entire Bible.

April 18
BE TENACIOUS

"Josiah removed all the detestable idols from all the territory belonging to the Israelites, and he had all who were present in Israel serve the LORD their God. As long as he lived, they did not fail to follow the LORD, the God of their fathers."
2 Chronicles 34:33 (NIV)

Be tenacious.

God used Josiah to bring forth a reformation in Israel. Here are a few of the reformation verbs found in 2 Kings 22-23 and 2 Chronicles 34-35: removed, burned, did away with, took, ground it to powder, scattered, tore, desecrated, pulled down, smashed, cut down, covered, defiled, slaughtered, got rid of, purged, cut to pieces, broke to pieces, tore down, and crushed. Josiah was willing to tenaciously follow God's lead and remove all the detestable idols.

Like his great-grandfather, Hezekiah, Josiah cleansed the nation of idolatry, repaired the temple, restored the worship, and celebrated a great nationwide Passover. Josiah tenaciously renewed the Covenant and reformed the culture.

What is keeping you from reaching your God-given potential? What are you giving your life to? Where does your life give evidence of tenaciously following God's lead?

God placed you right where you are so that you could be an irresistible influence for God's glory. God allowed you to wake up this morning so that you could spread the aroma of Christ through your conversation and your conduct. God did not call you to reflect the environment, but to set the environment. God did not save you so that you would embrace the way of the world. God saved you so that you would tenaciously follow the way of Christ.

THE RIGHT CHOICE

"'Enter through the narrow gate. For wide is the gate and broad is the road that leads to destruction, and many enter through it. But small is the gate and narrow the road that leads to life, and only a few find it.'" Matthew 7:13-14 (NIV)

How do you enter through the narrow gate that only a few find? What does it take to get in on what God has already made available?

Let's take a look at three steps to entering through the narrow gate:

Step 1: Admit that you are a sinner.
- *"For all have sinned and fall short of the glory of God."*
  Rom 3:23 (NIV)

Step 2: Believe that Jesus is God's Son.
- *"For God so loved the world that he gave his one and only Son, that whoever believes in hims shall not perish but have eternal life."*
  John 3:16 (NIV)

Step 3: Confess Jesus as Lord of your life.
- *"That if you confess with your mouth, 'Jesus is Lord,' and believe in your heart that God raised him from the dead, you will be saved. For it is with your heart that you believe and are justified, and it is with your mouth that you confess and are saved."*
  Rom 10:9-10 (NIV)

God loves us enough to make a way for us to be reconciled to Him. In fact, there is only one way to be restored to a right relationship with God. Jesus is the only way!

April 20
DAILY DECISIONS

"So then, just as you received Christ Jesus as Lord, continue to live in him, rooted and built up in him, strengthened in the faith as you were taught, and overflowing with thankfulness." Colossians 2:6-7 (NIV)

Continue to live in Christ.

Your daily decisions determine what you become. If you want to become a fully devoted follower of Christ, then you must make daily decisions that will produce that reality. If you want to be physically fit, then you must make daily decisions that will produce that reality.

- *"For physical training is of some value, but godliness has value for all things, holding promise for both the present life and the life to come."* 1 Tim 4:8 (NIV)
- *"Then Jesus said to his disciples, 'If anyone would come after me, he must deny himself and take up his cross and follow me.'"* Matt 16:24 (NIV)

A decision to follow Jesus daily as Lord requires discipline and devotion. Becoming a fully devoted follower of Christ demands a daily death, a daily denial, and a daily determination. The daily decision to continue in the life of full surrender to Jesus reaps immediate and eternal benefits.

Your passion should be to be conformed to the image of Christ. Whatever is in your life that does not reflect Christ has no right occupying space in your life. Your daily decisions include deciding what you are going to give your allegiance to and what you are not going to give your allegiance to. Deciding to continue to live in Christ means to give Him first place in your life.

YOUR BEST LIFE

"Enter through the narrow gate. For wide is the gate and broad is the road that leads to destruction, and many enter through it. But small is the gate and narrow the road that leads to life, and only a few find it." Matthew 7:13-14 (NIV)

Your best life is not your life. Your best life is God's life for you.

Who created you? What is the purpose of your existence? Why are you where you are right now? God created you to fulfill His purposes and His plan. You are not an accident. You have been appointed by God to join Him in His redemptive activity. Every thought you have today matters. Every conversation you engage in today matters. Every interaction you initiate today matters. God has saved you by His grace, sealed you with His Holy Spirit, and set you apart to serve others for His glory.

You could not dream of a better life than the one that God has for you on the narrow road. The same road that leads to eternal life leads to abundant life. God does not save you so that you can experience life once you get to Heaven. God saves you so that you can have eternal security and abundant life now on the narrow road. Your best life is not your life. God's life for you is truly your best life. There is not a better option. The best option is always God's option. The best way is always God's way. The best path is always God's path.

Are you living the life God has for you? If not, why not? What adjustments do you need to make in order to live the life God has for you?

April 22
SWIMMING UPSTREAM

"Therefore Jesus said again, 'I tell you the truth, I am the gate for the sheep. All who ever came before me were thieves and robbers, but the sheep did not listen to them. I am the gate; whoever enters through me will be saved. He will come in and go out, and find pasture. The thief comes only to steal and kill and destroy; I have come that they may have life, and have it to the full.'" John 10:7-10 (NIV)

Living the Christian life is living with opposition.

Motion causes friction. When you choose to follow Jesus and move in the direction of the narrow path, you will face opposition. Living the Christian life is like swimming upstream. The cultural current will work against you.

When you received God's gift of eternal life by placing your faith in Jesus alone for salvation, you were adopted into God's family. God placed you positionally in Christ and thus you became a recipient of the abundant life that Jesus gives. Along the way, you will have to overcome obstacles. Living in a fallen world as a Christ-follower does not exempt you from spiritual warfare. The reality is that your devotion to Christ will stir up a response from your adversaries.

Resistance is part of growth. Just as there is no growth in weight training without resistance, there is no growth spiritually without resistance. Your faith must be formed. Without a test, there is no testimony. Opposition provides you with the friction necessary to sharpen the blade of your faith in God.

Can you identify some obstacles to abundant life that you are facing personally? Will you allow God to use those in your life to conform you into the image of Christ?

GRAVITATIONAL PULL

"I do not understand what I do. For what I want to do I do not do, but what I hate I do." Romans 7:15 (NIV)

Sometimes your greatest obstacle is you.

Paul gave us insight into the civil war within him. Though a seasoned believer and a mature follower of Jesus Christ, Paul wrestled with his old sin patterns. His flesh kept calling him back to the old ways. He experienced the gravitational pull of the flesh.

In the Old Testament, the children of Israel had witnessed the mighty acts of God. Think about it. They participated in the crossing of the Red Sea on dry ground. They ate manna from Heaven and drank water from the rock. Their shoes did not wear out after forty years of wandering in the wilderness. The opportunity to enter the Land of Promise, the land flowing with milk and honey, was right before them. Yet, they were unwilling to embrace God's abundant life for them. They wanted to go back to Egypt where they were slaves.

- *"I have been crucified with Christ and I no longer live, but Christ lives in me. The life I live in the body, I live by faith in the Son of God, who loved me and gave himself for me."* Gal 2:20 (NIV)

Paul demonstrated the discipline of being crucified with Christ. When your flesh wants to go back to the bondage of Egypt and fulfill the cravings of your sin nature, choose to crucify the flesh. Remember, whatever you feed grows and whatever you starve dies. Starve the flesh! Feed your love relationship with God! Nourish the life of Christ in you!

April 24
OVERCOMING OBSTACLES

"Do not love the world or anything in the world. If anyone loves the world, the love of the Father is not in him. For everything in the world--the cravings of sinful man, the lust of his eyes and the boasting of what he has and does--comes not from the Father but from the world." 1 John 2:15-16 (NIV)

One obstacle to abundant life is the flesh within you. Another obstacle to abundant life is the world around you. The world around you is opposed to the Jesus in you. The cultural current is anti-Christian. The world's values will not be in alignment with the values of the follower of Christ. The way of Jesus is counter-culture. You will likely be in the minority as you live out your faith in a fallen world.

- *"'I have told you these things, so that in me you may have peace. In this world you will have trouble. But take heart! I have overcome the world.'" John 16:33 (NIV)*
- *"Dear friends, I urge you, as aliens and strangers in the world, to abstain from sinful desires, which war against your soul."* 1 Pet 2:11 (NIV)

God has called you to influence the culture instead of allowing the culture to influence you. The abundant life that God gives is not found on the broad road that leads to destruction. His abundant life is found on the narrow road. Consider the environments that God has placed you in to influence for His glory. Are you overcoming the obstacles and seizing the opportunities to make Jesus known?

"Be self-controlled and alert. Your enemy the devil prowls around like a roaring lion looking for someone to devour." 1 Peter 5:8 (NIV)

The devil beneath you is another obstacle to abundant life. Satan's mission is to disrupt and to dismantle God's agenda. As a result, the enemy seeks to attack that which is closest to God's heart, namely, God's children. Whenever you are under attack, remember that as a child of God you are a threat to Satan. When you choose to walk in the way of Jesus, you show up on Satan's radar.

- *"And no wonder, for Satan himself masquerades as an angel of light." 2 Cor 11:14 (NIV)*
- *"For our struggle is not against flesh and blood, but against the rulers, against the authorities, against the powers of this dark world and against the spiritual forces of evil in the heavenly realms." Eph 6:12 (NIV)*

The life God has for you will be opposed. Satan does not want you to experience the abundant life God has for you. Some of Satan's tools are: discouragement, disillusionment, distractions, depression, doubt, and drifting. The enemy's goal is to get you to drift from God's best. Often, the devil will sprinkle allurements along the way to try to get you to take a short cut or to bypass your allegiance to Christ.

Be alert! Be aware! Stand firm! You are a soldier in the Lord's army!

April 26
STAND FIRM

"Be on your guard; stand firm in the faith; be men of courage; be strong."
1 Corinthians 16:13 (NIV)

Get on your toes and be aware, be alert, and be armed.

The devil is real. Spiritual warfare is a reality of the life God has for you. This is not a time to embrace spiritual apathy or lethargy. Choose to live in the opposition readiness mode. God has given you everything you need to reign victoriously in this life.

> • *"And pray in the Spirit on all occasions with all kinds of prayers and requests. With this in mind, be alert and always keep on praying for all the saints." Eph 6:18 (NIV)*

Get on your knees and pray.

Praying is like flying; when you stop you drop! Nothing will keep you standing like kneeling before the Lord. Prayer is your life-line. Prayer is your communication connection to the Commander-in-Chief.

> • *"Fight the good fight of the faith. Take hold of the eternal life to which you were called when you made your good confession in the presence of many witnesses." 1 Tim 6:12 (NIV)*

Get on your feet and fight.

Move from the posture of kneeling in prayer to that of standing to your feet to face the enemy. God has armed you for battle. Stand firm! Fight the good fight! You may lose some battles, but as a child of the King, you win the war!

ASSESS YOUR WORSHIP

"And God said, 'I will be with you. And this will be the sign to you that it is I who have brought the people out of Egypt, you will worship God on this mountain.'" Exodus 3:12 (NIV)

How's your worship? Is God the object of your affection and the recipient of your relentless pursuit? God wants you to worship Him and no other. God wants you to display your love and affection for Him both in private worship and in public worship.

Moses encountered God at the burning bush. This divine appointment was a life-changing experience for Moses. God provided Moses with the blessing of an Egyptian upbringing and now God is teaching Moses some things in the desert that he couldn't learn in the palace. God reveals Himself to Moses. Moses comes to know God in His holiness and righteousness. God instructs Moses to deliver the children of Israel out of Egyptian bondage and to bring them to the mountain to worship God corporately.

God demands our worship. God deserves our worship. Spend some time in private worshiping God for who He is. Express your love to God by praising Him. Make a commitment to take your private worship to church. Join other believers in public worship. Seek to express your love to God with fellow believers in worship just like you do in your private worship. God alone is worthy of your worship and your praise!

Assess your worship. Is your private worship consistent and persistent? Do you draw near to God? How's your public worship? Are you joining other believers in a weekly celebration of God's Presence? Do you give God your best in your expression of worship?

April 28
VICTORY AND SURRENDER

"Jesus replied, 'The hour has come for the Son of Man to be glorified.'"
John 12:23 (NIV)

Victory comes through surrender.

Our culture teaches you to take control of your life. Be the best! Give it your all! Get all you can! Be happy! Win at all costs! Reality shows have glamorized the self-centered life. The persistent themes suggest that your best life is all about you and what you can acquire during your short stay on this planet.

Jesus demonstrated the opposite pursuit. Jesus left it all in Heaven so that He could come to earth, live and die a sinless death, be resurrected on the third day, and ascend back to His Father in Heaven. Jesus came not to be served, but to serve. Jesus oriented His life around the centrality of bringing glory to God.

Jesus willingly put others first. He willingly endured the agony of crucifixion and looked to the resulting outcome of saving mankind and bringing glory to God.

Your best life is not your life! Victory comes through surrender. Are you willing to follow the example of Christ and place God's agenda first in your life? Are you willing to reflect honor to God? Live in such a way that those who know you, but don't know God, will come to know God because they know you!

DYING TO SELF

"'I tell you the truth, unless a kernel of wheat falls to the ground and dies, it remains only a single seed. But if it dies, it produces many seeds.'"
John 12:24 (NIV)

Are you dying to live? God has placed within you unlimited potential. God created you to share His love and to shine His light. Your life purpose is to bring glory to God. There's no higher calling and there's no greater commission to give your life to than that of bringing glory to God. Are you living the life God has given?

The seed must die. In order for the potential within the seed to be unleashed, the seed must die. Without death, the seed will not germinate. Growth and development are dependent upon the seed dying.

In the life of the believer, death to self is vital. The child of God must surrender his or her personal agenda, personal aspirations, and personal ambitions. Choosing to sacrifice your personal preferences in light of God's best for you is a crucial decision.

> • *"Then God said, 'Take your son, your only son, Isaac, whom you love, and go to the region of Moriah. Sacrifice him there as a burnt offering on one of the mountains I will tell you about.'"*
> Gen 22:2 (NIV)

Is there an "Isaac" in your life that God wants you to be willing to sacrifice? Is there something in your life that needs to die in order for you to live the life God has for you?

April 30
ATTITUDE OF SERVITUDE

"The man who loves his life will lose it, while the man who hates his life in this world will keep it for eternal life. Whoever serves me must follow me; and where I am, my servant also will be. My Father will honor the one who serves me."
John 12:25-26 (NIV)

Victory comes through surrender.

Why did you wake up this morning? What are you giving your life to today? Who are you living for? God is working all things together for His glory and for your good. Today matters! God desires to conform you into the image of Christ. Christlikeness does not come without your willingness to fully surrender your life to the Holy Spirit's control. As you choose to lose your life, the life of Christ becomes more evident in you.

Consider embracing the attitude of servitude. Allow Jesus to live His life in you and through you. There's room only for one to take the reins to your life. Will you give Jesus His rightful place in your life? You cannot live the life God has for you apart from Christ in you. Even on your best day, you will come up short of God's perfection.

- *"I have been crucified with Christ and I no longer live, but Christ lives in me. The life I live in the body, I live by faith in the Son of God, who loved me and gave himself for me." Gal 2:20 (NIV)*
- *"To them God has chosen to make known among the Gentiles the glorious riches of this mystery, which is Christ in you, the hope of glory." Col 1:27 (NIV)*

Live by faith in the Son of God. Christ is in you and He is the hope of glory. Surrender to the Lordship of Christ and continue to follow His lead. Victory in this life comes through daily surrender to the One who gave His life for you.

GOD'S POWER

"At the time of sacrifice, the prophet Elijah stepped forward and prayed: 'O LORD, God of Abraham, Isaac and Israel, let it be known today that you are God in Israel and that I am your servant and have done all these things at your command. Answer me, O LORD, answer me, so these people will know that you, O LORD, are God, and that you are turning their hearts back again.'"
1 Kings 18:36-37 (NIV)

When you hear the name Elijah, your first inclination is to think of the major victory he experienced on Mt. Carmel. Elijah took on the four hundred and fifty prophets of Baal and the four hundred prophets of Asherah, who ate at Jezebel's table. Elijah is kind of like the "Rocky Balboa" of the Old Testament. He was not about to back down from the featured match between good and evil.

- *"Then the fire of the LORD fell and burned up the sacrifice, the wood, the stones and the soil, and also licked up the water in the trench." 1 Kings 18:38 (NIV)*
- *"When all the people saw this, they fell prostrate and cried, 'The LORD--he is God! The LORD--he is God!'" 1 Kings 18:39 (NIV)*

What a major demonstration of God's power! What a miraculous response to Elijah's prayer! God allowed Elijah to see and experience God's favor. Elijah truly had a mountain top experience on Mt. Carmel. How could Elijah ever doubt God or deny God's power after such a magnificent encounter?

You are most susceptible to sin after a major victory.

May 2
LOSING PERSPECTIVE

"Now Ahab told Jezebel everything Elijah had done and how he had killed all the prophets with the sword. So Jezebel sent a messenger to Elijah to say, 'May the gods deal with me, be it ever so severely, if by this time tomorrow I do not make your life like that of one of them.'" 1 Kings 19:1-2 (NIV)

Loss of perspective leads to confusion.

Elijah confronted idolatry and the forces of evil with courage and boldness. He aggressively opposed the prophets of Baal and Asherah. Elijah was able to raise his hands in victory after the fire of God fell on Mt. Carmel to consume the sacrifice. The public victory had been won.

Privately, Elijah shifted from faith in God to fear of the wicked woman, Jezebel. Elijah confronted the prophets with utter courage and now is running for his life as a coward because of a threat from Jezebel. Elijah displayed confusion as a result of losing his perspective. He falls into deep depression.

What are some causes of depression? Frustration can lead to depression. Frustration over the circumstances you find yourself in can lead to depression. Sometimes frustration related to a strained relationship can cause depression. Fear can certainly bring you down into the pit of despair. When you stop viewing life through the eyes of faith and start viewing life through the eyes of fear, depression seeps in. Fatigue has a way of opening the door to depression. When you are exhausted, you can quickly lose perspective. Then, of course, there is the bandit of financial pressure. That kind of perpetual pressure can lead you down the alley of depression.

Do you currently have God's perspective on your life and on your circumstances? Have you experienced any level of depression in recent days? There's hope!

Proper Diet and Exercise

"Elijah was afraid and ran for his life. When he came to Beersheba in Judah, he left his servant there, while he himself went a day's journey into the desert. He came to a broom tree, sat down under it and prayed that he might die. 'I have had enough, LORD,' he said. 'Take my life; I am no better than my ancestors.'"
1 Kings 19:3-4 (NIV)

Have you ever reached a point in your life where you had just had enough? In our fast paced culture, it is easy to reach the breaking point. Frustration, fear, fatigue, and financial pressure along with other stress in life can lead you to the place of depression. When you are depressed, your resistance to the stress of life weakens and your ability to bounce back may be inhibited.

What did God do to bring relief to the depression Elijah was experiencing?

- *"Then he lay down under the tree and fell asleep. All at once an angel touched him and said, 'Get up and eat.' He looked around, and there by his head was a cake of bread baked over hot coals, and a jar of water. He ate and drank and then lay down again."*
  1 Kings 19:5-6 (NIV)

Your body requires refreshment. God has designed your body to operate effectively and efficiently with the proper consumption of healthy food. Food is fuel for your body. What kind of fuel are you putting into your body?

Elijah ate the food God provided for his refreshment. You could call it Angel food cake. Sometimes you may feel depressed simply because of a nutritional deficit. Start experiencing God's refreshment by eating properly and exercising consistently.

May 4
ENSURING PROPER REST

"Then he lay down under the tree and fell asleep. All at once an angel touched him and said, 'Get up and eat.' He looked around, and there by his head was a cake of bread baked over hot coals, and a jar of water. He ate and drank and then lay down again." 1 Kings 19:5-6 (NIV)

When Elijah reached the lowest point of his life and prayed that he might die, God provided Elijah with physical nourishment and rest.

You will spend one-third of your life sleeping. For your body to operate at maximum capacity, rest is a nonnegotiable. So how's your sleep? Do you feel rested when you awake each morning? Sleep deprivation will negatively affect your mood, your energy, and your stress level.

To help ease your mind at night, have a notepad and pen close to your bed so you can jot down the items that are bothering you. Instead of counting sheep, talk to the Shepherd. Pray through whatever you are worrying about and anything that God brings to your mind. When your mind is at peace, your rest will be sweet.

Your pillow, mattress, sheets, and comforter do impact how well you sleep. If your room is too bright, you may want to think of ways to make your room darker. Another tip is to locate your alarm clock away from your face and place it across the room. If total silence helps you sleep better, then eliminate noise. If soft music helps you relax and fall asleep, then turn on the music.

God wants you to take care of your body, which is the temple of the Holy Spirit. Therefore, do whatever it takes to ensure a good night's rest. When you are well rested, you will feel the difference and you will have more energy to live for God's glory.

GROW THROUGH DEPRESSION

"The LORD said, 'Go out and stand on the mountain in the presence of the LORD, for the LORD is about to pass by.' Then a great and powerful wind tore the mountains apart and shattered the rocks before the LORD, but the LORD was not in the wind. After the wind there was an earthquake, but the LORD was not in the earthquake. After the earthquake came a fire, but the LORD was not in the fire. And after the fire came a gentle whisper." 1 Kings 19:11-12 (NIV)

God's revelation and relationships are antidotes to depression.

God has chosen to reveal Himself to us through His Word. As you read the Bible, you discover God's purpose and plan for your life. The ultimate revelation of God is His Son, Jesus. Jesus is God incarnate. Jesus became flesh, lived a sinless life, and died to purchase our salvation. God's Word is nourishment for your soul.

God has provided the way for us to walk in relationship with Himself and to walk in relationship with other believers. God revealed Himself to Elijah as a gentle whisper. God wanted to teach Elijah to be sensitive to His abiding Presence.

Elijah had chosen to leave his servant. As a result, his depression escalated in proportion to his isolation. One of Satan's most effective tools is that of isolation. He wants to remove you from relationships because God designed you for relationships. In fact, the first "not good" in the Bible is where God said that it was not good for man to be alone.

What are you currently doing for refreshment? What adjustments do you need to make in order to get more rest? Are you having a consistent intake of God's Word? Do you have a life-giving friend? Ask God to help you in these four specific areas to help you grow through depression.

May 6
TRUST GOD

"Do not let your hearts be troubled. Trust in God ; trust also in me."
John 14:1 (NIV)

God designed you for eternity.

Everybody will live somewhere forever. As Bruce Wilkinson says, "Your beliefs determine where you will spend eternity; your behavior determines how you will spend eternity." When you choose to live the life God has given, you experience abundant life on earth and you enjoy the reality of eternal life in Heaven. In this earthly existence, you live on a broken planet with the presence of sin. As a result, problems become part of the landscape of life.

The disciples were troubled as Jesus revealed the reality of His imminent death.

> • *"It was just before the Passover Feast. Jesus knew that the time had come for him to leave this world and go to the Father. Having loved his own who were in the world, he now showed them the full extent of his love." John 13:1 (NIV)*

As you can imagine, the disciples were grieving. Jesus offered them words of comfort by exhorting them to trust in God. They could trust God's timing and they could trust God's plan. Jesus included the appeal for the disciples to trust in Himself. Jesus had faithfully walked with them and taught them. The disciples had come to know Jesus in close proximity. Now they would have to trust in Jesus as He submitted to death on the cross.

Trust in God to do what He has promised. God keeps His word. God has provided the resolution for the problem of sin. Trust God to carry you through this life into the life to come.

GOD'S COMFORT

"No one will be able to stand up against you all the days of your life. As I was with Moses, so I will be with you; I will never leave you nor forsake you." Joshua 1:5 (NIV)

God's Presence brings comfort.

You will never go through anything that Jesus hasn't already endured on your behalf. Jesus knows grief, suffering, rejection, humiliation, betrayal, loneliness, and death on a first name basis. Yet, Jesus reigns in victory. If you will allow Jesus to reign in your life, you will reign in victory.

- *"For to me, to live is Christ and to die is gain."* Phil 1:21 (NIV)
- *"To him who is able to keep you from falling and to present you before his glorious presence without fault and with great joy--to the only God our Savior be glory, majesty, power and authority, through Jesus Christ our Lord, before all ages, now and forevermore! Amen."* Jude 1:24-25 (NIV)

Joshua, Paul, and Jude can testify with clarity and confidence that God's Presence sustains you while you live the life God has given on this earth. While you wait for your glorified body and your glorious reunion with Jesus and your loved ones in Heaven, God's abiding Presence enables you to endure the hard seasons of life.

What's troubling you today? Is there anything causing you to lose sleep or to agonize in the sea of worry? Has fear darkened your vision or diffused your passion? Surrender every fiber of your being to the Lord right now in prayer. Invite God to make His Presence known in your life.

May 8
YOUR ETERNAL HOME

"In my Father's house are many rooms; if it were not so, I would have told you. I am going there to prepare a place for you." John 14:2 (NIV)

Heaven is a place you can call home.

When Jesus spoke these words of comfort to His disciples, He affirmed the reality of Heaven and the specific rooms, mansions, or abodes in Heaven. Jesus was not going to build what was already in Heaven. Rather, Jesus was indicating that He was preparing a place for them and us in Heaven by going to the cross to pay the penalty of their sin and our sin.

- *"The Son is the radiance of God's glory and the exact representation of his being, sustaining all things by his powerful word. After he had provided purification for sins, he sat down at the right hand of the Majesty in heaven." Heb 1:3 (NIV)*
- *"But our citizenship is in heaven. And we eagerly await a Savior from there, the Lord Jesus Christ, who, by the power that enables him to bring everything under his control, will transform our lowly bodies so that they will be like his glorious body." Phil 3:20-21 (NIV)*

Jesus has prepared a place for you in Heaven by becoming the atoning sacrifice for your sin. Jesus has purchased your salvation with His death, burial, resurrection, and ascension. As a result, your citizenship is in Heaven. You are an alien on this earth. God made you not for time, but for eternity.

Don't get discouraged. Don't lose hope. Don't get too enamored by this life on planet earth. You aren't home yet. Heaven is your home!

READY FOR THE RAPTURE

"'And if I go and prepare a place for you, I will come back and take you to be with me that you also may be where I am.'" John 14:3 (NIV)

God has so much more in store for you than what you have currently in view. There's so much more on the other shore. God is growing you and grooming you in this life in preparation for the life to come. God's nature is that of integrity. God keeps His word. He is the real Promise Keeper.

As a follower of Christ, you will go to Heaven either through the doorway of death or the reality of the rapture. You will either go to Jesus upon your death or Jesus will come to you via the rapture of the church.

- *"Jesus answered him, 'I tell you the truth, today you will be with me in paradise.'" Luke 23:43 (NIV)*
- *"For the Lord himself will come down from heaven, with a loud command, with the voice of the archangel and with the trumpet call of God, and the dead in Christ will rise first. After that, we who are still alive and are left will be caught up together with them in the clouds to meet the Lord in the air. And so we will be with the Lord forever." 1 Thess 4:16-17 (NIV)*

You will experience the ultimate reunion with Christ and your believing loved ones who have gone before you. The ultimate trade-in will occur as you trade-in your current body for the glorified body that God has for you. There will be no more cancer, no more arthritis, no more heart disease, no more diabetes, no more multiple sclerosis, no more Alzheimer's, no more macular degeneration, no more mosquitoes, and no more humidity.

Are you ready for Jesus to come back?

May 10
THE ONLY WAY

"Jesus answered, 'I am the way and the truth and the life. No one comes to the Father except through me.'" John 14:6 (NIV)

There's only one way.

I have often heard people comment that we are all heading to the same place and that we are just taking different paths to get there. All paths do not lead to Heaven. There is only one path to Heaven. There is only one way to get to Heaven. It's not arrogant to say that Jesus is the only way. Actually, it is arrogant to say that there's another way. Jesus is the only way.

- *"'Salvation is found in no one else, for there is no other name under heaven given to men by which we must be saved.'" Acts 4:12 (NIV)*
- *"But these are written that you may believe that Jesus is the Christ, the Son of God, and that by believing you may have life in his name." John 20:31 (NIV)*

On March 28, 1979, I embraced Jesus as the way and the truth and the life by confessing my sin and inviting Jesus to take over my life. I surrendered to His Lordship and have sought to become more like Jesus day by day. I have the assurance of Heaven and eternal life, not because of who I am, but because of who He is. Long before I decided what to do with God, He decided what to do with me.

What's your decision? Have you had a life changing experience? Do you know for certain that if you were to die tonight that you would go to Heaven? If the rapture were to happen within the hour, are you ready? Are you rapture ready?

Her Children Arise

"Her children arise and call her blessed; her husband also, and he praises her: 'Many women do noble things, but you surpass them all.'"Proverbs 31:28-29 (NIV)

What a treasure to be surrounded by godly women: my wife, my mother, my mother-in-law, my mamaw, and my mawmaw! These five women in my immediate sphere of influence have modeled Jesus faithfully and served Him consistently. I see them in Scripture through the lives of Hannah, Lois, Eunice, Lydia, and Ruth.

- *"In bitterness of soul Hannah wept much and prayed to the LORD. And she made a vow, saying, 'O LORD Almighty, if you will only look upon your servant's misery and remember me, and not forget your servant but give her a son, then I will give him to the LORD for all the days of his life, and no razor will ever be used on his head.'" 1 Sam 1:10-11 (NIV)*
- *"I have been reminded of your sincere faith, which first lived in your grandmother Lois and in your mother Eunice and, I am persuaded, now lives in you also." 2 Tim 1:5 (NIV)*
- *"One of those listening was a woman named Lydia, a dealer in purple cloth from the city of Thyatira, who was a worshiper of God. The Lord opened her heart to respond to Paul's message." Acts 16:14-15 (NIV)*
- *"But Ruth replied, 'Don't urge me to leave you or to turn back from you. Where you go I will go, and where you stay I will stay. Your people will be my people and your God my God.'" Ruth 1:16 (NIV)*

Spend some time in prayer thanking God for the godly women that He has placed in your life. Some of them may have already gone to Heaven. It would still be proper to thank God for them and for their influence in your life that continues even after their departure.

May 12
SINCERE FAITH

"I have been reminded of your sincere faith, which first lived in your grandmother Lois and in your mother Eunice and, I am persuaded, now lives in you also."
2 Timothy 1:5 (NIV)

Would those who know you best say that you have a sincere faith? Is your faith genuine? Are you the real deal? If so, then how do you impart that kind of faith to those in your sphere of influence?

Paul affirmed Timothy for his faith. Without hesitation, Paul traced Timothy's sincere faith through both Timothy's mother and grandmother. Timothy was the recipient of seeing faith in action in a tangible form through the lifestyles exhibited by his mother and grandmother. They made their faith a daily priority. Each day Timothy examined the sincere faith that lived in his mother and grandmother. Now, Paul identifies that sincere faith in Timothy.

Are you imparting your sincere faith to others? Think about the spheres of influence that God has entrusted to your care. The environments may include home, school, work, athletics, recreation, church, and traveling. Your sphere of influence may include children. Is faith a daily priority in your life? Is your faith evident to those in your sphere of influence?

God brings people into your life so that you can influence them for His glory. What are you doing with the faith God has given you? Make faith a daily priority.

MODEL YOUR FAITH

"Don't let anyone look down on you because you are young, but set an example for the believers in speech, in life, in love, in faith and in purity."
1 Timothy 4:12 (NIV)

Did you know that you will multiply what you model? Now that is convicting! That means that it truly does matter how you live your life. It truly matters how you conduct your daily living. Your beliefs and your behavior both matter to God and impact others. So how do you impart your sincere faith to others?

Maybe you have heard parents remark that they want you to do as they say and not as they do. Of course, you would define that behavior as hypocrisy. God wants us to live in such a way that we encourage others to do as we say and as we do. We are to strive to live in such a way that the way we live lines up with what we say.

What kind of faith does God want you to model? God wants you to model sincere faith. God wants you to set an example for others to follow. In other words, be a model to follow. Model the kind of life that draws others to Christ. Live the kind of life that models the fruit of the Spirit: love, joy, peace, patience, kindness, goodness, faithfulness, gentleness, and self-control.

What are you multiplying? You know the answer: whatever you are modeling. Model what you want to multiply. May the whole earth be filled with fully devoted followers of Christ as a result of the sincere faith that you are modeling. Model sincere faith before others.

May 14
PROTECT THE FAITH

"What you heard from me, keep as the pattern of sound teaching, with faith and love in Christ Jesus. Guard the good deposit that was entrusted to you--guard it with the help of the Holy Spirit who lives in us." 2 Timothy 1:13-14 (NIV)

As you seek to impart your sincere faith, expect opposition. As a follower of Jesus Christ, you will be a threat to Satan and his agenda.

Your faith is worth fighting for. The faith of your family is worth fighting for. As you impart your faith to those in your sphere of influence, you will be impacting their lives for time and eternity. Because of the value God places on your sincere faith, Satan seeks to distract you.

- *"The Spirit clearly says that in later times some will abandon the faith and follow deceiving spirits and things taught by demons." 1 Tim 4:1 (NIV)*
- *"But mark this: There will be terrible times in the last days. People will be lovers of themselves, lovers of money, boastful, proud, abusive, disobedient to their parents, ungrateful, unholy, without love, unforgiving, slanderous, without self-control, brutal, not lovers of the good, treacherous, rash, conceited, lovers of pleasure rather than lovers of God--having a form of godliness but denying its power. Have nothing to do with them." 2 Tim 3:1-5 (NIV)*

Protect the faith God has given you.

INHERIT THE FAITH

"Children, obey your parents in the Lord, for this is right." Ephesians 6:1 (NIV)

Are your parents still alive? Have you inherited their faith? Maybe they modeled sincere faith before you consistently or maybe they did not make those kinds of deposits in your life. It could be that one of your parents faithfully handed down the faith while the other parent failed to maximize that opportunity.

As children, we are to obey our parents. God has given them the responsibility to model His love and His character before us. God has given them the privilege of knowing Him personally and making Him known relationally.

As children, we have the privilege of inheriting the faith. Our responsibility is to pay attention, listen, and obey. We don't get to Heaven by living vicariously through the faith of our parents. We must have a personal experience with God by confessing our sin and trusting in Jesus alone for salvation. Yet, the faith of our parents can be inherited as they model their sincere faith before us.

Assess your upbringing. What was your home life like? What part did faith play in your upbringing? Did you grow up in a home where Christ was honored and faith was a natural part of everyday life? Or, were you reared in an environment where sincere faith was invisible?

The good news is that you can learn from the deposits your parents made in your life. You can benefit from the presence of sincere faith or from the absence of sincere faith. You can choose to replicate in your life now the faith they demonstrated back then. Or you can choose to elevate a sincere faith that was absent in your upbringing. God can take you to a new level! Stay close to Him!

May 16
LEARN FROM YOUR PARENTS

"Honor your father and mother'--which is the first commandment with a promise--'that it may go well with you and that you may enjoy long life on the earth.'" Ephesians 6:2-3 (NIV)

One way to honor your parents is to learn what they know. Recently I visited my dad on the front porch of the nursing home where he resides. My parents have been divorced for over thirty years now. The beauty of the visit was the fact that my mom went with me to see my dad. It was very interesting and meaningful at the same time. One of the highlights of our visit took place when I asked my dad to tell about his upbringing and eventual marriage to my mom. I asked him to help me understand what caused him to take his first drink of alcohol and to help me understand what led him down the path to becoming an alcoholic.

Some of the most powerful lessons I have learned in life have come from being reared in a single-parent family since age seven. For me to fail to learn what my parents know would be cheating myself valuable life lessons that could enrich my life. It would be like swimming over an exotic reef without a snorkel and fins to capture the essence of aquatic life beneath the surface.

Learn what your parents know. Commit to grow by seeking to know. God has allowed your parents to live life years in advance of you so that you can benefit from their experience. You can honor your parents by learning what they know. Glean all you can from their faith journey. Your sincere faith always has room to grow.

"But as for you, continue in what you have learned and have become convinced of, because you know those from whom you learned it, and how from infancy you have known the holy Scriptures, which are able to make you wise for salvation through faith in Christ Jesus." 2 Timothy 3:14-15 (NIV)

Financial prosperity may not travel through your family tree, yet sincere faith can. Consider what your parents have left you in the realm of faith. What did they model before you as a child? How did they impart sincere faith throughout your upbringing? Were they instrumental in developing your appetite for reading God's Word? Did God use them to strengthen your prayer life and to fortify your faith in God?

Whatever your parents have left you in the realm of faith, make good on it. Maximize what you have been given. Standing on their shoulders, your sincere faith can grow and even multiply through the relationships in your sphere of influence.

Paul instructed Timothy to continue in what he had learned from the holy Scriptures. God's Word is your best teacher. If your parents pointed you to God's Word and demonstrated an abiding love for His Word, you are blessed. If your parents did not hand down that kind of passion for God's Word, don't allow their neglect to immobilize you. Commit to feeding your appetite for reading the Bible and choose to impart that lifestyle to others.

What are you doing with what you have been given? Eliminate excuses and embrace daily spiritual disciplines that will enhance your walk with God and impact others for God's glory. One of the most powerful investments in your day is the investment of time you allocate to reading the Bible.

May 18
Develop Sincere Faith

"The goal of this command is love, which comes from a pure heart and a good conscience and a sincere faith." 1 Timothy 1:5 (NIV)

Your reputation is based on what others say about you. Your character is based on what you really are when no one is looking. Nothing neutralizes your witness faster than hypocrisy. In reality, you can fool people by projecting a persona that does not line up with the reality of your personal character. However, God sees the unseen and knows the unknown.

Paul exhorted Timothy to operate in love from a heart that is pure, a conscience that is well informed, and a faith that is sincere. The value of a sincere faith is immeasurable.

Are you for real? Does your public life line up with your private life? Is your faith sincere? God knows the real you. God sees the sincerity of your faith.

- *"Search me, O God, and know my heart; test me and know my anxious thoughts. See if there is any offensive way in me, and lead me in the way everlasting." Psalm 139:23-24 (NIV)*
- *"All a man's ways seem innocent to him, but motives are weighed by the LORD." Prov 16:2 (NIV)*

Comparing yourself to others will not add value to your pursuit of becoming like Christ. Allow Jesus to be your standard for measurement. Confess any attitudes or actions that distract and damage your relentless pursuit of Christlikeness. Be willing to pray a dangerous prayer asking God to search your heart. Ask God to reveal anything in your life that brings Him displeasure.

A sincere faith is worth finding and worth following.

PRAY FOR YOUR PASTOR

"Devote yourselves to prayer, being watchful and thankful. And pray for us, too, that God may open a door for our message, so that we may proclaim the mystery of Christ, for which I am in chains. Pray that I may proclaim it clearly, as I should." Colossians 4:2-4 (NIV)

Do you ever pray for your pastor? If so, what exactly are you praying for? How do you pray for your pastor? What are his needs? Of course, your pastor has the same basic needs that you have. He has a need to be loved, accepted, and useful. Let's go beyond the basics and look inside your pastor's life on a positional level. In his role as pastor, how can you best pray for him?

As you devote yourself to prayer, being watchful and thankful, pray to God for an open door for your pastor's message. Pray that God will give your pastor opportunities to deliver God's message. Ask God to tear down walls of division and to build bridges of connection to enable your pastor to speak forth God's Word.

Where there is an opportunity for your pastor to deliver God's message, you can anticipate opposition. Satan does not want your pastor to preach the gospel. You can combat the spiritual forces of evil through prayer on behalf of your pastor. You can conduct warfare prayer for your pastor. Pray that he will preach with clarity. Pray that your pastor's message will spread rapidly and be honored. Pray to God for your pastor that he will make known the mystery of the gospel and to declare it fearlessly.

Why pray for your pastor? Pray for your pastor in order to create opportunities for the Lord's message to be heard and to combat opposition in the spirit realm. Pause right now to pray for your pastor by name.

WHEN YOU HAVE THE SON

"And this is the testimony: God has given us eternal life, and this life is in his Son. He who has the Son has life; he who does not have the Son of God does not have life. I write these things to you who believe in the name of the Son of God so that you may know that you have eternal life." 1 John 5:11-13 (NIV)

To have a dynamic worship experience, you must have a personal encounter. Do you have the Son? If you have the Son, then you have eternal life. So, how do you get the Son? The Bible teaches that belief in the completed work of Jesus on the cross is essential for salvation.

> • *"Though you have not seen him, you love him; and even though you do not see him now, you believe in him and are filled with an inexpressible and glorious joy, for you are receiving the goal of your faith, the salvation of your souls." 1 Pet 1:8-9 (NIV)*

Do you believe in the Person and work of Jesus on the cross? Jesus paid full price for your salvation so that you can know Him personally and eternally. Once you have a personal love relationship with Jesus, you have the wonderful privilege of worshiping Him. Express your love to Jesus in worship for who He is and for what He has done. Your personal encounter with Christ at salvation opens the door for you to experience the dynamic worship of Christ. Express your worship to God for sending Jesus to your rescue.

Rejoice in the personal encounter with Christ that changed your forever! Eternity in Heaven is your reality. Abundant life on earth is your blessing in Christ. Bring your worship of Him to Him! Jesus is worthy!

STAY CONNECTED

"Remain in me, and I will remain in you. No branch can bear fruit by itself; it must remain in the vine. Neither can you bear fruit unless you remain in me."
John 15:4 (NIV)

To nurture an abiding relationship with Christ involves a daily experience. Your private worship is vital to having an ongoing vibrant love relationship with Christ. Are you growing in your daily intimacy with God? It takes time to develop intimacy. You may say that you just don't have enough time to fit private worship into your schedule. The reality is that we make space for that which we value. Do you value intimacy with God? Are you willing to plan for and prepare for a daily experience with God?

If you go on a business trip or on a family vacation, you prepare for it. If you are anticipating a major exam in school or fulfilling a commitment to teach a small group Bible study, you prepare for it. The same is true in our daily walk with God. To have a meaningful and productive daily experience with God, you treat it as something you value and treasure. You prepare for your daily intimacy with God.

If my private worship time alone with God is important, then how should I prepare for it? Select a time each day when you are at your best. Find a physical location that enhances your experience with God. If you enjoy nature, then plan to have your quiet time outdoors. If you enjoy soft music playing as you spend time with God, then have the music ready for the moment. If you prefer solitude, then search for that room or closet or other environment that will provide that kind of atmosphere. Have a Bible reading plan in place whether it is to read through the Bible in one year, read one chapter, or read a few verses each day. Choose to jot down insights gleaned from your reading time. Reflect on what God is saying to you. Spend time in prayer sharing your heart with God and listening for His voice.

May 22
BRING YOUR WORSHIP

"Let us hold unswervingly to the hope we profess, for he who promised is faithful. And let us consider how we may spur one another on toward love and good deeds. Let us not give up meeting together, as some are in the habit of doing, but let us encourage one another--and all the more as you see the Day approaching." Hebrews 10:23-25 (NIV)

God desires a common expression of our worship to Him. You were made to worship God. Your private worship nurtures and expresses your abiding relationship with Christ. Your public worship with other believers is the common expression of worship. God is not looking for every believer to express worship the exact same way. God wants you to express your worship to Him based on your unique personality and temperament.

What does your public worship look like? How do you express your love to God in worship during a public gathering of believers? Are you reserved or outwardly expressive? Do you use physical gestures such as raising your hands in surrender or standing or kneeling? Does your corporate worship environment help you connect with God in worship or does it inhibit your worship?

I have often heard that you are not to come to church to worship, but to come to church worshiping. The corporate worship experience should be an outflow of your daily private worship experiences. The question then becomes: Are you bringing your worship to church?

Spend some time assessing the difference between your private and public worship. When do you feel most connected to God? When do you sense the most freedom and the most passion in expressing your love to God in worship? Maybe a worthy goal would be to bring your public worship up to where your private worship is or to bring your private worship up to where your public worship is depending on which one is more engaging.

"Let the word of Christ dwell in you richly as you teach and admonish one another with all wisdom, and as you sing psalms, hymns and spiritual songs with gratitude in your hearts to God." Colossians 3:16 (NIV)

Is God's Word at home in your heart? Your intake of God's Word will determine your level of living on mission with God. The primary tool of revelation that God uses for His children is the Bible. God reveals Himself through His Word. You can read the Bible. You can listen to the Bible. You can sit under the preaching and teaching of God's Word.

> • *"How, then, can they call on the one they have not believed in? And how can they believe in the one of whom they have not heard? And how can they hear without someone preaching to them? And how can they preach unless they are sent? As it is written, 'How beautiful are the feet of those who bring good news!'"*
> Rom 10:14-15 (NIV)

Your worship includes the intentional intake of God's Word. God has appointed and anointed pastors and teachers to communicate His Word in a creative and compelling way. Are you currently sitting under that kind of preaching and teaching? God speaks through human instrumentality.

There are many options out there. Make certain that you are connected to a Bible centered and Christ honoring local fellowship of believers led by a God fearing pastor. Don't compromise on this one. Be sure to find anointed Bible teachers to help you grow in your understanding and application of God's Word. Make room in your heart for God's Word!

May 24
LEVELS OF RECEPTIVITY

"But the one who received the seed that fell on good soil is the man who hears the word and understands it. He produces a crop, yielding a hundred, sixty or thirty times what was sown." Matthew 13:23 (NIV)

Have you noticed how you can read the Bible during a given season that you are in and then read the same passage of Scripture at another season of life and get something radically different from the very same passage? It has so much to do with your level of receptivity. I have noticed in my own life that when I am going through a season of brokenness, God's Word captures my heart at a different level. When I am longing for God's comfort, the Book of Psalm comes alive for me. When I am in need of direction and insight for a decision I need to make, Proverbs just delivers with clarity. If I am simply wanting to become more like Christ in how I treat others, reading the Gospels develops in me a new perspective on viewing others through the eyes of Christ.

The condition of your heart directly affects the level of revelation that takes root in your life. When your heart resembles the hard path, the thorny ground, or the rocky ground, your level of receptivity to God's Word diminishes exponentially.

Here's the good news: your heart can resemble good soil. Your heart can be tender and receptive to God's Word and yield a hundred, sixty, or thirty times what was sown. Your intake of God's Word can be beneficial, productive, and life changing if the condition of your heart is right.

HEART CONDITION

"Come near to God and he will come near to you. Wash your hands, you sinners, and purify your hearts, you double-minded." James 4:8 (NIV)

The condition of your heart before God affects your private and public worship. If you want to have a high level of receptivity to God's Word, your heart must be right before God. Sin will harden your heart towards God. Sin will hinder your capacity to hear from God.

> • *"The Lord says: 'These people come near to me with their mouth and honor me with their lips, but their hearts are far from me. Their worship of me is made up only of rules taught by men.'"*
> *Isaiah 29:13 (NIV)*

Keep your heart clean before God. Stay tender. Be teachable. Maintain purity in your thought life. Consistently confess known sin and live a life of moral purity. Surrender daily to the Lordship of Christ and do not give the devil a foothold in your life. At all costs, do not grieve or quench the Holy Spirit. Ask God to enable you to demonstrate a life of character and integrity. Crucify the flesh. Make no provision for the flesh. Keep your life in check. Weed the flowerbed of your life.

Sounds like a commitment to perpetual care doesn't it? Sin will create an immense deficit in bringing your worship to God. In fact, sin can easily become your worship. Guard your heart! Consecrate yourself before God and allow the light of His holiness to identify areas of your life that need to be surrendered.

Bring your worship of God to God with a heart of purity!

May 26
ASK THE RIGHT QUESTION

"Let the word of Christ dwell in you richly as you teach and admonish one another with all wisdom, and as you sing psalms, hymns and spiritual songs with gratitude in your hearts to God." Colossians 3:16 (NIV)

It is possible to worship the act of worship. When you become consumed with your personal preferences and neglect embracing the true focus of worship, you start worshiping worship. Often we ask the wrong question, "What do I like in worship?" If worshiping God becomes horizontal, the focus shifts to personal preferences.

The proper question to ask when it comes to worship is, "What moves the heart of God?" Worship is not about what I like but all about what moves the heart of God. My orientation moves from inward to upward. My focus becomes vertical. Does my expression of worship move the heart of God? Am I singing songs with gratitude in my heart to God?

Assess your private worship and your public worship. Think through what you are bringing to the worship experience. Is God the object of your expression of affection? Does God get your best? Put gratitude in your attitude and bring your worship to God.

AUTHENTIC WORSHIP

"And whatever you do, whether in word or deed, do it all in the name of the Lord Jesus, giving thanks to God the Father through him." Colossians 3:17 (NIV)

You have the power to conceal or reveal God's glory.

God reveals His glory to you as you worship Him privately and corporately. Whether you encounter God personally through private worship or in a setting with other believers, God reveals His glory. He wants you know His nature and His character. God wants you to come to know Him by experience.

As God reveals Himself to you, your relationship deepens. Your understanding of God's purposes and ways grows as you spend time with Him. The question becomes: What are you going to do with what God reveals to you? Are you going to conceal His glory or reveal His glory?

Authentic worship is a lifestyle. It is not what you come to on Sunday morning or what you go away from on Sunday afternoon. Worship is living a life that honors God as you are doing life. Everything you do should be an act of worship. Even menial tasks can be used to reveal God's glory.

- *"Therefore, I urge you, brothers, in view of God's mercy, to offer your bodies as living sacrifices, holy and pleasing to God--this is your spiritual act of worship." Rom 12:1 (NIV)*
- *"So whether you eat or drink or whatever you do, do it all for the glory of God." 1 Cor 10:31 (NIV)*

God will orchestrate opportunities today for you to reveal His glory to others. What will others come to know about God's nature and character through your willingness to reveal His glory?

May 28
UNCOVER YOUR CANDLE

"You are the light of the world. A city on a hill cannot be hidden. Neither do people light a lamp and put it under a bowl. Instead they put it on its stand, and it gives light to everyone in the house. In the same way, let your light shine before men, that they may see your good deeds and praise your Father in heaven."
Matthew 5:14-16 (NIV)

Uncover your candle.

Jesus has transformed your life so that you will become an agent of transformation in the world. Jesus has illuminated your life so that you will reflect His light and extend His love to a lost and dying world. As a child of God, you are the light of the world. God has strategically placed you in a dark culture in order to shine His light in you and through you. You are alive right now on purpose. You live, work, study, and play right where God has placed you to know Jesus and to make Him known.

Is your light shining? Is your candle burning brightly for the Lord? God has created people who need the light you have. God has brought them into your life and placed them in your sphere of influence so that you can let your light shine before them. Don't fear the open doors God places before you. Don't divert from the path God has placed you on. Don't neglect crossing the bridges God has built for you.

You will come into contact with people today who need the light God has placed within you. Will you uncover the candle? Will you allow the light of Jesus to shine through you in order to reveal His love to others?

Heightened Awareness

"In the year that King Uzziah died, I saw the Lord seated on a throne, high and exalted, and the train of his robe filled the temple." Isaiah 6:1 (NIV)

Authentic worship leads to sensitivity to God's activity.

When Isaiah saw the Lord high and lifted up, he encountered the holiness of God. As a result, Isaiah had a heightened awareness of both his personal sin and the sin of those around him. The light of God's holiness had exposed the darkness within him and around him. Isaiah was so overwhelmed by his encounter of God, that he said, "Woe is me."

Through his personal encounter with God, Isaiah heard the voice of God calling out to him. Isaiah was sensitive to God's activity. He made himself available for God's use by saying, "Here am I. Send me!" Have you reached that place in your walk with God? Have you encountered God's Presence at the level of hearing God's invitation to join Him in His redemptive activity?

Your worship of the One True Living God should result in a corresponding willingness to participate with God in His world redemption plan. Your heart aligns with the heart of God and you submit your will to God's will. His agenda becomes your passion.

Are you willing to place your yes on the altar unconditionally? Be willing to say to God, "Lord, I'm yours! Use me!"

May 30
GOD MOMENTS

"After six days Jesus took with him Peter, James and John the brother of James, and led them up a high mountain by themselves. There he was transfigured before them. His face shone like the sun, and his clothes became as white as the light." Matthew 17:1-2 (NIV)

God moments are difficult to transfer.

If only life was a perpetual mountaintop experience. Wouldn't it be wonderful to be on a constant spiritual high and never come down? Peter, James, and John had a once in a lifetime experience with Jesus on the top of a mountain. Jesus was transfigured before them. Peter wanted to build three shelters in order to stay on the mountaintop and live in the radiance of Jesus' glory.

Jesus used the experience to teach Peter, James, and John the necessity to come down the mountain to meet the needs of people in the valley. In other words, God surprises us with mountaintop experiences to reveal His glory so that we can go into the world to reveal God's glory to others.

Consider the terrain of your spiritual journey. Can you recall the mountaintop experiences you have had with God? Did God reveal His glory to you in those moments so that you would stay in the moment? No! God gave you those special glimpses into His nature and character so that you could go into the valley of life to connect with people in desperate need of God's salvation.

God moments can be difficult to transfer to others. Often, the God moments are for you to be encouraged and strengthened personally. The experience should motivate you to go into the world to declare the message of reconciliation to a world alienated from God.

MOVE WITH GOD

"They were looking intently up into the sky as he was going, when suddenly two men dressed in white stood beside them. 'Men of Galilee,' they said, 'why do you stand here looking into the sky? This same Jesus, who has been taken from you into heaven, will come back in the same way you have seen him go into heaven.'"
Acts 1:10-11 (NIV.)

The disciples experienced a monumental moment as they witnessed the ascension of Jesus. Jesus had walked with them and invested in them and mentored them. Jesus sacrificed His life upon the cross for them and was raised from the dead. Jesus interacted with the disciples during His forty days of post-resurrection appearances. Now, Jesus ascends before their eyes back into Heaven.

Can you imagine what they were feeling and thinking? How would you respond to such an experience? Where do you go after witnessing such a miraculous event?

It is possible to seek to live in a God-moment meant as an isolated experience and miss God's next assignment for you. God allows you to have special moments where He reveals more of Himself to you so that you can know Him more deeply and obey Him completely.

Keep moving with God. Had the disciples been unwilling to keep moving with God, they would have missed the outpouring of the Holy Spirit on the day of Pentecost. They had to go to Jerusalem and engage in a ten day prayer meeting in the upper room in order to have the experience of becoming Spirit-filled followers of Christ.

June 1
OUR MISSION

"Then Jesus came to them and said, 'All authority in heaven and on earth has been given to me. Therefore go and make disciples of all nations, baptizing them in the name of the Father and of the Son and of the Holy Spirit, and teaching them to obey everything I have commanded you. And surely I am with you always, to the very end of the age.'" Matthew 28:18-20 (NIV)

The Great Commission is our mission.

I live in awe of the reality that God would choose someone like to me to be adopted into His family, to be included in His redemption story, and to be empowered for His redemptive mission. If you have turned your life over to Jesus Christ and allowed Him to become the Lord of your life, you to have been adopted, included, and empowered by God and for God. Your life has true meaning. Your life matters to God and directly impacts the population of Heaven.

You have been given authority by Jesus to make disciples of all people groups. Now that's something worth giving your life to! Don't get distracted by materialism and the pursuit of prestige. Don't allow your passion for God and His redemptive activity to be dissolved by the pursuit of worldly pleasures. Laser focus your life on that which moves the heart of God. Give your life to influencing people for Christ. As you go, make disciples. Maximize every opportunity that God gives you to make Jesus known. You may be the only Jesus others see.

Reveal God's love to every person you come into contact with. Be an irresistible influence for Christ on this broken planet called earth. Reveal the grace you have been given by God to others. Reveal the mercy you have received through the atoning work of Jesus on the cross. Reveal the hope to others that you have come to know firsthand.

FISHING AND FOLLOWING

"As Jesus walked beside the Sea of Galilee, he saw Simon and his brother Andrew casting a net into the lake, for they were fishermen. 'Come, follow me,' Jesus said, 'and I will make you fishers of men.' At once they left their nets and followed him." Mark 1:16-18 (NIV)

If you're not fishing, you're not following.

To be a true follower of Jesus Christ, you must be fishing for souls. Jesus has called every follower of His to fish for men, women, boys, and girls. Our purpose for existence is to know Jesus personally, to grow in Jesus progressively, and to go for Jesus intentionally.

- Know: As a follower of Jesus Christ, your lifestyle should include both private and public worship. To know Jesus personally gives expression through your daily intimacy with Him in private worship. You bring your worship of Jesus with you to a gathering of fellow followers of Christ in public worship.

- Grow: Are you growing in your love relationship with Jesus? Are you connected to a small group of Christ-followers in order to grow progressively in community, in Bible knowledge and application, and in exercising your spiritual gifts? Are you growing in your knowing?

- Go: As you know Christ and grow in Christ, you are compelled to go into the world to represent Christ. Your lifestyle becomes intentional. Your soul-consciousness is elevated. Your passion to reach the lost at any cost is ignited.

Now, let's go fishing!

June 3
REJOICE IS A CHOICE

"Consider it pure joy, my brothers, whenever you face trials of many kinds, because you know that the testing of your faith develops perseverance."
James 1:2-3 (NIV)

Rejoice is a choice.

Living in a fallen world comes at a price. The consequences of sin have rippled throughout our family tree all the way back to Adam and Eve. When sin entered the human race, trials became the shadow. Trials are as much a part of life as the air we breathe. The question is not a matter of whether we will face trials or not in this life. The issue is how we choose to respond to the trials we face.

Trials are inevitable in a fallen world. However, we can choose to rejoice in the midst of the trials we navigate. We need not be surprised by the multifaceted trials that come our way. Instead, we need to live in the ready mode in order to anticipate trials and more specifically, plan our response to trials. Will you choose to rejoice? You cannot choose your trials, but you can choose your response to the trials.

- *"For it has been granted to you on behalf of Christ not only to believe on him, but also to suffer for him." Phil 1:29 (NIV)*
- *"Dear friends, do not be surprised at the painful trial you are suffering, as though something strange were happening to you. But rejoice that you participate in the sufferings of Christ, so that you may be overjoyed when his glory is revealed."*
  1 Pet 4:12-13 (NIV)

Consider the trials that you are currently experiencing. How will you respond today? Will your choice be to rejoice?

GAIN GOD'S PERSPECTIVE

"If any of you lacks wisdom, he should ask God, who gives generously to all without finding fault, and it will be given to him." James 1:5 (NIV)

View your trials from God's perspective.

Knowledge is needed to take things apart. Wisdom is needed to put things back together. When your life is coming apart, you need God's wisdom to put your life in order. Trials tend to skew our vision and stifle our passion. It is so easy to lose perspective when facing trials. Our tendency is to be captured by the immediate and bypass the future that God has in store for us.

Why do we wait so long in the process to turn to God in prayer? We try to figure out circumstances on our own and frantically search for answers apart from God. Nothing comes into our lives without God's permission. If God permits trials, then God will use those trials for our good and for His glory. If only we can embrace that reality earlier in the process of our trials. God is both the Creator and Sustainer of our lives. He knows where we are and what we are facing and where we are heading.

- *"Be still, and know that I am God; I will be exalted among the nations, I will be exalted in the earth." Psalm 46:10 (NIV)*
- *"Trust in the LORD with all your heart and lean not on your own understanding; in all your ways acknowledge him, and he will make your paths straight." Prov 3:5-6 (NIV)*

In faith, turn to God and ask for His wisdom. Seek to gain God's perspective on the trials you face.

June 5
BUILD YOUR TESTIMONY

"Consider it pure joy, my brothers, whenever you face trials of many kinds, because you know that the testing of your faith develops perseverance." James 1:2-3 (NIV)

Without a test, there is no testimony.

God allows trials to come into our lives in order to prove the authenticity of our faith. We are like a tube of toothpaste, when squeezed whatever is on the inside comes out. Trials have a way of revealing character. When our faith is tested, we have the opportunity to demonstrate the character of Christ being developed in us. Our testimony is enriched as our faith increases. Learning how to trust God when trials ensue is part of our spiritual formation. God does not waste the trauma that comes into our lives. When difficult circumstances are in view, our faith is fortified.

- *"Therefore, since we are surrounded by such a great cloud of witnesses, let us throw off everything that hinders and the sin that so easily entangles, and let us run with perseverance the race marked out for us."* Heb 12:1 (NIV)
- *"Therefore, among God's churches we boast about your perseverance and faith in all the persecutions and trials you are enduring."* 2 Thess 1:4 (NIV)

Review your spiritual journey and identify those hard places in your life that proved your faith. You will find that some of your most meaningful moments with God were during those seasons of intensity and adversity.

ADVERSITY AND MATURITY

"Perseverance must finish its work so that you may be mature and complete, not lacking anything." James 1:4 (NIV)

Spiritual maturity may involve adversity.

The child of God is not exempt from adversity. Often, God will allow adversity to enter our journey in order to move us toward spiritual maturity. God expects us to grow spiritually. Mediocrity, lethargy, and apathy are foreign to the maturation process. God enables us to grow through seasons of uncertainty and through seasons of drought. We are reminded of our inadequacy and our total dependency upon God. God's desire is for us to not lack anything. Trials produce the canvas upon which the providence of God is painted for our personal engagement.

- *"...until we all reach unity in the faith and in the knowledge of the Son of God and become mature, attaining to the whole measure of the fullness of Christ." Eph 4:13 (NIV)*
- *"Epaphras, who is one of you and a servant of Christ Jesus, sends greetings. He is always wrestling in prayer for you, that you may stand firm in all the will of God, mature and fully assured." Col 4:12 (NIV)*

Our response to adversity demonstrates our level of spiritual maturity. Our response to difficult circumstances can also propel our spiritual maturity to the next level. Here's the bottom line: Are you becoming more Christlike in the midst of the trials you face?

June 7
BEING MISUNDERSTOOD

"As she kept on praying to the LORD, Eli observed her mouth. Hannah was praying in her heart, and her lips were moving but her voice was not heard. Eli thought she was drunk and said to her, 'How long will you keep on getting drunk? Get rid of your wine.'" 1 Samuel 1:12-14 (NIV)

When you are hurting, your emotions may be expressed through anger, suppression, depression, or grief. At some point, your hurt will manifest. For Hannah, her pain was being expressed through heartfelt prayer. She was unveiling her broken heart before the Lord. Hannah was barren. Eli misinterpreted her pain as that of being drunk. She wasn't drunk. She was devastated with the reality of her circumstances. Can you relate?

- *"'Not so, my lord,' Hannah replied, 'I am a woman who is deeply troubled. I have not been drinking wine or beer; I was pouring out my soul to the LORD. Do not take your servant for a wicked woman; I have been praying here out of my great anguish and grief.'" 1 Sam 1:15-16 (NIV)*
- *"Early the next morning they arose and worshiped before the LORD and then went back to their home at Ramah. Elkanah lay with Hannah his wife, and the LORD remembered her. So in the course of time Hannah conceived and gave birth to a son. She named him Samuel, saying, 'Because I asked the LORD for him.'" 1 Sam 1:19-20 (NIV)*

God knows what you are feeling right now. God knows where you are and where you are headed. Nothing catches God by surprise. Maybe you are experiencing a delay that just doesn't make sense to you. Know that God has a purpose for every delay we endure. God understands our feelings and our frustrations even when others may not understand. God is all-knowing. God has the final say!

TRUST THE MASTER

"Without warning, a furious storm came up on the lake, so that the waves swept over the boat. But Jesus was sleeping." Matthew 8:24 (NIV)

Trials have a tendency to sneak up on us like weeds in a flowerbed. We can be living in the land of the familiar and enjoying our daily routine when all of the sudden, we get surprised by an unexpected interruption. Maybe we get an unwanted notice in the mail, or the check engine light in our car comes on, or the doctor walks in the room with a concerned look in his eyes. Life is filled with seasons of uncertainty.

Who do you turn to when trials come into your life? The disciples went to Jesus and woke Him and said, "Lord, save us! We're going to drown!" We must give them credit at this point. They knew to turn to Jesus. But, Jesus questioned them about their lack of faith and their pressing fear. Why would they be afraid of anything, knowing that Jesus was with them?

Jesus seized the opportunity to demonstrate His power over nature. Jesus rebuked the winds and the waves and it was completely calm. The disciples experienced the demonstration of Jesus' power.

Whatever trials come our way, remember that Jesus is our sufficiency. The storms of this life can never catch Jesus by surprise.

Jesus is in the boat!

June 9
GOD'S DISCIPLINARY PROCESS

"When he came to his senses, he said, 'How many of my father's hired men have food to spare, and here I am starving to death!'" Luke 15:17 (NIV)

Do you have someone in your life who is currently suffering the consequences of their poor choices? Everything within you wants to shift into rescue mode. You want to pull them out of reaping what they have sown. Their trial has become your trial because of the love you have for them.

The prodigal son traveled down the road filled with the potholes of selfish choices. The consequences of his sinful lifestyle were in full bloom. The fast lane had not delivered what it promised. What I admire most about his father, is that he allowed the natural consequences to flow. Instead of rescuing his son, the father gave God room to work and to produce deep conviction in his straying son's life.

Yes! It took a pigpen experience for the son to come to his senses. What if the father would have interrupted the process? What if the father would have chased the son down and prevented him from reaching the pigpen?

- *"No discipline seems pleasant at the time, but painful. Later on, however, it produces a harvest of righteousness and peace for those who have been trained by it." Heb 12:11 (NIV)*

Sometimes we just need to give God room to work to bring those He has created back to Himself. There are times when God wants to use us in the process of bringing a rebelling son or daughter back into alignment. Don't bypass God's disciplinary process.

RESPOND TO TEMPTATION

"No temptation has seized you except what is common to man. And God is faithful; he will not let you be tempted beyond what you can bear. But when you are tempted, he will also provide a way out so that you can stand up under it."
1 Corinthians 10:13 (NIV)

Temptation is an opportunity to honor God.

Our response to temptation will determine whether we honor God or dishonor God. As followers of Jesus Christ, we are not temptation exempt. Living in a fallen world and retaining our sin nature guarantee the presence of temptation. It is not a matter of if we will face temptation, but a matter of when we will face temptation. Even Jesus was tempted.

Temptation is a common feature in this life. Of course, temptation comes in different forms depending on where we are most susceptible. Satan knows what our weaknesses are and what will entice us toward sin.

We are not left alone to fend for ourselves. God is here! God is faithful! We can anchor our faith to the faithfulness of God. He will never leave us. He will not abandon us. In fact, God will not allow us to be tempted beyond what we can bear with Him. Temptation is a constant reminder of our dependency upon God. We need God!

God will also provide an exit strategy. When temptation knocks at our door, we don't have to submit to the temptation. God will always provide a way of escape so that we can stand up under the load and stress.

How will you respond when temptation comes your way? Will you seize the opportunity to honor God?

June 11
CHOOSE WISELY

"When tempted, no one should say, 'God is tempting me.' For God cannot be tempted by evil, nor does he tempt anyone; but each one is tempted when, by his own evil desire, he is dragged away and enticed." James 1:13-14 (NIV)

God is holy and God is love.

The nature of God will not allow temptation to be an instrument of Heaven. God cannot be tempted by evil because God is holy. As John MacArthur affirms, "God is aware of evil but untouched by it, like a sunbeam shining on a dump is untouched by the trash."

God is not the originator of temptation. God does not tempt anyone because God is love. In His love, God does not initiate temptation, but God will allow temptation to come into a person's life. The temptation provides the opportunity to choose the righteous path and to bring honor to God through the proper response.

When we choose to give in to temptation, we believe that it is the best option at that moment. Satan's goal is to get us to doubt God's Word and to doubt God's best.

- *"Now the serpent was more crafty than any of the wild animals the LORD God had made. He said to the woman, 'Did God really say, You must not eat from any tree in the garden?'" Gen 3:1 (NIV)*

God cannot be tempted by evil. God does not tempt anyone. How will you choose to respond to the temptation that God allows into your path? Will you take God at His Word and trust Him?

"Then, after desire has conceived, it gives birth to sin; and sin, when it is full-grown, gives birth to death." James 1:15 (NIV

Temptation has a predictable process.

James uses the metaphor of childbirth to capture the predictable process of temptation. In his letter to the Jews who were scattered outside of Palestine, James writes about the trials from without and the temptations from within.

We have God-given desires that are natural and are vital to life. For example, we have the desire for food. Without that desire we would die. We also have the desire for rest. Without that desire we would die. Yet, both desires can become sin when we take them beyond God's intended purpose. If we take our desire for food too far, we commit the sin of gluttony. In like manner, if we take our desire for rest too far, we commit the sin of laziness.

Arm yourself with the knowledge of the predictable process of temptation. We idolize something we desire. The next step is that we rationalize why we should have the desire fulfilled. In other words, we talked ourselves into compromising convictions. Then we strategize by coming up with a plan to obtain the object we are idolizing. Ultimately, we capitalize on the opportunity by seizing what we have desired. Remorse and guilt follow.

Look back over poor choices you have made in your lifetime. See if you can identify this predictable process. Here's the key to victory: The sooner in the process you avoid the sin, the more likely you will overcome the temptation.

June 13
MONITOR MEDIA INPUT

"Religion that God our Father accepts as pure and faultless is this: to look after orphans and widows in their distress and to keep oneself from being polluted by the world." James 1:27 (NIV)

God has called us to a lifestyle of moral purity. As followers of Jesus Christ, our constant assignment is to keep from being polluted by the world. Sin is rampant in our society and sin is present within our sin nature. As we battle temptation from within, we must establish guardrails to keep us on the straight and narrow path of holiness.

Let's consider using a MAP for walking in victory. The letter M will remind us to Monitor Media Input. In our age of technology, we have unprecedented access to images that dishonor God. High definition televisions, computers, and cell phones provide an array of images that pollute and contaminate the mind of the child of God. Filtering what we allow to come into our minds is a proactive step to walking in victory.

- *"Finally, brothers, whatever is true, whatever is noble, whatever is right, whatever is pure, whatever is lovely, whatever is admirable--if anything is excellent or praiseworthy--think about such things." Phil 4:8 (NIV)*
- *"Flee the evil desires of youth, and pursue righteousness, faith, love and peace, along with those who call on the Lord out of a pure heart." 2 Tim 2:22 (NIV)*

Take the initiative to monitor media input. When you put garbage in, you will get garbage out. When you put Christ in, you get Christ out. Fill your mind with that which brings honor to God.

"Avoid every kind of evil." 1 Thessalonians 5:22 (NIV)

Have you ever done something that compromised your convictions and broke the heart of God? When you look back on the experience, you still can't believe that you did such a thing. When you get too close to the edge, you slip down the slippery slope and immense guilt follows. Have you been there?

As we continue observing our MAP for walking in victory, let's use the letter A to remind us to Avoid Slippery Slopes. Because of our resident sin nature, we have a tendency to see how close we can get to the edge without slipping and falling. God's Word teaches us to guard our lives and to conduct our lives with caution. Slippery slopes abound. Opportunities to compromise our convictions are unlimited.

> • *"It is God's will that you should be sanctified: that you should avoid sexual immorality; that each of you should learn to control his own body in a way that is holy and honorable, not in passionate lust like the heathen, who do not know God." 1 Thess 4:3-5 (NIV)*
> • *"In your struggle against sin, you have not yet resisted to the point of shedding your blood." Heb 12:4 (NIV)*

God has called us to a lifestyle of self-control. Take the initiative to avoid slippery slopes. Ask God to give you wisdom to see the terrain as it is and to detect the slippery slopes awaiting your arrival. Living in a fallen world is a struggle. Resist sin at all costs.

June 15
PRACTICE BOUNCING EYES

"Let your eyes look straight ahead, fix your gaze directly before you."
Proverbs 4:25 (NIV)

Eyesight is an amazing feature of the human body. God's creation throughout the earth is awesome to behold whether taking in the sight of the blue sky in the day or the star filled sky at night or observing a butterfly dancing from leaf to leaf. From gazing at the flowing wildflowers in the open field to examining the intricacies of a cell under a microscope, eyesight is a gift from God.

As we seek to walk in victory in this life on planet earth, let's use the letter P in our MAP to remind us to Practice Bouncing Eyes. There is so much to look at from day to day. To walk in victory, we must be very selective in what we allow to come into our minds through the open window of our eyes.

- *"But I tell you that anyone who looks at a woman lustfully has already committed adultery with her in his heart." Matt 5:28 (NIV)*
- *"I made a covenant with my eyes not to look lustfully at a girl." Job 31:1 (NIV)*

Take the initiative to practice bouncing eyes. Train your eyes to bounce off of anything that does not honor God. As Billy Graham has said, "The first look is natural; the second look is sin."

WALK IN VICTORY

"For we do not have a high priest who is unable to sympathize with our weaknesses, but we have one who has been tempted in every way, just as we are--yet was without sin." Hebrews 4:15 (NIV)

Jesus understands your trials from without and your struggles from within.

In our contemporary vernacular: Jesus has been there and done that. Jesus has been tempted in every way, just as we are. He understands our struggles. Jesus endured temptation and chose to honor God throughout the process. Jesus entered the process and completed the process sinless. Our example is Jesus. Our pattern for victory is Jesus.

God never intended for us to live the Christian life outside of His enabling. In and of ourselves, we are insufficient. Our sufficiency is found in Christ. As we abide in Christ and submit to the Spirit's control in our life, victory results.

- *"I am the vine; you are the branches. If a man remains in me and I in him, he will bear much fruit; apart from me you can do nothing." John 15:5 (NIV)*
- *"Therefore do not be foolish, but understand what the Lord's will is. Do not get drunk on wine, which leads to debauchery. Instead, be filled with the Spirit." Eph 5:17-18 (NIV)*

Surrender to the Lordship of Christ. Surrender fully to the Spirit's control in your life. Jesus has been where you are and He knows what you need to walk in victory. Allow Jesus to live His life through you.

June 17
EXPRESS GRATITUDE

"He came to Derbe and then to Lystra, where a disciple named Timothy lived, whose mother was a Jewess and a believer, but whose father was a Greek." Acts 16:1 (NIV)

Timothy's father is not mentioned by name in the Bible. We only know that his dad was a Greek. However, Timothy's mother and grandmother are mentioned by name along with their spiritual influence in Timothy's life. We just don't know how long Timothy's father was in the picture. Maybe he was a disconnected dad or an absent father. Maybe he left Timothy's mother and separated himself from Timothy.

Everyone has a biological father. Some people have the privilege of knowing their dad and some grow up having never known their biological father. There are so many levels of proximity. What about your relationship with your biological father? At what level has your biological father been involved in your life? Do you know who he is? If so, do you have a growing relationship with him? Would you consider the relationship healthy? If you have never met your biological father, what would you want to say to him if you were to meet him? The truth is that your biological father has been influential in your life either directly or indirectly. You were created by God through your mom and dad. Your unique DNA includes both your mom and your dad.

Acknowledge your biological father's imperfections. He has never been perfect and will not be perfect until his transformation in glory. Be willing to extend forgiveness to him for the areas in your life where you feel neglected and maybe even betrayed. If you have a healthy relationship with your father, express your gratitude to him for his investment in your life. Maybe your biological father is no longer alive on earth. Spend some time expressing thanks to God for the biological father He gave to you.

SPIRITUAL INFLUENCE

"To Timothy, my dear son: Grace, mercy and peace from God the Father and Christ Jesus our Lord." 2 Timothy 1:2 (NIV)

Can you imagine having the Apostle Paul as a spiritual father? Timothy enjoyed the privilege of having Paul as an authentic spiritual father. Paul invested in Timothy's life. It is very likely that Paul led Timothy to faith in Jesus Christ. Paul provided Timothy with firsthand experience on his missionary journeys. Timothy observed Paul's faith in action. Their relationship was mutually beneficial and made a tremendous kingdom impact for the glory of God.

If you have had an authentic spiritual father in your life, then you are blessed with a special deposit. God has given you a tangible expression of His love and grace by allowing you to do life with a spiritual father who embodies the character of Christ. Think about the spiritual father that God has brought into your life. Think about the insights you have gleaned and the experiences you have captured through the relational velocity of a spiritual father. Perhaps you have more than one spiritual father. It is possible to have many spiritual fathers who have invested in your life over the years.

Give thanks to God for the influential spiritual relationships that have helped you in becoming a fully devoted follower of Christ.

June 19
YOUR HEAVENLY FATHER

"A father to the fatherless, a defender of widows, is God in his holy dwelling."
Psalm 68:5 (NIV)

Long before you decided what to do with God, God decided what to do with you. God took the initiative to reconcile you to Himself through the atoning work of Jesus on the cross. God is the both the Creator and Sustainer of life. God is love. God is holy. God is eternal. God is the ultimate Father. Your life is secure in His hands.

God has chosen you, redeemed you, forgiven you, included you, and sealed you by His Holy Spirit. You are the recipient of His unconditional love. You are the beneficiary of His mercy and grace. Your acceptance of God's gift of eternal life has transformed your status. You are now a child of God and your name has been written in the Lamb's Book of Life. Your standing before God is now made right by the imputed righteousness of Christ. God sees you through the blood of Jesus. You have been made acceptable in His sight.

- *"Because you are sons, God sent the Spirit of his Son into our hearts, the Spirit who calls out, 'Abba, Father.'" Gal 4:6 (NIV)*

The most influential person in your life should be God. The fatherhood of God has become a reality in your life as you have chosen to become a follower of Jesus Christ. Whether you have a godly biological father or not does not nullify the abiding relationship that you have with God. Your Heavenly Father will never let you down. He will never leave you nor forsake you. Your Heavenly Father is perfect.

THE PAIN GOD REDEEMS

"Praise be to the God and Father of our Lord Jesus Christ, the Father of compassion and the God of all comfort, who comforts us in all our troubles, so that we can comfort those in any trouble with the comfort we ourselves have received from God." 2 Corinthians 1:3-4 (NIV)

God redeems pain.

When you look into the rear view mirror of your life, you can probably recall painful experiences that you have had in your past. Some of those experiences may be the direct result of poor choices that you made and some of those experiences may be related to poor choices that someone else made. You may look back and recognize painful experiences that were not attached to poor choices at all. It may be that you simply encountered pain as a result of living in a fallen world.

Grief is an ongoing pain that resides within us as we try to navigate a path without someone who has meant so much to us. Grief can be encountered as a result of job loss, a shift in our personal health status, or a shattered dream. Are you currently experiencing any level of grief in your life?

God is the Father of compassion. He is the God of all comfort. God comforts us so that we can comfort others. We come to realize our dependency upon God and how desperate we really are for God.

God does not bring comfort into our lives so that we can become comfortable. God brings comfort into our lives during seasons of pain and difficulty so that we can comfort others who go through trying circumstances. Who has God brought into your path lately who simply needs to know God's comfort through you? That's one of the many ways that God redeems your pain.

June 21
THE POTTER'S TOUCH

"And we, who with unveiled faces all reflect the Lord's glory, are being transformed into his likeness with ever-increasing glory, which comes from the Lord, who is the Spirit." 2 Corinthians 3:18 (NIV)

We are still on the Potter's wheel.

How refreshing to know that we are still in the process of becoming who we are in Christ! God is not through with us. We are the clay and God is the Potter. His loving and corrective touch continues to mold and shape our lives for His glory. We are being transformed into the likeness of Christ.

- *"For those God foreknew he also predestined to be conformed to the likeness of his Son, that he might be the firstborn among many brothers." Rom 8:29 (NIV)*
- *"And just as we have borne the likeness of the earthly man, so shall we bear the likeness of the man from heaven." 1 Cor 15:49 (NIV)*

As we walk with God daily and stay close to Him in prayer and the reading of His Word, we are being transformed with an ever-increasing glory. The glory of God will be revealed in us and through us more and more as we abide in Christ. God draws near to us as we draw near to Him. The glow of God radiates from our life as we exhibit His love and express His life-saving message.

Are there any areas of your life that you have failed to surrender to the Lordship of Christ? Are there any habits or patterns of neglect that are currently hindering the process of transformation in your life? Yield to the Potter's touch. Allow God to perfect the image of Christ in you. May you become more like Christ today as a result of your willingness to fully surrender to the work of God in your life!

JUDGMENT SEAT OF CHRIST

"For we must all appear before the judgment seat of Christ, that each one may receive what is due him for the things done while in the body, whether good or bad." 2 Corinthians 5:10 (NIV)

Everyone will live forever somewhere.

What you do with Christ during your brief stay on planet earth will determine whether you spend eternity in Heaven or hell. Your response to God's offer of salvation is the deciding factor to your eternal destination.

- *"You, then, why do you judge your brother? Or why do you look down on your brother? For we will all stand before God's judgment seat." Rom 14:10 (NIV)*
- *"Therefore God exalted him to the highest place and gave him the name that is above every name, that at the name of Jesus every knee should bow, in heaven and on earth and under the earth, and every tongue confess that Jesus Christ is Lord, to the glory of God the Father." Phil 2:9-11 (NIV)*

Every human being will stand before God to give an account for his or her life. Every person will bow and confess that Jesus Christ is Lord! Those who reject God's offer of salvation while living on earth will still bow and confess that Jesus Christ is Lord, but it will be eternally too late. Believers will go to the Judgment Seat of Christ to receive reward and Heaven while unbelievers will go to the White Throne Judgment to receive punishment and hell (Rev 20:11-15).

Live circumspectly! Live in full awareness of God's holiness, purity, and justice! Take as many people with you to Heaven as you possibly can in full surrender to the Spirit's control. Make the most of every opportunity!

June 23
STAY CLEAN

"Since we have these promises, dear friends, let us purify ourselves from everything that contaminates body and spirit, perfecting holiness out of reverence for God." 2 Corinthians 7:1 (NIV)

Every possibility for contaminating our lives is available to us. Sin is rampant. We face trials from without and temptation from within. The cultural current is moving in the opposite direction of the Christ honoring flow. We must make a conscious and continuous decision to walk in purity.

- *"Come near to God and he will come near to you. Wash your hands, you sinners, and purify your hearts, you double-minded." James 4:8 (NIV)*
- *"Don't let anyone look down on you because you are young, but set an example for the believers in speech, in life, in love, in faith and in purity." 1 Tim 4:12 (NIV)*

Purify yourself in perfect holiness. Purify your heart and set an example for the believers in purity. In Christ, you are positionally pure. In Christ, you are a new creation. In Christ, you are adopted into God's family. Now live out practically what you are positionally in Christ. The only way to reign in this life is to allow Christ to reign in your life. Submit to His authority in your life. Allow Jesus to live His life through you.

Staying clean while living in a dirty world is only possible in the strength Christ provides. Jesus has already set the example. Jesus has demonstrated the life of purity in a sin-polluted culture. Jesus lived a sinless life and died a sacrificial death so that you can walk in victory.

"My dear brothers, take note of this: Everyone should be quick to listen, slow to speak and slow to become angry, for man's anger does not bring about the righteous life that God desires." James 1:19-20 (NIV)

Is your number one priority to obey God? Obeying God begins with surrendering to the Lordship of Christ and giving Him complete control of your life. God has given you two ears and one mouth. Be quick to listen. Listen to God's Word so that you can discover God's way.

Obeying God is always the best choice. Obedience to God is not only a mark of spiritual maturity; it is the birthmark of being born again. Obeying God is a non-negotiable.

- *"We know that we have come to know him if we obey his commands." 1 John 2:3 (NIV)*
- *"Then Samuel said, 'Speak, for your servant is listening.'" 1 Sam 3:10 (NIV)*

Are you in tune with the voice of God? God is a God of revelation. He chooses to reveal Himself to you. Are you listening? God reveals His ways so that you can obey Him.

Obedience to God is always the best option. Obey His way.

June 25
OBEY GOD

"So Abram left, as the LORD had told him; and Lot went with him. Abram was seventy-five years old when he set out from Haran." Genesis 12:4 (NIV)

What is keeping you from obeying God? Do you fear the unknown? Are you uncomfortable making a move without having more information? Maybe God has chosen to limit His revelation to match your obedience. Once you obey what He has already said, then He will show you the next step.

Abram took God at His word! He simply obeyed God. God told Abram to leave and go to a land that He would show him. Guess what? Abram left, as the Lord told him. He obeyed.

You can never go wrong obeying God. His way is always the best way. Even when it doesn't make sense or seem remotely logical, God's way is the right way. If you are confused about your next step, just obey what He has already said. Start there!

Identify what you are wrestling with right now? What is keeping you from taking the next step? Place that fear or frustration before the Lord in prayer and see how He helps you take the next step. You can trust God with your present circumstances and your future hopes and dreams.

PRACTICE INSTANT OBEDIENCE

"Do not merely listen to the word, and so deceive yourselves. Do what it says. Anyone who listens to the word but does not do what it says is like a man who looks at his face in a mirror and, after looking at himself, goes away and immediately forgets what he looks like." James 1:22-24 (NIV)

What does a life of instant obedience look like? It looks like humility, gentleness, patience, and forbearance in action. It is not enough to know to do right. You must place into action what you know. Application is the activation of faith. Notice how Jesus describes such a life.

- *"Therefore everyone who hears these words of mine and puts them into practice is like a wise man who built his house on the rock. The rain came down, the streams rose, and the winds blew and beat against that house; yet it did not fall, because it had its foundation on the rock. But everyone who hears these words of mine and does not put them into practice is like a foolish man who built his house on sand. The rain came down, the streams rose, and the winds blew and beat against that house, and it fell with a great crash."*
  Matt 7:24-27 (NIV)

Jesus authenticates that hearing God's Word is not enough. You must put feet to your faith by putting God's Word into practice. Application determines whether you are building on sand or on the rock.

Take a close look at your conduct both in private and in public. What does your conduct declare about your faith? Are you obeying what you know? Is your conduct consistent with the character of Christ? Are you building on the rock or on sand? Obey His way!

June 27
GO TO THE NEXT LEVEL

"Do not merely listen to the word, and so deceive yourselves. Do what it says."
James 1:22 (NIV)

We are bombarded with information. From billboards to books, from electronic media to engaging magazines, there is no void of information. The accessibility of information is literally at our fingertips. If you really want to know something, there are unlimited avenues of securing the information that you are seeking.

The Bible is still the most read book on planet earth. As you read God's Word, you have the opportunity to listen to what God is saying and then to do what He says. However, you also have the opportunity to keep God's Word at a distance. You can listen to God's Word for information purposes only. Your reading and hearing of God's Word becomes a cognitive exercise that yields minimal fruit in your life. God wants your level of listening to move beyond that of information. The reality is that we know more than we are doing. It is not that we need to know more at this point, but rather obey what we already know.

You can literally deceive yourself by listening to the Word of God at the level of information. God's Word is designed for more than just informing you about facts and trends. God's Word is to inform you about the nature and character of God. God's Word is to inform you about His world redemption plan and where you fit into the process. However, you can stay at the level of knowing about God and His plan without allowing the information to directly impact your life.

God wants you to go to the next level.

EXAMINE YOUR HEART

"Anyone who listens to the word but does not do what it says is like a man who looks at his face in a mirror and, after looking at himself, goes away and immediately forgets what he looks like." James 1:23-24 (NIV)

God's Word is a mirror. As we read and hear God's Word, we begin to see God for who He is and we begin to see ourselves as we really are in light of who God is. God's Word reveals God's holiness and our sinfulness. We have the opportunity to move from information to examination. In our spiritual growth, we seek to allow God's Word to penetrate our lives.

- *"Search me, O God, and know my heart; test me and know my anxious thoughts. See if there is any offensive way in me, and lead me in the way everlasting." Psalm 139:23-24 (NIV)*
- *"For the word of God is living and active. Sharper than any double-edged sword, it penetrates even to dividing soul and spirit, joints and marrow; it judges the thoughts and attitudes of the heart." Heb 4:12 (NIV)*

Are you willing to go to the next level and ask God to search your heart? Will you begin reading God's Word and hearing God's Word with the intent of examination? Invite the light of God's Word to expose areas of darkness or neglect that have embedded in your life. Confess known sin and fully surrender to the Spirit's control. Walk circumspectly in light of what God reveals to you through His Word.

God is for you. God has already demonstrated His unconditional love by giving His best, Jesus, to die on the cross to pay the penalty for your sin. You are forgiven! You are free to draw near to God and allow Him to draw near to you. Move from information to examination. Are you ready to go to the next level?

June 29
ACTIVATE GOD'S WORD

"But the man who looks intently into the perfect law that gives freedom, and continues to do this, not forgetting what he has heard, but doing it--he will be blessed in what he does." James 1:25 (NIV)

Information and examination without application will lead to frustration. God wants you to look intently into His Word. Pour your life into the reading and studying of God's Word. Don't neglect the discipline of investigation. Dive deep into God's Word. Be sure to come out of investigation with application. Personalize God's Word by asking: So what? Now what?

God reveals Himself to you through His Word so that you will do what He says. God reveals His heart and His agenda so that you can literally put feet to the faith God imparts. Move from being a hearer of the Word only, to being a doer of the Word. Activate God's Word in your life through practical living. Put God's Word into practice.

Start with loving God with all of your heart, mind, and strength. Launch into loving your neighbor as yourself. Begin forgiving others as God has forgiven you. Passionately serve others as Christ modeled faithfully. Be merciful. Be compassionate. Be gentle. Be faithful. Be considerate. Be patient.

Just do what God says! Move from information to examination and then to application. There's another level that has eternal implications.

SUCCESS IN GOD'S ECONOMY

"But the man who looks intently into the perfect law that gives freedom, and continues to do this, not forgetting what he has heard, but doing it--he will be blessed in what he does." James 1:25 (NIV)

How would you define success? The bumper sticker says, "He who dies with the most toys wins." Is that success? God's definition of success is summed up in one word: obedience. As you faithfully and consistently put God's Word into practice, you will be successful in God's economy.

Faithful application of God's Word will lead to transformation. Your obedience to God's Word will result in perpetual life change. You will become more and more like Christ. What does that transformation look like in the real world?

Both your conversation and conduct will be transformed by the consistent application of God's Word. The way you speak will be radically transformed. The way you view others and the way you treat others will be radically transformed. God's Word will be alive and active in you. Your relationship with God and your relationship with people will take on a new dimension proportionate to your obedience to God's Word.

Look within and detect areas of your life that need be come under the authority of God's Word. Yield to the call of God to consistently apply His Word in daily living. Allow all of your relationships to be transformed by the application of God's Word. Let God change you on the inside. Let Christ in you become evident to the watching world.

July 1
ELIMINATING FAVORITISM

"My brothers, as believers in our glorious Lord Jesus Christ, don't show favoritism." James 2:1 (NIV)

James gives perspective to the believers who have been dispersed by the persecution in Jerusalem. He is writing to the Jews of the Diaspora. They are living outside of their homeland. They are being exposed to different cultures and to different philosophies for living. James reminds them that they are believers in our glorious Lord Jesus Christ. Their position in Christ is to inform their behavior toward others.

We have been transformed by God's grace and adopted into His family. Our identity is that of being believers in our glorious Lord Jesus Christ. Our lives take on new meaning as we embrace the way of Jesus. His life and His mission become our reality. Jesus wants to transform the culture through us. Thus, we are not to show favoritism. We are not to value one person over another. We are not to favor one people group over another people group.

- *"Do not pervert justice; do not show partiality to the poor or favoritism to the great, but judge your neighbor fairly." Lev 19:15 (NIV)*
- *"I charge you, in the sight of God and Christ Jesus and the elect angels, to keep these instructions without partiality, and to do nothing out of favoritism." 1 Tim 5:21 (NIV)*

The spirit of favoritism does not reflect the heart of God. As His children, we are not to show favoritism. God has called us to extend His love to every people group on earth. That means to impartially radiate His love and compassion to every person regardless of their skin color or social status. A great start would be for you to begin praying for people who are not like you.

THE VALUE GOD BESTOWS

"Suppose a man comes into your meeting wearing a gold ring and fine clothes, and a poor man in shabby clothes also comes in. If you show special attention to the man wearing fine clothes and say, 'Here's a good seat for you,' but say to the poor man, 'You stand there' or 'Sit on the floor by my feet,' have you not discriminated among yourselves and become judges with evil thoughts?"
James 2:2-4 (NIV)

The corporate worship setting is sacred. When we gather with fellow believers to express our love to God in corporate worship, we are obeying God and demonstrating a reverence for His glory. The worship environment is conducive to encouraging each other and edifying the body of Christ. However, the corporate setting for worship can also be an environment where discrimination seeps in.

Making a judgment about one's appearance based on their attire is condescending to the very one Christ died for. For us to give preferential treatment to those endowed with financial prowess would be tragic in the eyes of God. For us to consider withholding our love, affirmation, acceptance, and inclusion of those less fortunate would break the heart of God.

Preferential treatment misrepresents the character of God. We need to embrace God's perspective on those He created and sent His Son to die for. God took the initiative to establish our value through the atoning work of Jesus on the cross. Every person matters to God. As followers of Jesus Christ, we are to place the same value on others that God does.

Is there anyone you are currently looking down on? Have you minimized the value God places on others? Let's be reminded of where we were when God found us in our sin.

July 3
GOD'S PERSPECTIVE

"Listen, my dear brothers: Has not God chosen those who are poor in the eyes of the world to be rich in faith and to inherit the kingdom he promised those who love him? But you have insulted the poor. Is it not the rich who are exploiting you? Are they not the ones who are dragging you into court? Are they not the ones who are slandering the noble name of him to whom you belong?"
James 2:5-7 (NIV)

What is your definition of rich? As you view those in your circles, whom would you identify as rich? In our materialistic culture, we tend to rank wealth based on the acquisition of possessions or the accumulation of exorbitant funds. If only we could operate from God's perspective.

God defines rich based on faith and not funds. In God's economy, the poor in the eyes of the world are made rich in faith and inherit the eternal riches of God's treasure by faith in Jesus. God is the equalizer. God elevates the poor. God can also easily dissipate the rich in the eyes of the world.

Maybe we just need to reflect on life from God's perspective. Maybe we need to contemplate what true wealth is. You can be rich as far as the world's standards are concerned and yet be destitute in God's economy. Forsaking God's offer of eternal life would keep a person in total desperation regardless of his or her earthly assets.

Calculate the value you currently place on others. Do you allow their social status to dictate how you treat them? Do you allow their appearance to formulate your view of them? What if you began to view others from God's perspective?

"If you really keep the royal law found in Scripture, 'Love your neighbor as yourself,' you are doing right." James 2:8 (NIV)

We are by nature self-absorbed, self-centered, and self-focused. When anything happens around us our first question is: How will this affect me? In many ways, we act as though the earth really does rotate around us. The reality of our fallen nature pops up from time to time like a ground hog trying to catch a glimpse of daylight.

Jesus acknowledges the presence of our self-love. We truly love ourselves. As one of my colleagues would often say, "Sometimes you just have to be good to yourself!" We have no problem being good to ourselves do we? We value comfort. We value pleasure. We value looking good and feeling good and sleeping good.

As we begin viewing others from God's perspective, we will begin to value others the way God values them. The resulting choice will be to love others as we love ourselves. In other words, we will begin to treat others the way we want to be treated. We will love others with the same kind of love that we desire to receive.

James identifies that we are doing right when we love others as we love ourselves. Longing to do right is not enough. Putting our faith in action by loving others brings honor to God.

Do you love others as much as you love yourself? Ouch! That's a painful question.

July 5
THE SIN OF FAVORITISM

"But if you show favoritism, you sin and are convicted by the law as lawbreakers. For whoever keeps the whole law and yet stumbles at just one point is guilty of breaking all of it. For he who said, 'Do not commit adultery,' also said, 'Do not murder.' If you do not commit adultery but do commit murder, you have become a lawbreaker." James 2:9-11 (NIV)

Have you ever heard of the domino effect? If you accidentally tip one domino, it triggers an effect that ultimately impacts every other domino. Tip-toeing through life in a fallen world is very similar to the domino effect. It doesn't take much to sin. One impure thought is sin. Failing to do what God wants you do is sin. Doing what God does not want you to do is sin.

- *"For all have sinned and fall short of the glory of God."*
  Rom 3:23 (NIV)
- *"If we claim to be without sin, we deceive ourselves and the truth is not in us." 1 John 1:8 (NIV)*

Our sin nature causes a chain reaction. The more we sin the more our sin nature craves sin. Whatever you feed grows and whatever you starve dies. Crucify the flesh! Make no provision for sin!

Favoritism is a sin that we can succumb to subtly. It can sneak up on us. We can drift from having God's perspective and fail to see others through His eyes.

Let's commit to stay sensitive to the presence of sin. Sometimes favoritism is not as tangible in our own lives. We may not even realize that we are showing favoritism. Let's ask God to help detect even a fraction of favoritism resident in our lives.

BEING MERCIFUL

"Speak and act as those who are going to be judged by the law that gives freedom, because judgment without mercy will be shown to anyone who has not been merciful. Mercy triumphs over judgment!" James 2:12-13 (NIV)

Imagine being transferred instantly before the throne of God. You are standing before God right now. You fall on your face before God and He asks you to give an account for your treatment of others. Where would that place you in the area of God's approval and affirmation? How would you measure up to God's standard of perfection?

God is a God of justice. And yes, God is a God of mercy. Without God's justice, mercy would not exist. Without God's mercy, justice would not exist. God declared His justice on your sin when Jesus took upon God's wrath for your sin on the cross. God demonstrated His mercy by providing for the forgiveness of your sin. How will you treat others in light of what God has done for you?

- *"Blessed are the merciful, for they will be shown mercy."* Matt 5:7 (NIV)
- *"Do not judge, or you too will be judged. For in the same way you judge others, you will be judged, and with the measure you use, it will be measured to you." Matt 7:1-2 (NIV)*

Our tendency is to use binoculars when judging our lives and using a microscope when judging the lives of others. Thank God for His mercy. God wants our conversation and our conduct to reflect the mercy we have received from Him. God is not asking us to do anything in our relationship with others that He has not already done for us.

July 7
THE FRAGRANCE OF MERCY

"Speak and act as those who are going to be judged by the law that gives freedom, because judgment without mercy will be shown to anyone who has not been merciful. Mercy triumphs over judgment!" James 2:12-13 (NIV)

Grace is getting what we do not deserve. We do not deserve God's love. We do not deserve God's gift of eternal life. We do not deserve our new identity in Christ. We do not deserve having our names written in the Lamb's Book of Life. Yet, God graced us with these and many other spiritual realities.

Mercy is not getting what we deserve. Because of our sin, we deserve separation, punishment, and alienation. Because of our sin, we deserve eternal damnation. Because of our sin, we deserve total isolation from God's abiding Presence. Yet, God extends His mercy to us and did not give us what we deserved. Instead, God has blessed us, redeemed us, included us, sealed us, and lavished us with His love.

Because of God's mercy, we have a song to sing and a message to declare. As recipients of God's mercy, we have been given a clean canvas upon which we join God in His redemptive activity.

May God's merciful treatment of us radically transform our conversation and our conduct! May our words and our walk exhibit mercy to others as God has exhibited to us!

> • *"May the words of my mouth and the meditation of my heart be pleasing in your sight, O LORD, my Rock and my Redeemer."*
> *Psalm 19:14 (NIV)*

Viewing others from God's perspective will produce the fragrance of mercy in our lives. May that aroma bring others closer to the love of God that we have found in Christ!

SAVING FAITH

"What good is it, my brothers, if a man claims to have faith but has no deeds? Can such faith save him?" James 2:14 (NIV)

You can profess Christ and not possess Christ.

What does it take for a person to be saved? Is it possible to have saving faith without deeds? Will my faith be demonstrated by my deeds? So many have embraced an "easy believism" theology which can produce a false sense of security. You can spend your entire life on the earth thinking that you are saved and in reality, be lost.

- *"'Not everyone who says to me, "Lord, Lord," will enter the kingdom of heaven, but only he who does the will of my Father who is in heaven.'" Matt 7:21 (NIV)*
- *"Therefore, my brothers, be all the more eager to make your calling and election sure. For if you do these things, you will never fall, and you will receive a rich welcome into the eternal kingdom of our Lord and Savior Jesus Christ." 2 Pet 1:10-11 (NIV)*

Your eternal destiny is determined by how you respond to God's offer of salvation found in Christ alone. Knowing about Christ is not sufficient for salvation. You must know Christ personally through faith in the completed work of Jesus on the cross. Take inventory of your spiritual condition. Don't rely on feelings. Trace your steps and identify the moment you had a life-changing experience. Clarify your conversion experience. When did you come to realize your sin and your need for God's forgiveness? When you did acknowledge that Jesus is God's Son and the only way to Heaven? When did you receive God's gift of eternal life?

July 9
PORTRAY YOUR FAITH

"Suppose a brother or sister is without clothes and daily food. If one of you says to him, 'Go, I wish you well; keep warm and well fed,' but does nothing about his physical needs, what good is it? In the same way, faith by itself, if it is not accompanied by action, is dead." James 2:15-17 (NIV)

Your actions speak so loudly I can't hear what you're saying.

If you have been born from above, adopted into God's family, and filled with the Holy Spirit, shouldn't the reality of your salvation be evidenced? If you have experienced transformation on the inside, shouldn't that show up on the outside? Faith void of action is dead. Your faith is to be demonstrated by action.

- *"In the same way, let your light shine before men, that they may see your good deeds and praise your Father in heaven."*
  Matt 5:16 (NIV)
- *"The Lord's message rang out from you not only in Macedonia and Achaia--your faith in God has become known everywhere.*
  Therefore we do not need to say anything about it, for they themselves report what kind of reception you gave us. They tell how you turned to God from idols to serve the living and true God, and to wait for his Son from heaven, whom he raised from the dead-- Jesus, who rescues us from the coming wrath."
  1 Thess 1:8-10 (NIV)

God has put you in the display window of life to demonstrate your faith in practical ways. Find a need and meet it. Shine the light of Jesus and share the love of Jesus. Pray continually, give sacrificially, and worship passionately. May those who know you but don't know Jesus, come to know Jesus because they know you. May your faith be that convincing! May your faith be activated and demonstrated to a watching world!

BELIEVE IN JESUS

"You believe that there is one God. Good! Even the demons believe that--and shudder." James 2:19 (NIV)

Believing in God will not get you to Heaven.

God has revealed Himself generally through nature and specifically through the incarnate Word, Jesus. To say that you believe in God is not sufficient for salvation. James asserts that even the demons believe there is one God. Their monotheism is not enough. Judaism, Islam, and Christianity embrace monotheism. However, believing in one God does not produce salvation.

- *"For since the creation of the world God's invisible qualities--his eternal power and divine nature--have been clearly seen, being understood from what has been made, so that men are without excuse." Rom 1:20 (NIV)*
- *"'Salvation is found in no one else, for there is no other name under heaven given to men by which we must be saved.'" Acts 4:12 (NIV)*
- *"Jesus answered, 'I am the way and the truth and the life. No one comes to the Father except through me.'" John 14:6 (NIV)*

God has revealed Himself to us in the Person of Jesus Christ. The question is: What will you do with Jesus? The atoning work of Jesus on the cross is sufficient to save anyone, but effective only for those who trust in Christ alone for salvation. The gift of eternal life doesn't become a gift to you until you personally receive it. Do you believe that Jesus is God's Son? Do you believe that Jesus died to pay your sin debt in full? Do you believe that Jesus is the only way to Heaven? Have you received the gift of eternal life?

July 11
SALVATION THAT WORKS

"You foolish man, do you want evidence that faith without deeds is useless? Was not our ancestor Abraham considered righteous for what he did when he offered his son Isaac on the altar? You see that his faith and his actions were working together, and his faith was made complete by what he did." James 2:20-22 (NIV)

Your good works will not produce salvation.

If only you could work your way to Heaven! Then the challenge would be knowing how much work would be required by God for you to deserve entrance into Heaven. How would you know if you have done enough to get there? What if you almost made it but fell short by one good deed? Fortunately, God does not base your salvation on your works.

The Bible does not present a works salvation, but a salvation that works. You cannot work for your salvation, but your salvation will be evidenced by good works. In response to God's gracious gift of salvation, you will want to express your appreciation to God through deeds of righteousness. Your deeds will not produce righteousness, but your righteousness in Christ will produce righteous deeds. Your "want to" changes as a result of your salvation.

- *"God made him who had no sin to be sin for us, so that in him we might become the righteousness of God." 2 Cor 5:21 (NIV)*
- *"Those who obey his commands live in him, and he in them. And this is how we know that he lives in us: We know it by the Spirit he gave us." 1 John 3:24 (NIV)*

Your salvation is a gift from God and is marked by a life of obedience.

FAITH WORKS

"And without faith it is impossible to please God, because anyone who comes to him must believe that he exists and that he rewards those who earnestly seek him." Hebrews 11:6 (NIV)

How does faith work?

Faith works for you. God is always at work to bring us to the point of recognizing our need for a saving relationship with Jesus. The Holy Spirit convicts us of sin and convinces us of our need for salvation. God enables us through faith to respond to His gift of eternal life. In faith, we choose to receive God's provision of forgiveness made available through the sacrifice of Jesus on the cross.

- *"For God so loved the world that he gave his one and only Son, that whoever believes in him shall not perish but have eternal life." John 3:16 (NIV)*
- *"That if you confess with your mouth, 'Jesus is Lord,' and believe in your heart that God raised him from the dead, you will be saved. For it is with your heart that you believe and are justified, and it is with your mouth that you confess and are saved." Rom 10:9-10 (NIV)*

Have you experienced faith working for you? God took the initiative to bring you into a right relationship with Himself. Jesus paid the ultimate price for the forgiveness of your sins. At salvation, you became the temple of the Holy Spirit. Faith is not a feeling. Faith is a fact of God's activity in your life.

July 13
FEED THE FAITH

"Perseverance must finish its work so that you may be mature and complete, not lacking anything." James 1:4 (NIV)

How does faith work?

Faith works in you. God's desire and design for you is to bring you to a point of maturity and completion. You are still in the process of becoming who you are in Christ. Each day, you are either becoming more like Christ or less like Christ. As John Eldredge says in his book, *Walking with God*, "We see the original and intended shape of our lives in Jesus." Jesus is the model to follow.

- *"Epaphras, who is one of you and a servant of Christ Jesus, sends greetings. He is always wrestling in prayer for you, that you may stand firm in all the will of God, mature and fully assured." Col 4:12 (NIV)*
- *"Anyone who lives on milk, being still an infant, is not acquainted with the teaching about righteousness. But solid food is for the mature, who by constant use have trained themselves to distinguish good from evil." Heb 5:13-14 (NIV)*

God wants you to develop the faith He has placed inside of you. The orientation of your entire life is to be focused on growing spiritually and being used of God perpetually. Feed the faith planted in you by nurturing your walk with God daily. Your moment by moment awareness of God's activity in you and around you will produce a desire to mature in the faith.

Are you working out the faith that God has put in you? Are you growing in your love relationship with Jesus?

"Therefore, my dear friends, as you have always obeyed--not only in my presence, but now much more in my absence--continue to work out your salvation with fear and trembling, for it is God who works in you to will and to act according to his good purpose." Philippians 2:12-13 (NIV)

Faith works through you. God works in you so that He can do a work through you. God's heart is for the nations to worship Him. Can you see it? Imagine every person on planet earth from every language confessing Jesus as Lord and joining God in His redemptive activity. Imagine being so in tune with God's work in you that you naturally allow God to work through you to touch the nations for His glory. As you pray, give, and go so that everyone may know of God's love personally, the kingdom of God expands. The number of people delivered from the clutches of hell and placed in the kingdom of light multiplies as you faithfully allow God to work through you.

> • *"For we are God's workmanship, created in Christ Jesus to do good works, which God prepared in advance for us to do."*
> *Eph 2:10 (NIV)*

You have been formed and fashioned by God to know Him personally through a saving relationship made possible by the redemptive work of Jesus on the cross. Now that you know Him personally, make Jesus known. Give your life to expressing your faith in Jesus in such a way that those who don't know Jesus will come to know Him personally. Let the faith that worked for you in salvation work in you and through you to bring others to a saving faith in Jesus.

July 15
OVERFLOW OF YOUR HEART

"Make a tree good and its fruit will be good, or make a tree bad and its fruit will be bad, for a tree is recognized by its fruit. You brood of vipers, how can you who are evil say anything good? For out of the overflow of the heart the mouth speaks." Matthew 12:33-34 (NIV)

Do you remember the days when the nurse would ask you to stick out your tongue in order to insert a thermometer? The process was to detect your physical temperature. Your tongue is also an indicator of your spiritual temperature. The words you speak reflect what's in your heart. Jesus affirmed that the mouth speaks out of the overflow of the heart.

Biting your tongue is not sufficient. It's really not about your tongue. It's about your heart. Whatever is in your heart will be displayed by your speech. The way you speak to others will exhibit what's in your heart. Just as a good tree will bear good fruit and a bad tree produces bad fruit, your words will bear fruit based on the spiritual condition of your heart.

Open your mouth and stick out your tongue. What has your tongue revealed about your heart this week? Examine the words you have spoken. Have you been gracious and kind in your conversations? Have your interactions revealed a heart aligned with God's heart?

WEIGH YOUR WORDS

"My dear brothers, take note of this: Everyone should be quick to listen, slow to speak and slow to become angry." James 1:19 (NIV)

Did you know that every chapter of James addresses your speech? Your conversation and your conduct will indicate the spiritual condition of your heart. Read through these verses slowly and allow God to speak to you about your speech.

- *"Speak and act as those who are going to be judged by the law that gives freedom, because judgment without mercy will be shown to anyone who has not been merciful. Mercy triumphs over judgment!" James 2:12-13 (NIV)*
- *"All kinds of animals, birds, reptiles and creatures of the sea are being tamed and have been tamed by man, but no man can tame the tongue. It is a restless evil, full of deadly poison." James 3:7-8 (NIV)*
- *"Brothers, do not slander one another. Anyone who speaks against his brother or judges him speaks against the law and judges it. When you judge the law, you are not keeping it, but sitting in judgment on it." James 4:11 (NIV)*
- *"Above all, my brothers, do not swear--not by heaven or by earth or by anything else. Let your 'Yes' be yes, and your 'No,' no, or you will be condemned." James 5:12 (NIV)*

God weighs our words specifically. Everything we say today matters in eternity. Maybe that's why God gave us two ears and one mouth.

July 17
THINK BEFORE YOU SPEAK

"If anyone considers himself religious and yet does not keep a tight rein on his tongue, he deceives himself and his religion is worthless." James 1:26 (NIV)

Have you ever said something that you wish you could retrieve? We have all been there. If only we could have thought about what we were going to say before we said it. Let's use the word THINK as an acrostic to give us some insightful questions to ask before we speak.

Is it **T**rue? Now that's a great question for us to consider before speaking. What would our world look like if everyone only spoke the truth? Instead of spreading lies and infusing suspicion, everyone would operate based on integrity and truth.

Is it **H**elpful? Consider your words. Are they beneficial to others? Does your conversation add value to the lives of other people? Let's commit to speak words that bless and build others up.

Is it **I**nspiring? God has sealed you by the Holy Spirit so that you can be a vessel of honor. Your life is designed by God to inspire others to come to a saving relationship with Jesus Christ and to mature spiritually. Do your words encourage others to reach their God-given potential?

Is it **N**ecessary? Sometimes silence is the best option. When we are about to say something that is not necessary, maybe that's a good time to hit the pause button.

Is it **K**ind? I remember hearing Dr. Jerry Vines, pastor emeritus of First Baptist Church of Jacksonville, Florida, say that "a Christian never has the luxury of being unkind." Will our words reflect the heart of Jesus?

CONTROL YOUR TONGUE

"We all stumble in many ways. If anyone is never at fault in what he says, he is a perfect man, able to keep his whole body in check." James 3:2 (NIV)

One of the marks of spiritual maturity is controlling the tongue. James is saying that if you control your tongue you will be able to control your whole body. The sin nature seeks to be gratified. One of the most susceptible instruments to sin is your tongue. Someone has commented that your tongue is located in an area that is slippery when wet and for that reason God has placed the tongue behind a cage of teeth walled in by the mouth.

We have learned that it's really not about the tongue but about the heart. Jesus said that out of the overflow of the heart, the mouth speaks. What does it take to align your heart with God's heart?

Step 1: Ask God to search your heart.

King David prayed, "Search me, O God, and know my heart; test me and know my anxious thoughts. See if there is any offensive way in me, and lead me in the way everlasting" (Psalm 139:23-24 NIV). Are you willing to pray such a bold prayer? When you ask God to search your heart, He will unearth sin that has been embedded in your heart. The light of God's holiness will penetrate and expose any dark areas of your heart that are not in alignment with His heart. You may want to consider having a pen and some paper handy to write down what God brings to your attention.

July 19
TRANSFORMED SPEECH

"For I know my transgressions, and my sin is always before me. Against you, you only, have I sinned and done what is evil in your sight, so that you are proved right when you speak and justified when you judge." Psalm 51:3-4 (NIV)

Aligning your heart with God's heart is vital if your are going to control your tongue. Your speech is a matter of the heart. Your transformed heart will produce transformed speech. After you have asked God to search your heart, you are ready for the next step in aligning your heart with God's heart.

Step 2: Confess the sin God reveals.

After King David committed adultery and murder, God brought deep conviction to David's heart in order to position him for confession and repentance. As God revealed the sin in King David's life, David acknowledged his sin before God.

- *"If we claim to be without sin, we deceive ourselves and the truth is not in us."* 1 John 1:8 (NIV)
- *"If we confess our sins, he is faithful and just and will forgive us our sins and purify us from all unrighteousness."* 1 John 1:9 (NIV)

As God reveals the sin in your life, be willing to confess your sin specifically. In the language of the New Testament, to confess means to say that same thing about your sin that God says about it. Don't try to neutralize your sin or water it down. Name it and say the same thing about your sin that God says about it. Once you have confessed your sin specifically, receive God's provision of forgiveness. Now embrace a lifestyle of moral purity. As your heart is transformed by the grace of God, your speech will be transformed.

SURRENDER YOUR TONGUE

"All kinds of animals, birds, reptiles and creatures of the sea are being tamed and have been tamed by man, but no man can tame the tongue. It is a restless evil, full of deadly poison." James 3:7-8 (NIV)

As a child, my favorite part of the circus was watching the lions do tricks at their master's command. To see the lions that normally would devour a human being for an afternoon snack, now obeying their master, was breath taking. The lions had been tamed.

James says that no man can tame the tongue. He goes on to say that the tongue is a restless evil and full of deadly poison. That doesn't sound too good, does it? Is it even possible to control the tongue? The answer is "no." You cannot control the tongue on your own. That brings us to the final step in aligning your heart with God's heart.

Step 3: Surrender to the Holy Spirit's control.

Your body is the temple of the Holy Spirit. By refusing to give the Holy Spirit full control of your life, you will grieve and quench the Holy Spirit. You do not have the power in and of yourself to tame your tongue. Only the convicting, convincing, and comforting work of the Holy Spirit in your heart can produce lasting life change. To surrender to the Holy Spirit's control is a perpetual process of yielding to His prompting.

Jesus modeled this concept of yielding in the garden of Gethsemane when He yielded to the Father's will by saying, "My Father, if it is possible, may this cup be taken from me. Yet not as I will but as you will" (Matt 26:39 NIV). Jesus is our model to follow.

July 21
WOUNDED WITH WORDS

"If you have been trapped by what you said, ensnared by the words of your mouth, then do this, my son, to free yourself, since you have fallen into your neighbor's hands: Go and humble yourself; press your plea with your neighbor!"
Proverbs 6:2-3 (NIV)

Has your tongue ever gotten you in trouble? Examine the following verses to get a glimpse of how God views the words you speak.

- *"Whoever of you loves life and desires to see many good days, keep your tongue from evil and your lips from speaking lies."*
  Psalm 34:12-13 (NIV)
- *"He who guards his lips guards his life, but he who speaks rashly will come to ruin." Prov 13:3 (NIV)*
- *"The tongue has the power of life and death, and those who love it will eat its fruit." Prov 18:21 (NIV)*
- *"When words are many, sin is not absent, but he who holds his tongue is wise." Prov 10:19 (NIV)*
- *"A man of knowledge uses words with restraint, and a man of understanding is even-tempered." Prov 17:27 (NIV)*

In light of these verses, let's open another door. Have you wounded anyone with your words? Words have the power to build up or tear down. Words have the power to encourage or to deflate. Your words can bring healing or your words can bring harm.

In humility, go to the person you have wounded with your words and acknowledge your guilt. Ask for their forgiveness and watch God do a reconciling work in your relationship. Even if the person does not respond like you desire, do the right thing to honor God. God's way is always the best option!

DOING LIFE GOD'S WAY

"Who is wise and understanding among you? Let him show it by his good life, by deeds done in the humility that comes from wisdom." James 3:13 (NIV)

What does the good life look like? The good life is doing life God's way. God has created you for His glory. You are here to fulfill God's will. God has included you in His master plan. In order to do life God's way, you will need God's wisdom. Moses felt overwhelmed by God's assignment to deliver the children of Israel out of Egyptian bondage. Notice what Moses requested of God.

- *"If you are pleased with me, teach me your ways so I may know you and continue to find favor with you. Remember that this nation is your people." Ex 33:13 (NIV)*
- *"Wisdom is supreme; therefore get wisdom. Though it cost all you have, get understanding." Prov 4:7 (NIV)*

Wisdom is something that is given by God and is also something that you seek. What you will discover in your love relationship with God through the saving work of Jesus on the cross is that God invites you to participate with Him in doing life His way. Would others consider you wise and understanding? Have you demonstrated the good life by doing life God's way?

July 23
HEAVENLY WISDOM

"But if you harbor bitter envy and selfish ambition in your hearts, do not boast about it or deny the truth. Such 'wisdom' does not come down from heaven but is earthly, unspiritual, of the devil. For where you have envy and selfish ambition, there you find disorder and every evil practice." James 3:14-16 (NIV)

James distinguishes between earthly wisdom and heavenly wisdom. Your conversation and your conduct will demonstrate the kind of wisdom you are operating from. The way you treat others will indicate the wisdom you draw from. The earthly wisdom that James identifies comes naturally. Heavenly wisdom is supernatural and is reserved for the child of God. However, it is possible for a believer to operate in the realm of earthly wisdom and neglect the wisdom from Heaven.

The poison of envy and the toxin of selfish ambition are earthly, unspiritual, and of the devil. The good life that God calls us to is not rooted in earthly wisdom which is marked by selfishness. Earthly wisdom feeds the cravings of the sin nature. The gratification of the flesh is centered in earthly wisdom. The devil seeks to get people to resist heavenly wisdom and to settle for the vanity of envy and selfish ambition. Disorder and every evil practice are the byproduct of a self-centered life steeped in earthly wisdom.

Take personal inventory. What kind of wisdom are you drawing from? Does your life give evidence to the good life God has designed for you?

Employ Heavenly Wisdom

"But the wisdom that comes from heaven is first of all pure; then peace-loving, considerate, submissive, full of mercy and good fruit, impartial and sincere." James 3:17 (NIV)

Doing life God's way involves obtaining and employing heavenly wisdom. What does that kind of wisdom look like? James has already explained the components of earthly wisdom in the previous three verses. We learned that earthly wisdom is characterized by selfishness while heavenly wisdom is characterized by selflessness. Selfishness is an expression of earthly wisdom. Selflessness is an expression of heavenly wisdom. Jesus, of course, is our model to follow.

- *"Do nothing out of selfish ambition or vain conceit, but in humility consider others better than yourselves. Each of you should look not only to your own interests, but also to the interests of others."* Phil 2:3-4 (NIV)
- *"Your attitude should be the same as that of Christ Jesus: Who, being in very nature God, did not consider equality with God something to be grasped, but made himself nothing, taking the very nature of a servant, being made in human likeness. And being found in appearance as a man, he humbled himself and became obedient to death--even death on a cross!"* Phil 2:5-8 (NIV)

Heavenly wisdom becomes a practical expression in your daily living. As you do life God's way, you will live a life of moral purity. You will be peace-loving, considerate of others, and submissive to God's agenda. Heavenly wisdom will be evidenced through your lifestyle of mercy and good fruit, being impartial and sincere. What kind of wisdom are you exhibiting through your conversation and your conduct? Will others be drawn to Christ or repelled from Christ?

July 25
REVERE GOD

"Now all has been heard; here is the conclusion of the matter: Fear God and keep his commandments, for this is the whole duty of man." Ecclesiastes 12:13 (NIV)

Imagine enjoying a cup of coffee at Starbuck's with one of the wisest men to ever live, Solomon. That's right! You are sitting across from Solomon and you ask him to share with you what he has learned after experiencing life in a way that few would ever experience in a lifetime. Solomon pursued wealth, wisdom, and women. At the end of his life, he looks into the rear view mirror and captures what matters most.

Let me share the first essential to doing life God's way: Revere God.

Solomon says to "fear God." In the language of the Old Testament, to fear God means to revere God. It means to hold God in high esteem. We are to place the worth and value on God that He deserves. We are to reverence God for who He is and for what He has done.

Revering God involves giving Him first place in your life. Your ambition is to honor God with your life. His agenda becomes the focus of your life. You revere God by aligning your heart with His heart. Revering God is demonstrated by loving what God loves and by hating what God hates.

In his book, *Walking with God*, John Eldredge writes, "I assume that an intimate, conversational walk with God is available, and is meant to be normal." As you walk with God and revere Him, your love relationship with God will become intimate. Doing life God's way always produces intimacy with God and brings Him pleasure.

TRUE SUCCESS

"Now all has been heard; here is the conclusion of the matter: Fear God and keep his commandments, for this is the whole duty of man." Ecclesiastes 12:13 (NIV)

Another essential to doing life God's way is obedience. Revering God is demonstrated through obeying God. Solomon recognized the priority of doing life God's way. After experiencing life in the fast lane and having access to the wealth of the world, Solomon embraced the value of making God his top priority. Keeping God's commandments became the central focus of Solomon's life.

- *"Therefore everyone who hears these words of mine and puts them into practice is like a wise man who built his house on the rock. The rain came down, the streams rose, and the winds blew and beat against that house; yet it did not fall, because it had its foundation on the rock." Matt 7:24-25 (NIV)*
- *"We know that we have come to know him if we obey his commands." 1 John 2:3 (NIV)*

Let me encourage you to obey what you know. As you grow in your knowledge of God's Word and as you grow in your love relationship with God, seek to obey what God has already revealed to you. Seek to love God and to love others the way God has loved you.

How would you define success in this life? Consider the bumper sticker I have seen recently: He who dies with the most toys wins! Is that true success? Success is obedience! Let's do life God's way.

July 27
SEIZE OPPORTUNITIES

"For God will bring every deed into judgment, including every hidden thing, whether it is good or evil." Ecclesiastes 12:14 (NIV)

As you revere God and obey Him, you will be obtaining and employing heavenly wisdom. Another essential to doing life God's way is portraying the life of Christ. God pursued you with His love and rescued you so that you would portray the life of Christ on earth. You are to bloom where God has planted you so that others will be drawn to Christ through your witness. Think of the people God has placed in your sphere of influence. Why do you think God brings such people into your life? God wants you to live in such a way as to model Christ before them.

- *"Don't let anyone look down on you because you are young, but set an example for the believers in speech, in life, in love, in faith and in purity." 1 Tim 4:12 (NIV)*
- *"Be very careful, then, how you live--not as unwise but as wise, making the most of every opportunity, because the days are evil." Eph 5:15-16 (NIV)*

One day you will stand before God to give an account for your life. Seize the opportunities that God gives you to make Jesus known. Do life God's way so that you will bring honor to God and populate the kingdom of Heaven.

FULL SURRENDER

"If any of you lacks wisdom, he should ask God, who gives generously to all without finding fault, and it will be given to him." James 1:5 (NIV)

Here's an overview of what we have learned from the first three chapters of James.

- Respond properly to trials from without.

- Respond properly to temptations from within.

- Apply God's Word consistently in daily living.

- Value others as God does.

- Demonstrate a faith that works.

- Control your speech.

- Employ God's wisdom in daily decisions.

- Do life God's way by revering, obeying, and portraying Christ.

The good life is marked by full surrender to God's agenda. Allow God to work in you so that He can work through you to bring others to Christ. Your conversation and your conduct have eternal implications. The way you treat others is a direct reflection of your love relationship with Christ.

Don't hesitate to ask God for wisdom each day. God is generous and wants to shower you with heavenly wisdom for doing life His way. Trust God to be your sufficiency!

July 29
TAKE PRIDE FOR A RIDE

"What causes fights and quarrels among you? Don't they come from your desires that battle within you?" James 4:1 (NIV)

Have you ever been in a fight? Have you ever quarreled with someone and sought to get your way at any cost? Can you imagine that kind of behavior among believers? James identifies the reality of infighting among the believers who have been dispersed as a result of persecution. Now they are persecuting each other with improper behavior. It can happen to good people who are seeking to follow God.

Even after we profess Christ as Lord of our lives, we continue to battle the sin nature. The old patterns that God delivered us from seek to pop up from time to time. We have three enemies that we combat: the devil, the world, and the flesh. What if the devil eased up on us and the tugs of the world lessened their appeal? The truth is, we would still have to combat the cravings of our flesh.

James points to the culprit of fights and quarrels, namely, our desires that battle from within. Selfish desires and behavior steeped in pride come from within. The outward expression of our inward desires can bring harm to the Body of Christ and contaminate our witness. Attacking other believers through our words and our deeds is an indicator of selfishness and pride.

What's the opposite of pride? Humility! God gave us a portrait of humility by allowing Jesus to pay full price for the sin debt of the world. If God was willing to do that for us, what should we be willing to do for Him? Let's start with treating others the way God has treated us.

PURE MOTIVES

"You want something but don't get it. You kill and covet, but you cannot have what you want. You quarrel and fight. You do not have, because you do not ask God. When you ask, you do not receive, because you ask with wrong motives, that you may spend what you get on your pleasures." James 4:2-3 (NIV)

Motives matter to God.

Have you ever been the recipient of a gift that was given with impure motives? When motives are not right, the gift loses its impact. How you give is just as important as what you give. How you serve is just as important as the act of serving. How you do life is just as important as what you do with your life.

God is all-knowing and all-seeing. In His omniscience, God detects the motives in which you operate your life. God looks beneath the surface of your good deeds to identify your true motives. Selfishness is an indicator of impure motives. Wrong motives will cause you to mistreat others in order to get what you want.

- *"All a man's ways seem innocent to him, but motives are weighed by the LORD." Prov 16:2 (NIV)*
- *"'Ask and it will be given to you; seek and you will find; knock and the door will be opened to you. For everyone who asks receives; he who seeks finds; and to him who knocks, the door will be opened.'" Matt 7:7-8 (NIV)*

What if we started with a boldness to simply ask God? If there is something we need, what keeps us from asking God who is the Creator and Sustainer of life? Why do we try to take life into our own hands and allow impure motives to infiltrate our decisions? Let's commit to go to God! He is our sufficiency!

July 31
SUBMIT TO GOD

"Submit yourselves, then, to God. Resist the devil, and he will flee from you."
James 4:7 (NIV)

Rebellion against God is rooted in pride. Submission to God is rooted in humility. Rebellion brings harm and punishment. Submission brings relief and reward. Knowing that God opposes the proud and gives grace to the humble, the child of God benefits from submission. To submit to God is not a sign of weakness, but a sign of wisdom.

When you recognize that God is the Creator and that you are the created, you relinquish the pursuit of control. Submitting to God is allowing God to have complete control of your life. When you submit to God, you are acknowledging His supremacy and your dependency. The posture of submission resonates with the life of Christ.

- *"'My food,' said Jesus, 'is to do the will of him who sent me and to finish his work.'" John 4:34 (NIV)*
- *"Going a little farther, he fell with his face to the ground and prayed, 'My Father, if it is possible, may this cup be taken from me. Yet not as I will, but as you will.'" Matt 26:39 (NIV)*

How will you respond to life today? Will you submit to God? Are you in tune with God's purpose and plan for your life? Has God's agenda become your passion?

"Submit yourselves, then, to God. Resist the devil, and he will flee from you."
James 4:7 (NIV)

Jesus is our portrait of humility. The devil is our portrait of pride. Jesus came to earth to fulfill the Father's will. The devil came in rebellion to thwart God's agenda. As an angel of God, the devil pridefully sought to dethrone God. It backfired on him! God de-heavened the devil!

- *"You said in your heart, 'I will ascend to heaven; I will raise my throne above the stars of God; I will sit enthroned on the mount of assembly, on the utmost heights of the sacred mountain. I will ascend above the tops of the clouds; I will make myself like the Most High.' But you are brought down to the grave, to the depths of the pit." Isaiah 14:13-15 (NIV)*
- *"Be self-controlled and alert. Your enemy the devil prowls around like a roaring lion looking for someone to devour. Resist him, standing firm in the faith, because you know that your brothers throughout the world are undergoing the same kind of sufferings." 1 Pet 5:8-9 (NIV)*

The devil is real. However, as you submit to God and choose to resist the devil, he will flee from you. As a child of God, you have everything you need to defeat the enemy. In Christ, you are the victor! In order to reign in this life, allow Jesus to reign in your life! Submit and resist!

August 2
DRAWING NEAR

"Come near to God and he will come near to you. Wash your hands, you sinners, and purify your hearts, you double-minded." James 4:8 (NIV)

Over the years I have experimented with different ways to enhance my daily intimacy with God. I have utilized the daily devotional by Oswald Chambers, *My Utmost for His Highest* and also *Experiencing God Day by Day* written by Henry Blackaby. The most vital element in my spiritual development has been a consistent intake of God's Word such as reading through the entire Bible in one year. Sometimes I commit to reading a chapter of Proverbs each day for an entire year. Thus, I read the book of Proverbs all the way through each month. That's been an incredible adventure. The following verses are my favorite from the fourth chapter of Proverbs. When I think of drawing near to God and living wisely, this passage immediately rises to the surface.

- *"Above all else, guard your heart, for it is the wellspring of life. Put away perversity from your mouth; keep corrupt talk far from your lips. Let your eyes look straight ahead, fix your gaze directly before you. Make level paths for your feet and take only ways that are firm. Do not swerve to the right or the left; keep your foot from evil." Prov 4:23-27 (NIV)*

There are so many options for you to embrace in this world. Countless paths await your selection. Careless living will grant you unlimited choices that will never deliver what they promise. Are you guarding your heart? Is your speech laced with purity? Is your vision focused on the way that brings honor to God? Are you taking paths that are pleasing to God? Do you consistently avoid evil? Are you choosing to draw near to God and to live a life of moral purity?

"But he gives us more grace. That is why Scripture says: 'God opposes the proud but gives grace to the humble.'" James 4:6 (NIV)

Grace is getting what we do not deserve. We do not deserve God's forgiveness, salvation, reconciliation, favor, blessing, and Heaven. But God demonstrates His love by gracing us with that which we do not deserve. God stands in opposition to the proud but responds with grace to the humble. So what does humility look like? As we examine the life of Jesus, we see humility defined. Jesus willingly put others before Himself. Jesus lived selflessly and died sacrificially. Jesus came to this earth to serve and to save. How will you respond?

- *"Humble yourselves before the Lord, and he will lift you up."* James 4:10 (NIV)
- *"Humble yourselves, therefore, under God's mighty hand, that he may lift you up in due time."* 1 Pet 5:6 (NIV)

We are to humble ourselves. As an act of the will, we are to choose to humble ourselves. God can navigate circumstances to bring humility into our lives to remind us of our dependency upon Him. Yet, God wants to us choose the way of humility without the influence of outward circumstances. Based on our love relationship with God, we are to respond to His grace by exemplifying a life of humility.

Is there an element of pride in your life? Have you exhibited the sin of pride through your conversation or your conduct? Trying to do life your way instead of God's way is an expression of pride. Embrace the way of humility which places God's agenda above your own agenda. Anticipate God's grace to flow like a river!

August 4
OBTAIN A PROPER VIEW

"For by the grace given me I say to every one of you: Do not think of yourself more highly than you ought, but rather think of yourself with sober judgment, in accordance with the measure of faith God has given you." Romans 12:3 (NIV)

Do you have a skewed view of yourself? When you examine your life, what do you see? Perhaps you have a low view of yourself. It may be that you have an inflated view of yourself. Someone has remarked that we view others based on their actions and we view ourselves based on our intentions.

How does God want you to view yourself? The proper way to view yourself is in accordance with the measure of faith God has given you. How do you measure that faith? You need a standard! The wonderful news is that Jesus is our standard. He is the benchmark for our assessment. God wants you to use sober judgment. In other words, you are to measure your life with accuracy. Instead of comparing yourself to others, examine your life in light of Christ.

Assess your current reality using Jesus as your standard. He is the model to follow. Jesus is the example to emulate. Obtain a proper view of yourself. Allow the standard of Christ's life to produce an element of brokenness and humility inside of you. Embrace the desperation and invite Jesus to take you to the place of being more like Him.

Begin to view others through the lens of the journey you are on. Recognize that you haven't arrived. Start viewing others through the prospect of their life fully yielded to Christ. What if they became like Christ? View yourself and others through the measure of faith God has given you. You are in Christ because of God's unconditional love.

"Therefore, since we have a great high priest who has gone through the heavens, Jesus the Son of God, let us hold firmly to the faith we profess. For we do not have a high priest who is unable to sympathize with our weaknesses, but we have one who has been tempted in every way, just as we are yet was without sin. Let us then approach the throne of grace with confidence, so that we may receive mercy and find grace to help us in our time of need."
Hebrews 4:14-16 (NIV)

As believers, we commune with God through Jesus. As a Christ follower, you have direct access to God through Jesus. Are you aligned with God's agenda? God's will includes you.

God's will involves prayer. Prayer is aligning your life with God's agenda. God has a plan for your life. He has a purpose for you to fulfill. How do you get connected to that purpose and plan? Through alignment!

Prayer is the avenue through which we connect with God. He has already broken down the barriers that separated us. God grants us access to Him through prayer based on the atonement of Christ. Because Jesus paid the penalty for our sin, we have the privilege of communing with God through prayer.

The Israelites communed with God through the use of the Tabernacle.

- *"'Then have them make a sanctuary for me, and I will dwell among them. Make this tabernacle and all its furnishings exactly like the pattern I will show you.'"* Ex 25:8-9 (NIV)

August 6
LIVE IN THE NOW

"Do not boast about tomorrow, for you do not know what a day may bring forth."
Proverbs 27:1 (NIV)

We may not know what tomorrow holds, but we know who holds tomorrow. God is eternal. God was never born and He will never die. God is infinite and we are finite. God is all-knowing and we are limited in our knowing. God is the Creator and we are the created. In other words, God is the potter and we are the clay.

- *"For you created my inmost being; you knit me together in my mother's womb. I praise you because I am fearfully and wonderfully made; your works are wonderful, I know that full well."* Psalm 139:13-14 (NIV)
- *"'For I know the plans I have for you,' declares the LORD, 'plans to prosper you and not to harm you, plans to give you hope and a future.'" Jer 29:11 (NIV)*

We have no room to boast about tomorrow. We cannot see tomorrow, but God can. In our humanity, we have a limited view of tomorrow, but God's view is complete. God formed us and fashioned us for His glory. God's plans are to prosper us and not to harm us. God's plans include giving us hope and a future.

SENSITIVITY TO GOD'S ACTIVITY

"Jesus said to them, 'My Father is always at his work to this very day, and I, too, am working.'" John 5:17 (NIV)

God's will involves identifying where God is at work. Jesus said that God is always at work. The question is not, is God at work, but where is God at work. As Henry Blackaby says, "Look to see where God is at work so that you can join Him in what He is doing." In your current situation, God is at work. In your neighborhood, God is at work. In your community, your country, and on every continent, God is at work. Are you willing to look to see where God is at work and choose to join Him in His activity?

Detecting where God is at work requires sensitivity. You must be sensitive to God's activity. You can get so busy in life and so distracted by the things of this world that you become numb toward the activity of God. Sensitivity to God's activity comes through a life of full surrender. As you surrender your agenda to God's agenda and surrender your desires to God's desires, you will begin seeing God's activity. Your sensitvity to God's activity will continue to grow as you join God in what He is doing.

There's no place on earth like being in the center of God's will. Take some time today to evaluate your level of sensitivity to God's activity. Have you become anesthetized to the things of God? Have you become numb toward the activity of God? Surrender completely to the Lord and ask Him to give you a special sensitivity to His activity.

August 8
LIVE OUT GOD'S WORD

"Do not merely listen to the word, and so deceive yourselves. Do what it says."
James 1:22 (NIV)

God's will involves listening. God speaks to us through the Bible. As you read the Bible, you read God's revelation. God's will is that you obey His Word. God also speaks through prayer. As you connect with God through prayer, He reveals His will to you. In order to hear God's voice, you must listen with expectation and anticipation of God's revelation. You learn to recognize God's voice as you walk with God.

- *"When he has brought out all his own, he goes on ahead of them, and his sheep follow him because they know his voice."*
  John 10:4 (NIV)
- *"My sheep listen to my voice; I know them, and they follow me."*
  John 10:27 (NIV)

Listening to God's Word is not enough. You must do what it says. Put God's Word into practice by obeying what God reveals to you. Sometimes God will wait for you to obey what He has already revealed to you before unveiling His next layer of revelation. Are you obeying what God has already revealed to you?

Obey what you know. As you obey, God will show you more and more of His way.

WORLD REDEMPTION ACTIVITY

"The Lord is not slow in keeping his promise, as some understand slowness. He is patient with you, not wanting anyone to perish, but everyone to come to repentance." 2 Peter 3:9 (NIV)

God's will is that you be saved. The heart of God is for world redemption. The ultimate price has been paid for world redemption to be made possible. That price was paid by the substitutionary death of Jesus on the cross. Jesus paid the debt we could not pay to purchase the salvation we could not earn.

Universalism teaches that all will be saved. However, the Bible is clear that only those who confess Jesus as Lord will be saved. Only those who have been born again will enter the kingdom of Heaven. Without receiving the gift of eternal life through Jesus Christ, a person is without hope and without Heaven. This would be an ideal time to take spiritual inventory of your own life and solidify your own salvation. It is God's will that you be saved. Have you received God's gift of eternal life?

- *"For the wages of sin is death, but the gift of God is eternal life in Christ Jesus our Lord." Rom 6:23 (NIV)*
- *"That if you confess with your mouth, 'Jesus is Lord,' and believe in your heart that God raised him from the dead, you will be saved. For it is with your heart that you believe and are justified, and it is with your mouth that you confess and are saved."*
  Rom 10:9-10 (NIV)

God saves you to secure you for eternity in Heaven and to empower you to shine His light and to share His love with the lost and dying world that He has placed you in. You are rescued by God so that you can join God in His world redemption activity.

August 10
RECOGNIZE GOD'S SOVEREIGNTY

"Now listen, you who say, 'Today or tomorrow we will go to this or that city, spend a year there, carry on business and make money.' Why, you do not even know what will happen tomorrow. What is your life? You are a mist that appears for a little while and then vanishes. Instead, you ought to say, 'If it is the Lord's will, we will live and do this or that.'" James 4:13-15 (NIV)

God's will is that you grow spiritually. The process of sanctification includes your obedience to God's plan. As you submit to God's will, your spiritual maturity continues to develop. One mark of spiritual maturity is the recognition of the sovereignty of God. Instead of presuming upon the grace of God and His plan, you acknowledge that God has the final say in what each day holds for you. His plans supersede your plans. God's agenda becomes the priority of your life.

James reminds us of the brevity of life. Another mark of spiritual maturity is recognizing how fragile life is. In light of eternity, your life on planet earth is brief. God made you not for time, but for eternity. Living in light of eternity not only helps you develop spiritual maturity, but also helps to measure your level of spiritual maturity. Your view of life on earth will determine how you invest your time, treasures, and talents.

Learn to live each day with the "if" of God's will. If it is God's will, you will do this or that.

Just Do It

"Anyone, then, who knows the good he ought to do and doesn't do it, sins."
James 4:17 (NIV)

What would God have you do today? Did you know that God has a "to-do" list for you for today? God wants you to be saved! God wants you to grow spiritually! God wants you to share His love and to shine His light! God created you to be relational, not robotic. As you walk with God, He invites you to be in such relational intimacy with Him that you respond to His voice with instant obedience.

You know the good that you ought to do. It's not that you need more information or more imperatives. Start doing what God has already told you to do. Instant obedience demonstrates your allegiance and loyalty to God's will. There are times when you may desire God to simply write His will on the wall so that you can read it and obey. It just so happens that the wall is the pages upon which God's Word is written for you to read personally and obey instantly.

You may be waiting for God's direction concerning a specific decision that you need to make. Walk in the light God gives you. If you are not at peace about a certain direction, don't make a move. Wait until God gives you the release to move into that particular direction. Remember that God has been at work long before your specific situation showed up on your radar. Nothing catches God by surprise. God has a purpose for anything and everything that surprises us. Wait on God's timing and practice instant obedience. God's way is always the best way!

August 12

FINISH STRONG

"I have fought the good fight, I have finished the race, I have kept the faith. Now there is in store for me the crown of righteousness, which the Lord, the righteous Judge, will award to me on that day--and not only to me, but also to all who have longed for his appearing." 2 Timothy 4:7-8 (NIV)

This verse comes to life when you bury someone close to you. There's something about funerals that remind us of the brevity of life and the reality of Heaven. Maybe it causes us to move closer to the reality of our mortality. The pace of life on earth can sometimes numb our emotions and keep us from dealing with life beyond the grave. Seeing your loved one in a casket is a stark reminder that we are one breath away from eternity.

Paul was at the end of his life and wrote a final letter to his son in the ministry, Timothy. Paul had truly fought the good fight. Paul had finished the race and kept the faith. He finished strong! Paul reminded Timothy of the crown of righteousness that Jesus would be awarding at the finish line.

Think about your life. How are you doing? When you look into the rear view mirror of life, do you have any regrets? Remember, it's not how you start; it's how you finish that matters most! Fight the good fight of the faith. Yes! It is a fight because we are in a spiritual battle that has eternal implications. Your life has eternity written all over it. Finish strong!

"I have been reminded of your sincere faith, which first lived in your grandmother Lois and in your mother Eunice and, I am persuaded, now lives in you also."
2 Timothy 1:5 (NIV)

Does your faith come across to others as sincere? Do others detect the genuineness of your faith? That kind of faith is a positive witness for Christ. Think about those who have modeled that kind of faith for you. Perhaps you can look within your immediate family to find a sincere faith. You may have to go beyond those relationships to identify a sincere faith depending on the spiritual reality found within your family.

Paul recognized the sincere faith that lived in Timothy. Paul traced Timothy's sincere faith through his mother, Eunice, and his grandmother, Lois. The sincere faith was modeled faithfully and handed down intentionally. Timothy was blessed to have a godly grandmother and a godly mother committed to the sincere faith that is the fruit of a transformed life.

Are you modeling a sincere faith? Are you intentionally handing down the faith to others? Spend a few moments thanking God for the individuals He has placed in your life in the past and in the present who have modeled a sincere faith before you. Consider the impact they have made on your life and give God the glory!

August 14
WITNESS THROUGH ADVERSITY

"Now I want you to know, brothers, that what has happened to me has really served to advance the gospel. As a result, it has become clear throughout the whole palace guard and to everyone else that I am in chains for Christ. Because of my chains, most of the brothers in the Lord have been encouraged to speak the word of God more courageously and fearlessly." Philippians 1:12-14 (NIV)

Adversity creates opportunity.

The Apostle Paul knew adversity on a first name basis. He experienced the fangs of adversity as he served God and sought to spread the gospel message. During his first imprisonment in Rome, Paul wrote a letter to the church he started in Philippi. Paul acknowledged how God used the adversity in his life to advance the gospel. Instead of Paul's imprisonment halting the movement of the gospel, God utilized Paul's adversity as an avenue for the gospel to saturate the land.

One of my favorite quotes from Rick Warren is, "Everything that happens to a child of God is father-filtered." If God permits something to come into your life, He will use it for your good and for His glory. God does not waste pain. God does not waste the trauma we experience while living in this fallen world. God redeems our pain and creates opportunities through our adversity to spread the gospel.

What kind of adversity are you currently experiencing? Don't ask "why", but ask "what" is God wanting to accomplish through the adversity He has allowed into your life.

GROW THROUGH ADVERSITY

"In this you greatly rejoice, though now for a little while you may have had to suffer grief in all kinds of trials. These have come so that your faith--of greater worth than gold, which perishes even though refined by fire--may be proved genuine and may result in praise, glory and honor when Jesus Christ is revealed."
1 Peter 1:6-7 (NIV)

Adversity is as normal in this life as the rising and setting of the sun. Living in a fallen world accentuates the instability of morality. Selfishness and sinfulness permeate the global landscape. Since the Fall of man, we have combated our three enemies: Satan, our flesh, and the world. Eliminate Satan and you still have to contend with the cravings of the sin nature and the gravitational pull of the world. Yet, all three enemies are alive and well.

Jesus prayed that God would protect us from the evil one (John 15:17). The enemy is at work seeking to destroy the work of God in us and the work of God through us. In the midst of the battle, God converts what the enemy meant for evil into good (Gen 50:20). Remember, if God allows adversity into your life, He will use it for your good and His glory.

Will you grow through adversity as you go through adversity? Will you allow God to build your character and develop your faith through the assembly line of adversity? Your faith is of greater worth than gold to God. God's goal is that your faith be proved genuine so that it may bring glory to God when Jesus Christ is revealed.

August 16
SERVE IN ADVERSITY

"And when the centurion, who stood there in front of Jesus, heard his cry and saw how he died, he said, 'Surely this man was the Son of God!'" Mark 15:39 (NIV)

What was it about the final hours of Jesus' life that made an eternal impact on the centurion who approved of the punishment Jesus endured? What were the features of Jesus' death that convinced the centurion that Jesus was the Son of God? I wonder how many crucifixions this centurion had witnessed before he even knew Jesus existed. Perhaps the centurion had personally witnessed hundreds or thousands of these executions.

There was something about the way Jesus died that changed everything for this centurion. Maybe the centurion overheard the conversation between Jesus and the thief on the cross who said to Jesus, "Remember me when you come into your kingdom" (Luke 23:42 NIV). Jesus responded to the thief, "I tell you the truth, today you will be with me in paradise" (Luke 23:43 NIV). Perhaps the centurion saw the grace of God in action as Jesus put the needs of someone else before His own.

The centurion could have been standing close enough to overhear Jesus say to His mother, "Dear woman, here is your son" and to the disciple whom Jesus loved, "Here is your mother" (John 19:26-27 NIV). Maybe the centurion detected the deep love that Jesus had for His mother and the compassion He extended from the cross as He made sure His mother's needs would be met. Of all the crucifixions the centurion assisted in, perhaps he had never seen such love.

Adversity creates unique opportunities to show the love of Jesus as you serve others. Jesus exemplified servitude in the midst of extreme adversity. Are you watching for opportunities to serve others while you navigate the terrain of adversity?

"But the fruit of the Spirit is love, joy, peace, patience, kindness, goodness, faithfulness, gentleness and self-control. Against such things there is no law."
Galatians 5:22-23 (NIV)

In my journey of walking with God, I have discovered that God will focus on the fruit of the Spirit in your life that is most neglected. Whichever fruit of the Spirit you are least evidencing is the fruit that God will seek to develop in you through the university of adversity. I've taken many courses in that particular university.

If you lack the fruit of the Spirit, love, then God will allow difficult people to come into your life in order to give you opportunities to develop that specific fruit of the Spirit. If you lack patience, God will allow trying circumstances to come into the domain of your daily life in order to produce patience in you. That's why I never ask anyone to pray that God would give me patience. If you lack gentleness, God will orchestrate situations which will give you relational opportunities to develop that particular fruit of the Spirit.

In all things God works for your good (Rom 8:28) and God's goal for your life is conformity to Christ (Rom 8:29). Anything in your life that doesn't look like Christ will be removed through God's loving hammer and chisel of adversity. Don't be surprised by the adversity God allows into your path. God is building you into a portrait of His grace. Christlikeness is God's goal for your life!

So how do you look? Do you look like Christ? Is there any attitude or behavior that is not Christlike? Are you drifting from God or drawing near to God? Is the fruit of the Spirit evident in your conversation and your conduct?

August 18
CESSATION OF ADVERSITY

"Therefore we do not lose heart. Though outwardly we are wasting away, yet inwardly we are being renewed day by day. For our light and momentary troubles are achieving for us an eternal glory that far outweighs them all. So we fix our eyes not on what is seen, but on what is unseen. For what is seen is temporary, but what is unseen is eternal." 2 Corinthians 4:16-18 (NIV)

Adversity is not terminal, but it produces eternal results. Our current adversity is achieving for us an eternal glory. One day we will receive our glorified body. We will be delivered from this fallen world. We have been justified by God's grace. We are being transformed into the likeness of Christ and we will be glorified. The best is yet to come. Don't give up! Don't throw in the towel!

- *"Listen, I tell you a mystery: We will not all sleep, but we will all be changed--in a flash, in the twinkling of an eye, at the last trumpet. For the trumpet will sound, the dead will be raised imperishable, and we will be changed. For the perishable must clothe itself with the imperishable, and the mortal with immortality." 1 Cor 15:51-53 (NIV)*
- *"No longer will there be any curse. The throne of God and of the Lamb will be in the city, and his servants will serve him. They will see his face, and his name will be on their foreheads. There will be no more night. They will not need the light of a lamp or the light of the sun, for the Lord God will give them light. And they will reign for ever and ever." Rev 22:3-5 (NIV)*

Adversity will cease and God's peace will reign. Our battle with sin, sorrow, and sickness will end. God's glory will be revealed and we will reign with Him forever and ever! Are you ready for Heaven? Fix your eyes on Jesus!

Pray Through the Pain

"Is any one of you in trouble? He should pray. Is anyone happy? Let him sing songs of praise." James 5:13 (NIV)

Independence is valued in our society. Being strong and self-sufficient tend to be the marks of success by the world's standards. However, God's economy has a much different value system. It's not about personal strength, but reliance upon God's strength. Self-sufficiency is replaced with dependency upon God and His provision. Success in God's economy is marked by instant obedience and alignment with God's plan.

Part of God's plan includes our relational connection to God through an abiding relationship with Jesus Christ. The love relationship that God has made available to us in Christ is nurtured by our daily communion with God in prayer. The prayer connection flows from God to us and from us to God. God invites us into an intimate prayer connection that radiates from His heart of love and our response of awe and wonder. Imagine being able to share your heart as well as your heartaches with the God of the universe. We have that amazing privilege to bring everything to God in prayer. In Christ, we have been given access to the Creator of the universe.

Are you in trouble? Are you experiencing challenging circumstances or strained relationships? Don't delay! Take your burdens to the Lord in prayer. Empty the contents of your heart before the loving and faithful God that you have come to know by experience. God has provided you with the ultimate communication instrument called prayer. Just pray! Begin to articulate to God whatever is perplexing you and whatever is bothering you. God can handle your hurt. God can make the fog lift. Be still and know that He is God (Psalm 46:10). God's line is never busy and yes, He can hear you now!

August 20
ASKING FOR PRAYER

"Is any one of you sick? He should call the elders of the church to pray over him and anoint him with oil in the name of the Lord." James 5:14 (NIV)

The Christian life is not a solo flight. God never intended for us to live out our faith in isolation. As followers of Christ, we have Jesus at the right hand of the Father making intercession for us (Rom 8:34) and we have the Holy Spirit interceding for us with groans that words cannot express (Rom 8:26-27). God has also given us fellow believers who can stand in the gap for us in prayer.

The Apostle Paul asked for the believers in the church at Ephesus to pray that he would fearlessly make known the mystery of the gospel (Eph 6:19). Paul asked the church at Colosse to pray that God would open a door for his message so that he could proclaim the mystery of Christ (Col 4:3). Paul asked the church at Thessalonica to pray for he and his ministry partners that the message of the Lord would spread rapidly and be honored and that they would be delivered from evil and wicked men (2 Thess 3:1-2).

James affirms the need for outside prayer support for our lives. If you are experiencing spiritual weakness or even a physical illness, ask a spiritual leader to pray for you. If you are walking through a challenging situation or combating a difficult season, ask a spiritual leader to pray for you. Surround yourself with prayer warriors who will do warfare praying on your behalf. Don't be afraid to ask for prayer support. God has placed people within your sphere of influence who can stand in the gap for you in prayer.

Do you have someone praying you through?

"And the prayer offered in faith will make the sick person well; the Lord will raise him up. If he has sinned, he will be forgiven." James 5:15 (NIV)

Did you know that even godly people who have a vibrant faith in God can go through seasons of adversity? Often these difficult seasons can strengthen your faith and also cause you to become weary. As you fight the good fight of the faith (1 Tim 6:12), you may experience spiritual exhaustion. Battle fatigue is a potential reality for the follower of Christ.

James wrote to believers who had experienced severe persecution. Their faith had been tested and many of them had become emotionally depleted and spiritually exhausted. In some cases, their spiritual weakness caused them to be unable to call on God.

We need each other. God does not expect you to live the Christian life on your own. God wants you to live out your faith as you connect with your spiritual family. God adopted you into His family. Allow other believers who are spiritually strong to come alongside to help you through seasons of spiritual lethargy and warfare.

The spiritually strong will offer their prayer in faith, fully trusting that God is able to do what He says (Rom 4:21), and you will be restored. God will raise you up from a condition of spiritual weakness to a state of spiritual strength and stability.

Will you invite a spiritually mature follower of Christ to offer a prayer in faith on your behalf? Don't walk alone through the seasons of adversity. Allow your spiritual family to intercede for you.

August 22
PRAYING FOR OTHERS

"Therefore confess your sins to each other and pray for each other so that you may be healed. The prayer of a righteous man is powerful and effective."
James 5:16 (NIV)

You may have been taught to not air out your dirty laundry. In other words, you may have been taught that some things are to be kept within the confines of secrecy. However, in God's economy, confessing sin to a trusted fellow believer is healthy and demonstrates obedience to God's Word. We are commanded to confess our sins to each other. Confide in a mature follower of Christ who cares about you and who wants to see you reach your God-given potential. That trusted friend who is yoked with you in Christ will help you experience the liberation from the bondage of sin that you are confessing.

Doing life together with fellow believers who have the heart of Christ and the love of Christ will be an encouraging journey. We are to walk in such community and fellowship with other believers that confessing sin to each other and praying for each other becomes normal. Of course, the need to confess sin to others will decrease as you turn from sin and embrace the life God has for you. Pray for others with the same passion that you have when you are praying for God's wisdom for something you are facing personally. Try to get in their skin to feel what they are feeling and to pray with compassion.

Think about a safe and spiritually mature person in your life who would be the person you would go to in order to confess sin. Begin asking God who He would have you to be praying for.

Praying In Power

"Therefore confess your sins to each other and pray for each other so that you may be healed. The prayer of a righteous man is powerful and effective."
James 5:16 (NIV)

How can the prayer of one person be powerful and effective and the prayer of another person be weak and ineffective? The power hinges on the level of righteousness. When a person is positionally in a right standing before Almighty God, the prayer is infused with power. When a person is living in sin and chooses to rebel against God, the prayer is contaminated by the poison of sin.

God rewards righteous living. God is holy and expects His children to be holy (1 Pet 1:16) and to live a life of moral purity. Where there is purity, there is power!

- *"Who may ascend the hill of the LORD? Who may stand in his holy place? He who has clean hands and a pure heart, who does not lift up his soul to an idol or swear by what is false."* Psalm 24:3-4 (NIV)
- *"I want men everywhere to lift up holy hands in prayer, without anger or disputing."* 1 Tim 2:8 (NIV)

Do you want your prayer to be powerful and effective? Examine your life and ask God to search your heart (Psalm 139:23). God wants you to have a vibrant prayer life. What is keeping you from having that kind of prayer life? Are you clean before God? Is there any unconfessed sin in your life? Are you harboring even a fraction of bitterness or resentment? Confess the sin God reveals and surrender to the Holy Spirit's full control of your life. Walk in the purity you have found in Christ.

August 24
SECURING A PRAYER CLOSET

"But when you pray, go into your room, close the door and pray to your Father, who is unseen. Then your Father, who sees what is done in secret, will reward you." Matthew 6:6 (NIV)

When you look into the rear view mirror of your life, where were you when you had the most meaningful times of prayer with the Lord? Can you identify a literal location? What was the environment like? Was it in the morning, at mid-day, in the evening, or into the night? When and where you connect with God matters. Of course, we know that God is omnipresent. There is nowhere God is not. God is everywhere all the time.

Jesus solidifies the discipline of securing a location to connect with God in prayer. Why would the location matter? Can't you connect with God in prayer from any location? Yes! God can retrieve your prayer from any location, but Jesus is affirming the value of having a special place for communion in addition to practicing God's Presence throughout the day.

Maybe you already have that special place where you meet with God to read His Word and to spend time in unbroken fellowship with God in prayer. Perhaps you have not selected that special place yet. Think about your schedule and think about a location that will enhance your daily quiet time alone with God. If you prefer solitude, then find a place that will ensure an environment of solitude. If you love the outdoors, find a place outside that helps you best connect with God. If you enjoy worship music playing softly while you commune with God, then have the music ready.

Remember that God will reward you for your private time alone with Him. God desires intimacy with you and has made that level of connection available to you. What will you do with the opportunity God has given you to know Him more?

"Be joyful always; pray continually; give thanks in all circumstances, for this is God's will for you in Christ Jesus." 1 Thessalonians 5:16-18 (NIV)

Are you too busy to pray? Then, you are too busy. Make room for your relationship with God to be nurtured and developed through daily intimacy with God. Guard that special time and place to connect with God through Bible reading, meditating on God's Word, and prayer. Once you leave that special time and place designed for your daily quiet time, commit to practice God's Presence throughout the day.

To pray continually or to pray without ceasing is to operate your life throughout the day cognizant of God's activity. You can enjoy unbroken fellowship with God throughout the day as you remain in an abiding relationship with Christ. As you maintain a level of relational bonding with God through being fully surrendered to His leadership and Lordship, you will enjoy an open line of communication with God.

The Holy Spirit indwelling you will be your constant Companion. You have the privilege and the honor of maintaining a perpetual awareness of God's Presence in your life. Staying sensitive to the Holy Spirit's prompting moment by moment will enable you to experience the work of God in you and around you. Your heightened sensitivity to God's activity will result in deeper intimacy with God.

August 26
CONSIDER YOUR OPTIONS

"This day I call heaven and earth as witnesses against you that I have set before you life and death, blessings and curses. Now choose life, so that you and your children may live and that you may love the LORD your God, listen to his voice, and hold fast to him. For the LORD is your life, and he will give you many years in the land he swore to give to your fathers, Abraham, Isaac and Jacob."
Deuteronomy 30:19-20 (NIV)

God demonstrates His love and security by giving us options to consider. God does not force us to love Him. Allowing us to choose or refuse Him, God presents us with opportunities to come to know Him by experience. Every human being is on a journey of discovery. Some will ignore God's revelation and some will choose to come to know God personally through an abiding relationship with Jesus.

Life and death are set before you. You have the freedom to choose the path that leads to life or you can choose the path that leads to death. Consider your options. If you choose life, then you are choosing to orient your life in alignment with God's agenda. If you choose death, your path will be marked by rebellion against God and His plan for your life.

Choose life so that you will fulfill the purpose for which God created you. Choose life so that the next generation can examine your life and be convinced to follow in your steps on the path of life. Choose life so that you may love God with all your heart, soul, mind, and strength (Mark 12:30). Learn to listen to His voice and to practice instant obedience (John 10:27).

Have you allowed Jesus to be your life? Consider your options. Now, choose life!

"As Jesus walked beside the Sea of Galilee, he saw Simon and his brother Andrew casting a net into the lake, for they were fishermen. 'Come, follow me,' Jesus said, 'and I will make you fishers of men.'" Mark 1:16-17 (NIV)

Have you come to know Christ? When did that eternal transaction take place in your life? Where were you when you recognized your sinfulness and your desperate need for Jesus to come to your rescue?

Conversion is the redemptive work of God in a person's life. Your conversion is the event of being delivered from the kingdom of darkness and brought into the kingdom of light. Your conversion is the event of being adopted into God's family and being filled with the Holy Spirit.

As a child of God, you have received the ultimate invitation to know Jesus personally. Jesus invites you to come to Him and enjoy an abiding love relationship with Him that is eternal. Your salvation event is followed by a process of knowing Jesus more intimately. Your conversion is followed by ongoing transformation and spiritual maturation. After you have been adopted into God's family, you walk with Jesus to work out what God has worked in (Phil 2:12). You are yoked up with Christ to fulfill God's mission on earth.

August 28
THE GREENHOUSE

"Come, follow me,' Jesus said, 'and I will make you fishers of men.'"
Mark 1:17 (NIV)

Jesus invites us into a relationship that is progressive. We move from just believing that Jesus is God's Son and the Savior of the world to following Him as Lord. We follow Jesus in order to do what He did. Our belief determines where we will spend eternity.

Think about the spiritual environments you are in on a daily and weekly basis. The greenhouse for spiritual maturity is found in private devotion and small group connection. You grow spiritually as you engage in daily communion with the Lord through a daily quiet time. Reading God's Word, meditating on God's Word, praying, listening to God's voice, journaling, and obeying God's directives form a greenhouse for maturation. Are you making room for unhurried time alone with God? Are you guarding your daily intimacy with God?

A healthy relationship with God and with other believers will produce growth. Are you in a small group with other believers? Are you doing life with a small group of followers of Christ? That small group is made up of vital members of your spiritual family who impact your spiritual development. The environment of small group interaction allows you the opportunity to love and be loved, to know and to be known, to care and to be cared for. Jesus modeled the value of having a small group as He did life with His disciples.

What condition is your greenhouse in? Are you connecting with God daily through private devotion? Are you connecting with a small group of believers weekly in order to inspire and to experience life transformation? Nurture your relationship with Jesus and your relationships with other believers for the glory of God.

Blooming

"For we are God's workmanship, created in Christ Jesus to do good works, which God prepared in advance for us to do." Ephesians 2:10 (NIV)

Bloom where God has planted you.

What are you waiting for? Don't put off what God wants to do in you and through you. Don't delay in being and portraying what God has created you for. The time is now. God wants you to shine His light and share His love right where you are. You don't have to wait another moment. God knows where you are and what are you experiencing. God knows the spiritual condition of every person you will come in contact with this week.

You have been saved by knowing Jesus. Now that you are saved, you grow by connecting with Jesus and doing life with other believers. You grow in order to bloom for God's glory. God has strategically placed you right where you are so that you can be an irresistible influence for Christ.

- *"And God is able to make all grace abound to you, so that in all things at all times, having all that you need, you will abound in every good work." 2 Cor 9:8 (NIV)*
- *"And we pray this in order that you may live a life worthy of the Lord and may please him in every way: bearing fruit in every good work, growing in the knowledge of God." Col 1:10 (NIV)*

Are you growing? Are you allowing Jesus to live His life in you and through you to draw others to a saving relationship with Jesus? Will the population of Heaven be increased by your life on earth? Your life matters for eternity.

August 30
FISHING

"'Come, follow me,' Jesus said, 'and I will make you fishers of men.'"
Mark 1:17 (NIV)

If you aren't fishing, you aren't following.

Jesus invites us into a love relationship with Himself that is immediate and eternal. Our relationship with Jesus is to be marked by spiritual maturity and a passion for souls. Once you have been delivered from the flames of hell and graciously positioned on the path that leads to life eternal, you will want to share the Good News with others who don't know Christ. You will want those who are hellbound to become a new creation in Christ. When your citizenship has been transferred to Heaven at conversion, you will want others to have the same gift that you have received. You will not be ashamed of the gospel for you will recognize it as the power of God unto salvation (Rom 1:16).

- *"The fruit of the righteous is a tree of life, and he who wins souls is wise." Prov 11:30 (NIV)*
- *"I pray that you may be active in sharing your faith, so that you will have a full understanding of every good thing we have in Christ." Philem 1:6 (NIV)*

Watch for divine appointments ochestrated by God. The fish will be attracted by the lure of your life transformation in Christ. The glow of God on your countenance and the "Living Water" you splash as you interact with others will draw people to Christ. Let others see Jesus in you. Infuse your conversation with spiritual questions that prompt people to think about their eternal destination. There's no lack of fish, only a lack of fishers of men, women, boys, and girls (Matt 9:38). What will you do with the opportunities God gives you this week to make Jesus known?

"Now that I, your Lord and Teacher, have washed your feet, you also should wash one another's feet. I have set you an example that you should do as I have done for you." John 13:14-15 (NIV)

You are never more like Jesus than when you are serving.

A few years ago, I had the privilege of spending three days with Dr. Adrian Rogers who was the pastor of Bellevue Baptist Church in Memphis, Tennessee, and is now in Heaven. He walked a few of us pastors into the courtyard of Bellevue to show us the statue of Jesus bending down to wash a man's feet. As we stood to behold the magnitude of the statue, Dr. Rogers said to us, "Men, it's hard to look down on someone when you are washing his feet."

God has not saved you to sit, but to serve. Jesus was not obedient to death on the cross so that you could embrace a consumer mindset of wanting to be served by others. Jesus took on the full wrath of God for your sin in order to save you from your sin and to propel you into a life of serving others. Jesus is not asking us to do anything He has not already done. Jesus is not asking us to give anything He has not already given. Jesus is our model to follow.

Are you doing as Jesus has done? Are you placing the needs of others before your own? Are you seizing the opportunities that God gives you to serve others? Are you serving your family? Are you serving your classmates or co-workers? Are you serving strangers?

Have you washed any feet lately?

September 1
FAMILY BUSINESS

"So God created man in his own image, in the image of God he created him; male and female he created them." Genesis 1:27 (NIV)

God designed the family and God defines the family. The family business is God's business. God created Adam and Eve in His image. God created them for His pleasure. He blessed them and commanded them to fill the earth and subdue it (Gen 1:28). Their assignment was to love God, to love each other, and to be fruitful and increase in number.

What comes to your mind when you think of the word, family? You may have warm feelings of special memories that where made in the context of a loving environment. Perhaps the concept of family for you may surface feelings that are less desirable due to neglect or fractured relationships. Think about your current reality. What does your current family scenario look like?

God has a plan for you and for your family. His plan includes your need for loving relationships. God's desire is that you know Him personally and then express His love within your family and to a lost world.

LEADING YOUR FAMILY

"So we make it our goal to please him, whether we are at home in the body or away from it." 2 Corinthians 5:9 (NIV)

Have you ever wondered what the purpose of your family is? Have you discovered why you exist? God wants your family to maintain a vertical orientation. You exist to please God. In his letter to the church at Corinth, Paul reminded the church family that their goal was to please God. Are you a God pleaser?

The enemy assaults the family. You have to fight for your family and you have to guard your passion to please God. You will have to combat the attempts the enemy makes to diffuse your focus on pleasing God. You have a choice to make. Joshua faced the onslaught of attacks which sought to erode the commitment to God embraced by the children of Israel. On behalf of his family, Joshua made the right choice.

- *"'But if serving the LORD seems undesirable to you, then choose for yourselves this day whom you will serve, whether the gods your forefathers served beyond the River, or the gods of the Amorites, in whose land you are living. But as for me and my household, we will serve the LORD.'" Josh 24:15 (NIV)*

Will you lead the way for your family to please God? Will you make the bold commitment to serve the Lord? Let me encourage you to keep your eyes on Jesus. Stay vertical!

September 3
FAMILY LIFE

"So whether you eat or drink or whatever you do, do it all for the glory of God."
1 Corinthians 10:31 (NIV)

What motivates you to live the Christian life? Do you live the Christian life to get others to think highly of you or to generate words of affirmation? No, you live the Christian life to bring glory to God. The same is true for your family business. Your family exists to bring glory to God.

It gets personal when you begin to assess the reason for your family's existence. Your family does not exist to accumulate wealth and parade personal acclaim. Instead, your family exists to operate in such a fashion as to bring glory to God during every season of family life.

Think about your home. Does your home bring honor to God? Is your home life a testimony to God's faithfulness and holiness? Maybe you are the only believer in your home or maybe your entire family has known the Lord. As a unit, would you say that your family brings glory to God?

Examine your home life this week and take note of ways that your family honors God. If you identify areas of your life at home that dishonor God, confess those things to God and ask for His help in bringing everything under His care. Make the smile of God the goal of your home and family!

"My people will live in peaceful dwelling places, in secure homes, in undisturbed places of rest." Isaiah 32:18 (NIV)

We exist as a family to love each other unconditionally in an atmosphere of acceptance and trust. Now that statement is loaded with meaning and with life-giving principles. Is your family characterized by love? Does your family consistently extend unconditional love? Love is the mark of a mature follower of Jesus Christ. If our home and family are going to bring honor to God, love must be the supreme demonstration. The unconditional love God has shown us in Christ is to be duplicated in our home. Love is also a fruit of the Spirit which is evidenced through our treatment of others.

- *"Do not let any unwholesome talk come out of your mouths, but only what is helpful for building others up according to their needs, that it may benefit those who listen." Eph 4:29 (NIV)*
- *"Be kind and compassionate to one another, forgiving each other, just as in Christ God forgave you." Eph 4:32 (NIV)*

Seize opportunities within your home this week to demonstrate the unconditional love of God. Whenever you go through seasons of not wanting to love that way, just remember how God has lavished you with His unconditional love. God is not asking us to do anything He has not already done for us in Christ.

September 5
NO PLACE LIKE HOME

"Accept one another, then, just as Christ accepted you, in order to bring praise to God." Romans 15:7 (NIV)

What kind of home environment did you grow up in? Was your home a safe place where love was extended unconditionally and where acceptance was granted freely? Do you recall if your home was filled with an atmosphere of trust? We exist as a family to love each other unconditionally in an atmosphere of acceptance and trust.

What about now? What's your home life like? Have you nurtured an atmosphere of acceptance? When you accept God's acceptance of you, every relationship takes on a new dimension. Drawing from what God has done in your life, you will be able to extend acceptance of others. When you accept others, it does not mean that you condone their behavior or affirm inappropriate conduct. Rather, you are demonstrating that your acceptance of them is not based upon performance.

> • *"Therefore, as God's chosen people, holy and dearly loved, clothe yourselves with compassion, kindness, humility, gentleness and patience. Bear with each other and forgive whatever grievances you may have against one another. Forgive as the Lord forgave you. And over all these virtues put on love, which binds them all together in perfect unity." Col 3:12-14 (NIV)*

Clothe yourself with the garment of God's love and acceptance. Treat your family members the way God has so graciously treated you. God has already given us so much more than we deserve. God simply wants us to let His life flow through us to influence our home for His glory!

"Follow my example, as I follow the example of Christ." 1 Corinthians 11:1 (NIV)

Your home should be a place to run to, not run from. God wants your home to be an oasis. Your home should be the safest place on earth to be yourself. Trust is essential. In fact, without trust there is no relationship. Without trust, your home will not be an oasis.

Relationships are built on trust. Your love relationship with Jesus is in your response to your trusting in Jesus alone for salvation. God has entrusted you with the gospel message and spiritual gifts to serve others. God has demonstrated His trust in you which makes your unbroken fellowship with God possible.

In order to be trusted by others, you must be trustworthy. To create an environment of trust within your home, the members of your family must be trustworthy. Living a life of integrity elevates the level of trust within your home.

- *"Dear friend, do not imitate what is evil but what is good. Anyone who does what is good is from God. Anyone who does what is evil has not seen God." 3 John 1:11 (NIV)*
- *"Join with others in following my example, brothers, and take note of those who live according to the pattern we gave you." Phil 3:17 (NIV)*

You can be the example for other family members to follow. If you want to be encouraged, spend a few moments thanking God for the family members who have modeled Christ before you. You may even consider sending them a note or an email expressing your gratitude for their example in your life.

September 7
FAMILY MISSION STATEMENT

"'My food,' said Jesus, 'is to do the will of him who sent me and to finish his work.'" John 4:34 (NIV)

Jesus focused His life on God's agenda. He didn't allow anyone or anything to distract Him from living a life pleasing to God and a life faithful to God's work. Use the following content as a guide to formulate a family mission statement.

Family Mission Statement

We The _____ Family

Hereby Declare That

> We exist as a family to please God and to bring glory, honor, and praise to His name. (1 Cor 10:31; Col 3:17-4:1; Josh 24:15)
>
> We exist as a family to love each other unconditionally in an atmosphere of acceptance and trust. (Isaiah 32:18; Eph. 4:29-5:2; Col 3:12-17; Phil 2:1-11)
>
> We exist as a family to learn, live and model Christian values and a biblical worldview. (Deu 6:4-6; Matt 5:13-16; Acts 1:8)

Signed By _____

On The Day Of _____

Personalize this family mission statement to fit your family. Seek input from your family members so that they can be part of the process. Ask God to enable your family to focus on His agenda.

CLARITY AND COMMUNICATION

"My dear brothers, take note of this: Everyone should be quick to listen, slow to speak and slow to become angry, for man's anger does not bring about the righteous life that God desires." James 1:19-20 (NIV)

Communication is vital for the home and family to operate in a way that pleases God. Relationships deepen as communication strengthens. The more effective we are in communicating understanding and communicating love within our home, the more effective our witness for Christ will be. God magnifies the witness of the family that communicates effectively within the home. Your home becomes a testimony before the Lord.

When it comes to communication, how well do you listen? Are you intentional in listening empathetically and compassionately? Do you seek to understand and communicate that understanding?

- *"Then Samuel said, 'Speak, for your servant is listening.'"*
  1 Sam 3:10 (NIV)
- *"He who answers before listening--that is his folly and his shame."*
  Prov 18:13 (NIV)

Let's commit to be quick to listen. Remember, God has given us one mouth and two ears. What would happen if we intentionally listen twice as much as we speak? Our level of effective communication may very well increase. Thank God for the listening ears He has sprinkled throughout your life to help you along the way. People who came alongside you with a compassionate ear are worthy of your thanksgiving. Now be that kind of person in the lives of others for the glory of God. Start with your family and become a good listener.

September 9
USING WORDS TO EDIFY

"May the words of my mouth and the meditation of my heart be pleasing in your sight, O LORD, my Rock and my Redeemer." Psalm 19:14 (NIV)

Have you weighed your words lately? Your words have the potential to crush or to mend. Your words have the power to destroy relationships or to restore relationships. Every word you speak matters to God. Every word you speak aloud or mutter under your breath is captured by God

- *"Do not be quick with your mouth, do not be hasty in your heart to utter anything before God. God is in heaven and you are on earth, so let your words be few." Eccl 5:2 (NIV)*
- *"Do not let any unwholesome talk come out of your mouths, but only what is helpful for building others up according to their needs, that it may benefit those who listen." Eph 4:29 (NIV)*

Give the Lord full control of your speech. May your words be pleasing to God. When you yield to His control, your communication within the home will be a blessing to your family. Your communication outside of the home will benefit others, too. Seek to please God and to build others up with your words.

FAMILY BOARD MEETING

"Listen to advice and accept instruction, and in the end you will be wise."
Proverbs 19:20 (NIV)

Has God ever used a child to teach you a valuable lesson in life? It happened to me last night. We had a family board meeting last night at our kitchen table. In response to our pastor's Sunday morning message, we were working through the five questions included in the sermon listening guide. Take a look at these five questions:

1. In your opinion, what are the two biggest barriers to our communication?

2. Of the five levels of communication (cliché, facts, opinions, feelings, needs), which level typically represents our communication?

3. On a scale of 1-10, with 10 being the highest, how well do I listen when others are speaking?

4. On a scale of 1-10, with 10 being the highest, how "understood" do I feel when we talk?

5. What is one specific thing we can do to improve the quality of our communication?

Through our family board meeting experience, God spoke through my son Austin to show me how my Blackberry was a barrier to communication. Isn't that interesting? The purpose behind the technology of my Blackberry is actually to enhance communication. However, the very instrument which enhances communication can become a communication barrier.

God is honored when you take the time to have a family chat to discuss ways to improve communication.

September 11
PRIVATE WORSHIP

"God, who has called you into fellowship with his Son Jesus Christ our Lord, is faithful." 1 Corinthians 1:9 (NIV)

Every believer is called by God and for God. The highest calling on a believer's life is not to become a preacher or an international missionary. The highest calling on a believer's life is to live in unbroken fellowship with Jesus Christ. What we do vocationally and relationally flows out of that calling to perpetually fellowship with Jesus. Being united with Christ and nurturing His life in us is our ongoing assignment.

God is faithful! You can anchor your faith to His faithfulness. God created you for intimacy with His Son and our Savior, Jesus Christ. You have been chosen by God to enter into the most dynamic, meaningful, and purpose driven relationship ever established. The redemptive work of Christ on the cross has given you access to the one relationship that will change your forever. Your life will never operate in the center of God's will until you come into fellowship with Jesus.

Now that you are in Christ, grow in your love relationship with Him. Enjoy daily intimacy with the Lord through having a daily quiet time. Make a standing appointment with the Lord each day. Give Him your undivided attention. Spend unhurried time alone with Him as you read His Word and sit at His feet. Encounter His abiding Presence as you pour out your heart in prayer. Share your fears, frustrations, and failures. Express your appreciation for all that Jesus has done to set you free and to empower you to live in victory.

Fellowship with Jesus is not only a specific amount of time carved out to have a daily devotion, but also an ongoing relationship. You can walk with Jesus moment-by-moment in full awareness of His Presence. You can talk to Jesus throughout the day. Invite Jesus to live His life through you.

WHEN STORMS COME

"The LORD is my rock, my fortress and my deliverer; my God is my rock, in whom I take refuge." Psalm 18:2 (NIV)

Who are you relying upon? What is your faith anchored to? Where do you run when the storm comes? Where do you go when life doesn't make sense? Can you affirm these words?

> The LORD is my rock. He provides my stability!
> The LORD is my fortress. He provides my serenity!
> The LORD is my deliverer. He provides my solidarity!

The LORD God is my rock, in whom I take refuge. He provides my safety!

We are in desperate need of God's moment-by-moment provision. He is still on His throne and has given us everything we need to live out His plan and fulfill His purpose. God is not limited by our limitations. God is eternal, holy, immutable, omnipotent, omniscient, and omnipresent. He is sovereign. His love endures forever and His mercies are new every morning. You can take refuge in Him.

What is currently causing you to lose sleep? What are you worrying about? Anchor your faith to the Rock. God will see you through. When storms come He is all you need.

September 13
OUR SUFFICIENCY IN CHRIST

"For we do not have a high priest who is unable to sympathize with our weaknesses, but we have one who has been tempted in every way, just as we are--yet was without sin." Hebrews 4:15 (NIV)

Are you struggling? Are you hurting? Do you ever go through seasons of loneliness? Have you encountered frustration or disappointment? Have your dreams been shattered?

Jesus is more than enough! He can identify with our heartache and pain. He knows what it feels like to be misunderstood. His life was marked by ridicule, unfair treatment, and betrayal. Jesus is well acquainted with the onslaught of temptation. Was He tempted? Yes! Did He commit sin? No! Can He relate to the gravitational pull of sin? Yes!

Our insufficiency is transformed by the sufficiency of Christ. When we are weak, He is strong! When we are most susceptible to sin, Jesus consistently stands as the model to follow.

Remember, Jesus became like us so that we could become like Him.

REMOVE DISTRACTIONS

"Not long after that, the younger son got together all he had, set off for a distant country and there squandered his wealth in wild living." Luke 15:13 (NIV)

How does a runner prepare for a marathon? He removes distractions that would impede his progress and focuses his energy and effort on intentional training.

One of Satan's primary tools is to keep us distracted from God's plan. We begin to major on the minors and minor on the majors. We drift from our core values and seek to embrace superfluous agendas.

The prodigal son allowed the allurements of the distant country to distract him from his father's plan. He sought to bypass his father's protection and provision in order to court a cheap but appealing substitute. Sin never delivers what it promises!

What's the antidote to distractions? How do you overcome the lure of leaving the straight life? Here it is: Make up your mind!

> • *"Since, then, you have been raised with Christ, set your hearts on things above, where Christ is seated at the right hand of God. Set your minds on things above, not on earthly things. For you died, and your life is now hidden with Christ in God." Col 3:1-3 (NIV)*

Pray this prayer with me: "Lord, I have made up my mind. Since I have been raised with You, I will set my heart on things above where You are seated at the right hand of God. Lord, I have made up my mind. I will set my mind on things above and not on earthly things. I have made up my mind. Since You died on the cross for me, my life is now hidden with You in God. I have made up my mind in Jesus' Name, Amen."

September 15
RECOGNITION

"The son said to him, 'Father, I have sinned against heaven and against you. I am no longer worthy to be called your son.'"Luke 15:21 (NIV)

There is power in the recognition of your true disposition. You can shroud your persona with a facade that exudes perfection while your inner life embodies disarray. Disguising the reality of your inner self has the potential to delay being found out. However, the manifestation of your true disposition will appear at some point. God has a way of exposing our current reality.

When God asked Adam and Eve, "Where are you?", He was not perplexed that He had misplaced the crown of His creation. His question was not one of confusion related to an inability to find the couple that He created. His question was to heighten their recognition of their true disposition. God wanted Adam and Eve to recognize their current reality.

After Isaiah encountered God's holiness, he came face to face with his true disposition. A new standard of measurement became his conscious defining moment. Notice Isaiah's response:

> • *"'Woe to me!' I cried. 'I am ruined! For I am a man of unclean lips, and I live among a people of unclean lips, and my eyes have seen the King, the LORD Almighty.'" Isaiah 6:5 (NIV)*

The prodigal son identified his true disposition and responded with the confession, "Father, I have sinned against heaven and against you. I am no longer worthy to be called your son."

Consider the holiness of God. Are you sensing a need for confession in light of His holiness and your true disposition? His purity exposes our sinfulness. He graciously offers forgiveness.

"When Jesus heard what had happened, he withdrew by boat privately to a solitary place. Hearing of this, the crowds followed him on foot from the towns. When Jesus landed and saw a large crowd, he had compassion on them and healed their sick." Matthew 14:13-14 (NIV)

Has your life ever been interrupted by a hurricane? Storms have a way of intruding your normal routine and invading the conveniences of life. Your whole world of normal comes to an abrupt halt as you navigate the rugged terrain of survival.

Jesus experienced a painful interruption that hit close to home. Jesus received news that His cousin, John the Baptist, had been beheaded. Remember, John had baptized Jesus to inaugurate Jesus' public ministry. John was the forerunner of Christ. Now Jesus had to deal with grieving the unfortunate loss of John.

Our lives here in the Houston area were interrupted by Hurricane Ike. What if we could turn this interruption into an opportunity to identify what matters most in life? In times like these, we are reminded of the value of our faith, our family, and our friends. Spend some time in prayer thanking God for what you do have, including the life-giving relationships that God has blessed you with.

September 17
EMBRACE SOLITUDE

"When Jesus heard what had happened, he withdrew by boat privately to a solitary place. Hearing of this, the crowds followed him on foot from the towns. When Jesus landed and saw a large crowd, he had compassion on them and healed their sick." Matthew 14:13-14 (NIV)

After hearing of John the Baptist's death, Jesus chose to embrace solitude in order to connect with our Heavenly Father. Jesus modeled the value of knowing God intimately.

When interruptions arise, turn them into opportunities to take your love relationship with God to the next level. Hurricane Ike gave many of us in the Houston area the necessity to embrace a different pace. Our entire region shifted into survival mode. Families were coming together and working together to do life together through the backside of this storm. What an opportunity to know Christ more!

- *"I want to know Christ and the power of his resurrection and the fellowship of sharing in his sufferings, becoming like him in his death, and so, somehow, to attain to the resurrection from the dead." Phil 3:10-11 (NIV)*
- *"Come near to God and he will come near to you." James 4:8 (NIV)*

As followers of Christ, we have the privilege of determining our level of intimacy with God. God invites us to know Him personally and intimately through our relationship with Jesus. Whatever you are facing during this season of life, make the choice to daily draw near to God. There's more to explore!

SERVE OTHERS INTENTIONALLY

"When Jesus landed and saw a large crowd, he had compassion on them and healed their sick." Matthew 14:14 (NIV)

What if you turned an interruption into an opportunity to express God's love by serving others? Jesus faithfully served others during His earthly ministry. He put His compassion in action. The ultimate demonstration of servitude is the atoning work of Jesus on the cross. Jesus put our needs before His own.

- *"You, my brothers, were called to be free. But do not use your freedom to indulge the sinful nature ; rather, serve one another in love." Gal 5:13 (NIV)*
- *"Each of you should look not only to your own interests, but also to the interests of others." Phil 2:4 (NIV)*

Look to see where God is at work and take the initiative to join Him in His activity. Be the hands, feet, and voice of Jesus this week and serve others. Find a need and meet it. Put the needs of others before your own. Treat the next person you come into contact with as the most important person on the planet. Explore ways to be a blessing to that person. Express God's love by serving others. May others see Jesus in you!

The Power of Availability

"Do not forget to entertain strangers, for by so doing some people have entertained angels without knowing it." Hebrews 13:2 (NIV)

God uses ordinary people to accomplish the extraordinary.

Did you know that God receives glory as you make yourself available for His use? God is not restricted by your ability. God chooses to use you based on your availability. His plan includes His power. When you align your life with God's agenda, God's power is unleashed in you and through you.

Don't limit God! If you only reach out to people you know, you will constrict the impact God wants to make through your life. Choose to engage people outside of your normal sphere of influence. Be available to be used by God to touch people you would normally not cross paths with. Pray the prayer of Jabez (1 Chron 4:10): Lord, bless me, enlarge my territory, let Your hand be upon me, and keep me from harm. Allow God to enlarge your territory by being available to go places you have never gone and meet people you have never met. It may involve a short-term mission trip overseas or simply a walk across the street to meet the neighbor you don't know.

Are you willing to place your "yes" on the altar? Say to the Lord, "I'm yours! Use me!" Don't put conditions on God. Make yourself completely available for God's use in God's timing for God's glory.

THE POWER OF SENSITIVITY

"Remember those in prison as if you were their fellow prisoners, and those who are mistreated as if you yourselves were suffering." Hebrews 13:3 (NIV)

Be sensitive to God's activity.

God wants us to express His love to His creation. People matter to God. Our value was clearly demonstrated by the ultimate love bridge ever built. "But God demonstrates his own love for us in this: While we were still sinners, Christ died for us" (Rom 5:8 NIV). The Bible is God's love letter to us portraying His constant pursuit to restore fallen mankind.

Being on mission with God requires sensitivity to God's activity. We will never live for the global glory of God if we are insensitive to what He values. God wants to use us in His redemptive activity. What does this kind of sensitivity look like? It looks like remembering those who are mistreated as if you were suffering. It looks like remembering those in prison as if you were their fellow prisoner. It looks like remembering the poor as if you were living in poverty. It looks like remembering those who are lonely as if you were lonely.

Are you willing to ask God to sensitize you to His activity? God is not through with you. Your light can still shine for His glory. His love can still be expressed through you to bring others into a saving relationship with Jesus.

September 21
THE POWER OF INTENTIONALITY

"And do not forget to do good and to share with others, for with such sacrifices God is pleased." Hebrews 13:16 (NIV)

Be intentional.

What moves the heart of God? What brings God pleasure? What makes God smile? Doing good and sharing with others! We have the freedom to choose to do good or to exit from the highway of holiness. We can embrace God's best or settle for less. The choice is ours to share with others or to operate in the currency of selfishness. God is pleased when we choose to do good and to share with others.

- *"For the kingdom of God is not a matter of eating and drinking, but of righteousness, peace and joy in the Holy Spirit, because anyone who serves Christ in this way is pleasing to God and approved by men."* Rom 14:17-18 (NIV)
- *"Finally, brothers, we instructed you how to live in order to please God, as in fact you are living. Now we ask you and urge you in the Lord Jesus to do this more and more."* 1 Thess 4:1 (NIV)

Live your life with intentionality. Abandon to God's will. Surrender to the Lordship of Christ. Yield to the prompting of the Holy Spirit. Love God and love others. Serve God by serving others. Put the needs of others before your own. Share Christ faithfully. Give sacrificially. Trust completely. Express God's love intentionally.

JOY TO THE HEART

"The precepts of the LORD are right, giving joy to the heart. The commands of the LORD are radiant, giving light to the eyes." Psalm 19:8 (NIV)

God honors our obedience to His Word. One of the benefits of obedience is joy. Joy is not connected to our circumstances. As followers of Jesus Christ, we experience joy as a result of our abiding relationship with Christ marked by obedience.

- *"Blessed is the man who does not walk in the counsel of the wicked or stand in the way of sinners or sit in the seat of mockers. But his delight is in the law of the LORD, and on his law he meditates day and night." Psalm 1:1-2 (NIV)*
- *"But the man who looks intently into the perfect law that gives freedom, and continues to do this, not forgetting what he has heard, but doing it--he will be blessed in what he does." James 1:25 (NIV)*

Are you receiving joy to the heart? Take a look at your level of obedience to God's Word. Your joy will be proportionate to your level of obedience. Obey what God has shown you. Obey what you already know and enjoy the benefit of joy.

September 23
JOY IN GOD'S PRESENCE

"You have made known to me the path of life; you will fill me with joy in your presence, with eternal pleasures at your right hand." Psalm 16:11 (NIV)

God fills you with joy in His Presence.

The thought of having access to the Presence of God is still amazing. God has made known the path of life. Jesus is the way, the truth, and the life (John 14:6). We have gained access to God through the shed blood of Jesus on the cross. Our sin debt has been paid in full. In Christ, we have been reconciled to God. God chooses to fill us with joy in His Presence. We don't have to wait until we get to Heaven to enjoy God's Presence. We don't have to wait until we get to Heaven to enjoy the eternal pleasures.

God is for us. He created us. God is with us. Jesus redeemed us. God is in us. The Holy Spirit indwells us. The Presence of God is no longer confined to the Old Testament Tabernacle or Temple. God's Presence is no longer confined to the Ark of the Covenant. God has chosen to take up residence in us.

- *"Do you not know that your body is a temple of the Holy Spirit, who is in you, whom you have received from God? You are not your own; you were bought at a price. Therefore honor God with your body." 1 Cor 6:19-20 (NIV)*
- *"May the God of hope fill you with all joy and peace as you trust in him, so that you may overflow with hope by the power of the Holy Spirit." Rom 15:13 (NIV)*

Are you walking in the joy of God's Presence?

Express Your Union

"And I tell you that you are Peter, and on this rock I will build my church, and the gates of Hades will not overcome it." Matthew 16:18 (NIV)

God ordained marriage and God ordained the church. We are married to Christ and our union is expressed through His Body, the church. Peter confessed that Jesus was the Christ, the Son of the living God. Jesus affirmed that He would build His church on that reality.

In order to become a follower of Jesus Christ and become a member of His Body, the church, a person must confess Jesus as the Christ, the Son of the living God. This profession of our faith is essential to salvation (Rom 10:9-10). Jesus builds His church by adopting us into His family (Eph 1:5). Only those who are born again enter into His Kingdom (John 3:3).

Jesus builds His church. Our job is to be the church. Jesus saves people from their sin. Our job is to share the Good News of Jesus so that others can know Jesus personally and eternally. Jesus saves us, not sit, but to serve. Our role in the Body of Christ, the church, is to empty hell and to populate Heaven.

How many people will be in Heaven because of you?

September 25
LEARN TO WAIT

"'I am going to send you what my Father has promised; but stay in the city until you have been clothed with power from on high.'" Luke 24:49 (NIV)

God's will often includes waiting.

Jesus instructed the believers to wait in Jerusalem until they had received what His Father had promised, namely, power from on high. Jesus had to ascend back to the Father so that He could send the Counselor, the promised Holy Spirit (John 16:7). Yet, Jesus did not give them an exact time or date for the Holy Spirit's arrival. They had to wait!

The 120 believers waited ten days to be clothed with power from on high (Acts 1:15). Have you ever wondered why it took ten days? During that time, they replaced Judas by adding Matthias to the eleven apostles (Acts 1:26). But why did it take ten days? Perhaps the 120 believers had some internal issues to resolve. Maybe they had to confess sin and remove jealously, bitterness, and envy. Maybe it took ten days to come to the place of complete unity as a community of Christ-followers.

Are you currently waiting for God to reveal His next step for your life? Is there anything in your life that God wants you to deal with before He shows you what's next? Ask the Lord to search your heart (Psalm 139:23).

"When the day of Pentecost came, they were all together in one place. Suddenly a sound like the blowing of a violent wind came from heaven and filled the whole house where they were sitting. They saw what seemed to be tongues of fire that separated and came to rest on each of them. All of them were filled with the Holy Spirit and began to speak in other tongues as the Spirit enabled them."
Acts 2:1-4 (NIV)

God empowers us for participation in His redemptive activity.

We cannot operate in God's kingdom economy without God's kingdom resources. God's agenda can only be fulfilled by God's enabling. Without God's power, we cannot fulfill God's mission. On the day of Pentecost, the Holy Spirit indwelt the believers and enabled them to speak forth the gospel. Everyone heard the Good News in their own heart language. This miraculous communication of the gospel was God's demonstration that the gospel is for everyone!

What is your spiritual story? How did you come to know Christ personally? What has your life been like since being filled with the Holy Spirit? What does God's Word say about how a person can be saved? If you have experienced the gospel firsthand, then you are now ready to witness to Christ's saving power. You are now ready to share your faith with others. Read Romans 3:23, 5:8, 6:23, 10:9-10, and 10:13.

God has reconciled you to Himself so that you can join God in reconciling others to Himself. Build bridges to those who don't know Jesus so that they can have the saving relationship that you enjoy in Christ. There's no greater task on planet earth!

September 27
AUTHENTIC COMMUNITY

"Those who accepted his message were baptized, and about three thousand were added to their number that day." Acts 2:41 (NIV)

Wow! On the day of Pentecost, three thousand were adopted into God's family. Three thousand were delivered from the clutches of hell and placed on the path that leads to Heaven. Three thousand were saved by God and for God. They became followers of Jesus Christ and were added to His Body, the church. An eternal transaction took place!

What's next? Now that the three thousand are in Christ, how are they to function as a community of Christ-followers? What will be different about their conversation and their conduct? Do they go back to business as usual or do they embrace a new way of living?

Notice how their lifestyle radically changed. On this side of their salvation, the three thousand along with the other 120 believers start doing life together. They begin to operate as a community of believers. They are walking together in unity. Their priorities have shifted and their time allocation reflects the heart of God.

Take a moment to examine your life in light of Acts 2:42-43. Are you devoted to the reading, study, hearing, and application of God's Word? Are you in fellowship with a group of believers you can do life with? Are you consistently embracing the privilege of prayer? Are you in awe of the redemptive activity of God?

ADD VALUE TO THE TEAM

"All the believers were together and had everything in common. Selling their possessions and goods, they gave to anyone as he had need. Every day they continued to meet together in the temple courts. They broke bread in their homes and ate together with glad and sincere hearts, praising God and enjoying the favor of all the people. And the Lord added to their number daily those who were being saved." Acts 2:44-47 (NIV)

God's team is made up of those who have been saved by His grace. God's team members wear the Jesus jersey and play for His glory. His team is characterized by unity, community, selflessness, generosity, compassion, loyalty, fellowship, gladness, sincerity, evangelism, and growth.

Doing church first involves being the church. Our doing flows out of our being. It is possible to become so busy doing church that you bypass the relational aspect of being the church. God has called us, the church, to an abiding relationship with Christ.

As a member of God's household, you are called to abide in Christ. Your perpetual connection to Christ and His resources will result in bearing fruit. However, don't focus on bearing fruit. Focus on abiding. As you abide in Christ, fruit will be born. Apart from Christ, you can do nothing. His is your Source and He is your Life! As you abide in Christ, you will instantly add more value to the team, the Body of Christ.

September 29
RESOLVE CONFLICT

"You said in your heart, 'I will ascend to heaven; I will raise my throne above the stars of God; I will sit enthroned on the mount of assembly, on the utmost heights of the sacred mountain. I will ascend above the tops of the clouds; I will make myself like the Most High.' But you are brought down to the grave, to the depths of the pit." Isaiah 14:13-15 (NIV)

Every conflict has pride at its root.

Before God created man in His own image, God had to resolve conflict that erupted in Heaven. Pride infused Lucifer (Satan, the devil), the angel of God. In pride, Lucifer sought to lead a rebellion against God and thought he could dethrone God. However, God is holy and does not tolerate sin. Thus, God "de-Heavened" Lucifer. Jesus spoke of this fall and John recorded the fall of Satan in Revelation 12:9.

Pride causes us to think of ourselves before thinking of others. Pride causes us to embrace selfishness and self-centeredness. In pride, we forfeit God's agenda and become absorbed in our own personal agenda. Pride is evidenced by our pursuit of gratifying our sinful nature (Gal 5:16).

If pride seeps into your home, your family will experience major conflict. Pride corrupts and erodes relationships. Satan is the mascot of pride. He does not want your family to operate in peace, unity, and trust.

Examine the weeds inside your home. Don't try to cut the weeds off at ground level by dealing with the symptoms of pride. Get to the root of the conflict within your home. As you trace the origin of conflict, you will find the root of pride.

CREATED FOR COMPANIONSHIP

"The LORD God said, 'It is not good for the man to be alone. I will make a helper suitable for him.'" Genesis 2:18 (NIV)

God created us for relationship.

The first "not good" in the Bible is connected to aloneness. God created us for companionship. We do better together. God designed us to be relational, not robotic. God's desire is for us to be rightly related to Him and rightly related to each other.

God created Eve to complete Adam. Adam transitioned from "me" to "we" and from "mine" to "our's" in response to God's gracious creation activity. God knew what Adam needed most! Adam needed companionship. As you read God's Word, you will discover that the Bible is the story of God's relationship with His creation and their relationship with each other.

- *"God made him who had no sin to be sin for us, so that in him we might become the righteousness of God." 2 Cor 5:21 (NIV)*
- *"Finally, all of you, live in harmony with one another; be sympathetic, love as brothers, be compassionate and humble." 1 Pet 3:8 (NIV)*

Satan is anti-relationship. Satan is anti-companionship. Satan is anti-family. The devil does not want you to be in a right relationship with God and he does not want you to be in a right relationship with others. Don't allow the enemy to keep you from enjoying a loving relationship with God and with others. You are made for relationship. If you are battling aloneness, ask God to bring some life-giving relationships into your life.

October 1
RESOLVE CONFLICT TOGETHER

"Finally, all of you, live in harmony with one another; be sympathetic, love as brothers, be compassionate and humble." 1 Peter 3:8 (NIV)

Families that resolve conflict together stay together.

If the devil came to you for counsel on how to destroy families, what would your advice entail? Perhaps you would recommend the weapon of mass destruction, unforgiveness. Unforgiveness poisons harmony and erodes trust. Unforgiveness perpetuates suspicion and fertilizes bitterness. As a result of living in a fallen world among fallen people, conflict is inevitable. In other words, motion causes friction. It is not a matter of "if" conflict will happen, but a matter of "when" conflict will occur. Conflict is a natural part of life on a broken planet. Conflict is the normal confetti of living in a fallen world.

Every relationship at some point will hit the wall of conflict. As my pastor, Dr. David Fleming says, "Every wall of conflict has a door which leads to conflict resolution, meaningful conversation, and intimacy." Unfortunately, we often react to the wall of conflict by withdrawing or attacking. Instead of patiently pursuing the door of conflict resolution, we take a shortcut and forfeit the potential on the other side of the wall of conflict.

What if we were willing to risk the pursuit? What if we were willing to allow God to navigate us through the process of locating the door positioned at every wall of conflict? What if we decided to resolve conflict together as a family? Could it be that revival would come to the home through the doorway of conflict resolution?

Forgiveness unlocks the door!

CHOOSE TO RESPOND

"John said to the crowds coming out to be baptized by him, 'You brood of vipers! Who warned you to flee from the coming wrath? Produce fruit in keeping with repentance. And do not begin to say to yourselves, "We have Abraham as our father." For I tell you that out of these stones God can raise up children for Abraham. The ax is already at the root of the trees, and every tree that does not produce good fruit will be cut down and thrown into the fire.'" Luke 3:7-9 (NIV)

When conflict arises, we can choose to react or respond.

John the Baptist confronted his hearers with the reality of their spiritual condition and exhorted them to product fruit in keeping with repentance. Of course, this created a major conflict for the hearers to resolve in their own lives. They could react to the conflict or respond to the conflict. Fortunately, they responded with an appropriate question: "What should we do then?" John instructed them to share what they had with others including food and clothing. To the tax collectors, John exhorted them not to collect more than required. To some soldiers, John told them to stop extorting money and accusing people falsely and to be content with their pay (Luke 3:10-14).

You have a choice. You can react in the flesh or respond to the conflict God's way. If God has allowed conflict to enter your domain, then God will use it to conform you into the image of Christ and to strengthen your faith. God will use the immediate conflict you are confronting by giving you the grace you need to experience a personal breakthrough.

Are you teachable? Are you willing to hear from God in the midst of your circumstances? Is your heart tender enough to ask God, "What should I do?"

October 3
WHEEL OF CONFLICT

"Do not let any unwholesome talk come out of your mouths, but only what is helpful for building others up according to their needs, that it may benefit those who listen." Ephesians 4:29 (NIV)

Our words have such power. With our words we can encourage and comfort or we can shatter hearts and dreams. God wants our words to benefit others.

Let's talk about the wheel of conflict. Now, let's imagine that conflict enters your path. You experience hurt feelings which may lead to anger. Someone has wounded you. You have a choice to make. You can flee and withdraw which leads to isolation and unresolved conflict. Or you can choose to face the conflict. Once you make that decision, two more options arise: fight or invite. You can go head-to-head with that person and launch a verbal assault and fight. Or you can take the better option: invite the person into dialogue. Simply say, "Let's talk." Then be willing to extend or receive forgiveness. When you respond to conflict this way, you experience growth in your relationship. The very conflict that could have destroyed the relationship actually takes the relationship to the next level based on how you respond.

Would you be willing to allow the wheel of conflict to roll in a healthy direction? Ask God to give you the wisdom to make proper decisions to navigate through the tunnel of conflict and come to the place of healing, restoration, and growth for His glory.

BEYOND THE SPECK

"Why do you look at the speck of sawdust in your brother's eye and pay no attention to the plank in your own eye? How can you say to your brother, 'Let me take the speck out of your eye,' when all the time there is a plank in your own eye? You hypocrite, first take the plank out of your own eye, and then you will see clearly to remove the speck from your brother's eye." Matthew 7:3-5 (NIV)

If we want to find fault in someone, we won't have to look far. It is so easy to discover inconsistencies in others. When it comes to examining the lives of others, we have the eyes of an eagle. Detecting defects in others has a way of boosting our self image and stroking our ego. We tend to look through the microscope to view others and then choose to view ourselves through rose colored glasses.

Jesus uncovered our human tendency to view others critically while viewing ourselves gently. Jesus even used the explosive word, hypocrite. When we critique others unfairly and then hide behind a mask that conceals our authentic current reality, Jesus exposes our hypocrisy.

What if we began viewing ourselves in light of the holiness of God? What if we began to view ourselves in light of God's Word? Our response would be like that of Isaiah, "Woe to me! I am a man of unclean lips!" (Isaiah 6:5). Remember, man looks at the externals, but God looks at the heart (1 Sam 16:7).

.

Let's deal with the gigantic log in our own eye and stop judging others for the speck in their eye. To help us find what God wants us to look for, consider praying daily through the Ten Commandments (Ex 20:3-17) and praying daily through the fruit of the Spirit (Gal 5:22-23).

October 5
PEACEFUL DWELLING PLACE

"My people will live in peaceful dwelling places, in secure homes, in undisturbed places of rest." Isaiah 32:18 (NIV)

Do you dread going home or do you look forward to it each day? Is your home a war zone or an oasis? Does your home drain the life out of you or impart life to you? Is your home characterized by conflict, tension, and chaos or meaningful communication, refreshment, and peace? What's your home like?

God desires that our home be a peaceful dwelling place. Don't you just love that word, peaceful? It is so soothing and so inviting. God's portrait for our home includes security. Our home is to be a place of refuge and safety from the venom of our fallen world. Our home is to be an undisturbed place of rest. That opens a whole new level of living.

How far off is your home compared to the home God desires for you? The environment in which you call home is so much more than brick, stucco, and paint. Home is all about relationships and how we interact with each other and how we treat each other. Home is all about how we do life together as a family.

- Make personal spiritual growth a priority.
- Model what you want to multiply in your home.
- Mobilize your family to radiate God's love beyond your home.

My prayer is that your home will become a holy place where Jesus is honored and spiritual maturity is nurtured so that the population of Heaven will be increased and the population of hell decreased. Now that's the family business!

PROXIMITY FOR OBJECTIVITY

"Moses' father-in-law replied, 'What you are doing is not good. You and these people who come to you will only wear yourselves out. The work is too heavy for you; you cannot handle it alone.'" Exodus 18:17-18 (NIV)

You are structured for the results you are getting.

How's life? Are you stressed out? Are you overextended, over-scheduled, or overwhelmed? Are you getting enough rest at night? Are you still tired the next day? Do you feel that you have too many plates spinning? As you assess your current reality, what is God showing you about your life?

The truth is that you are simply getting the results that your life is currently structured for. The way you have chosen to live and the way you have chosen to allocate your time has determined your current reality. Moses slipped right into a harmful lifestyle because his life was structured for results he was getting. The way he was doing life and the way he was fulfilling his role as leader of the nation of Israel produced the results he was getting.

Jethro was willing to get involved! Moses was willing to allow Jethro into his life at a proximity for objectivity. Moses was also willing to allow Jethro to speak into his life. Jethro spoke these words to Moses with clarity, "What you are doing is not good."

Let's begin there. As you take a close look at your life, what do you sense a "Jethro" in your life would say about your current reality? Would that person acknowledge that what you are doing is not good?

Be still before the Lord for a few moments and ask God to help you uncover your current reality. You may even want to ask God to show you a Jethro that you can invite into close proximity to express objectively concerning your current reality.

October 7
SIT AT HIS FEET

"As Jesus and his disciples were on their way, he came to a village where a woman named Martha opened her home to him. She had a sister called Mary, who sat at the Lord's feet listening to what he said. But Martha was distracted by all the preparations that had to be made. She came to him and asked, 'Lord, don't you care that my sister has left me to do the work by myself? Tell her to help me!'" Luke 10:38-40 (NIV)

Busyness is one of Satan's most effective tools to fragment the life of a believer. We have places to go, things to do, and people to see. The activity never ends and the deadlines never cease. We are never finished! There are always more hills to conquer and mountains to climb. The opportunities to get swept up by the current of activity are endless. Busyness abounds!

It is possible to get so busy doing life and fulfilling expectations that you bypass meaningful communication with people. You can become so task oriented that you neglect the relationships that God sprinkles along your path. The most vital relationship that gets hindered by the culprit of busyness is our love relationship with Jesus.

Martha was exercising her gift of hospitality to benefit Jesus within her home. However, she got lost in her busyness and missed the opportunity to simply abide at Jesus' feet. Martha thought the most important activity was extending hospitality. Yet, Jesus brought clarity to the confusion by affirming that Mary had chosen what was better (Luke 10:42).

What if we replaced busyness with abiding in Christ? Sometimes the most spiritual activity we can embrace is sitting at the feet of Jesus! But, it's hard to sit at His feet when you are sprinting!

BEFORE YOU WERE BORN

"'Before I formed you in the womb I knew you, before you were born I set you apart; I appointed you as a prophet to the nations.'" Jeremiah 1:5 (NIV)

Allow God's agenda to become your agenda.

Before you were born, God existed. God is eternal. That means that God has always been and God will always be. God was never born and God will never die. Yet, you have a beginning. You have a birth date! Nine months before your birth date, you were conceived. Thus, you have a date of conception. To know the heart of God for you, we must travel even further back into time. Before God formed you, He knew you. Wow! That means that you were not an accident. You were created by God for a divine purpose.

Before you were born, God set you apart. The concept in the language of the Old Testament is that of being sanctified. Before you were born, God had in mind exactly what He wanted you to become and God had in mind exactly when He wanted to introduce you to life on planet earth. God orchestrated all of this before you were born. Before you were born, God set you apart to participate in His kingdom activity.

God loves you and has a purpose for your life. God's purpose for your life is for you to experience His redemptive love personally and then for you to join Him in expressing His redemptive love locally and globally. You have a massive mission to fulfill on this planet during the time God gives you. Don't waste it! Don't allow anything to steal your passion for God and your passion to be on mission with God!

October 9
TECHNOLOGY FAST

"Then Saul dressed David in his own tunic. He put a coat of armor on him and a bronze helmet on his head." 1 Samuel 17:38 (NIV)

Technology can become a space invader.

As you can imagine, King Saul had the latest in warfare technology. His armor was the best of the best and fit for a king. Yet, Saul tried to shroud the shepherd boy, David, with this state of the art technology and it just didn't fit. The armor that was to enhance David's ability to combat and defeat Goliath actually became a major hindrance.

Technology has a way of enhancing our lives doesn't it? We have more technology at our fingertips than at any other time in history. We are in the fast lane when it comes to our technology. Yet, it seems that over the years we have not really had technology; technology has had us. Instead of technology enhancing our lives, it has the potential of hindering us from the living the life God has given us.

Maybe we need to find ourselves once again. Maybe it's time to go back to the One who Created us and ask Him to show us our five smooth stones and sling. God created us to fulfill His agenda in His power with the technology of His choosing. Could it be that we have replaced our dependency upon God with an obsessive dependency upon technology?

What if God called us to a technology fast? Can we really make it without email, cell phones, text messaging, and the Internet? Can life continue if we aren't connected to our technology?

MAKE ROOM FOR REST

"For in six days the LORD made the heavens and the earth, the sea, and all that is in them, but he rested on the seventh day. Therefore the LORD blessed the Sabbath day and made it holy." Exodus 20:11 (NIV)

Work can become a space invader.

Do you have room in your life for rest? Of course not! You have too much to do and work is calling your name. "I owe, I owe, so off to work I go!" Work is demanding your time, energy, and attention. Work is biblical isn't it? Doesn't God expect you to work? Isn't work God's idea?

Consider the reality that the Creator of the universe established a divine guideline for both work and rest. God was not tired after the six days of creation activity. God chose to model the value of working and resting. God established a pattern for us in order to keep life in balance and to do life God's way.

When your work becomes a space invader, your life is out of balance. God does not want your work to rule your life and to dominate your energy allocation. God wants you to set aside a day each week to cease creating, forming, fashioning, meeting deadlines, and pushing yourself through the performance trap. You need a day to allow God to put you back together. That's why God created the Sabbath day. You need a Sabbath. You need a day to allow God to re-create you. You need to transition off of the racetrack down pit road and allow God to change your spiritual tires, remove the debris from your spiritual windshield, and to refuel your spiritual tank. You need a weekly pit stop!

October 11
PARENTAL ALIGNMENT

"Train a child in the way he should go, and when he is old he will not turn from it." Proverbs 22:6 (NIV)

Child-centered parenting is not in alignment with God's economy.

God values order. God established the home for our benefit and for His glory. God's blueprint for the home includes order. God expects the husband and father to be the spiritual leader of the home. During my upbringing, my parents divorced, and as a result, my mother became the spiritual leader of our home. The spiritual leader of the home is responsible to set the spiritual temperature for the home. Thus, the spiritual leader of the home is to be the spiritual thermostat for the home.

When our children are elevated to the place of setting the environment for the home, something is out of order. When parenting becomes child-centered, in that everything centers around the wants and wishes of the child, something is out of order.

Excessive extra-curricular activities for our children can become space invaders. When our lives and our schedules resemble a perpetual rat race, then something is out of order. We can overload and overwhelm our home by being overextended and overcommitted to too many activities.

Who is making the tough choices in your home to keep your family in alignment with God's economy? Who is guarding the priorities and the order ordained by God for your home? The decisions you make to create space for doing life together as a family will serve as a tangible model for your children to emulate when they become parents one day.

SPIRITUAL ACTIVITY

"Let us not give up meeting together, as some are in the habit of doing, but let us encourage one another--and all the more as you see the Day approaching."
Hebrews 10:25 (NIV)

Excessive church activities can become a space invader.

You have probably heard people say that they were in church every time the church doors were open. That sounds really spiritual at first. However, it is possible to be at church too much. Be careful not to equate spiritual activity with spiritual maturity. Having an abundance of church activities does not ensure personal spiritual growth. You can get spread too thin saying "yes" to too many church functions.

The writer of Hebrews is affirming the value of doing life together with other believers in community. You have the privilege of encouraging each other in the faith as you meet together to study God's Word and to build meaningful relationships. God wants you to be in fellowship with other believers at the level of meeting regularly to develop your relationship with God and with each other.

How can you keep from overloading your calendar with church activities? Learn to say "yes" to the right things. For example, you should be connected to three environments on a weekly basis. You need to be involved in a Christ exalting corporate worship environment, a small group Bible study where you can experience authentic community, and an area of service where you can exercise your spiritual gifts. Focus on those three environments and you will not only simplify your life, but also experience a new measure of spiritual growth.

October 13
LIVING THE DASH

"Why, you do not even know what will happen tomorrow. What is your life? You are a mist that appears for a little while and then vanishes." James 4:14 (NIV)

In light of eternity, life on earth is marked by brevity.

When you examine your life up close, what really matters in this life is how you live the dash. The dash represents the time you spend on earth. God has given you a certain amount of time to fulfill His plan upon the earth. It comes down to two dates and a dash. The date of your birth, the date of your death, and the dash in between capture your earthly existence. It's hard to believe that your entire life can be placed on a marble tombstone with two dates and a dash.

Is your life only a mist that appears for a little while and then vanishes? If you have the privilege of living over seventy years on this earth, would that be considered a mist? In light of eternity, your seventy years of earthly existence is only a mist.

Here's the good news! We get to choose how we spend our dash. We get to make choices each day which determine how we live. God created us with the sacred trust of decision making. We can choose to invest our life or we can choose to waste our life.

Ponder your dash. Invite God into your dash and ask Him to make adjustments in your life to help you live in light of eternity.

FAITH JOURNEY

"The LORD had said to Abram, 'Leave your country, your people and your father's household and go to the land I will show you.'" Genesis 12:1 (NIV)

Leave room for mystery.

How would you respond if God told you to leave everything familiar and go to a land that He would show you? What if God asked you to uproot and relocate? The only catch is, you have to trust God for the details. God's instruction to you is to simply leave and go. That's it! So you start packing and you launch out to pursue God's will and wait for Him to show you the next step. You do not know exactly where you are going. The destination has not been communicated to you. You are simply leaving and going.

God's will includes an element of mystery. God created you to be relational and to learn how to enter into communication with Him. God communicates His will to you. God reveals His purpose and plan for your life. You have the freedom to respond with instant obedience.

Living the dash involves a faith journey. You are the creature whom God created. You are finite and God is infinite. You are seeking to know the heart and will of the Creator of the universe. Leave room for mystery as you walk with God. As God reveals His plan to you, obey what God shows you. As you spend time in His Word, obey what God says to you. You will discover that your obedience unlocks God's next step. As you obey what you know, God will show you what to do next.

Abraham had to trust God to show him the next step. As Abraham obeyed God, God revealed the next step to Abraham. Are you willing to obey God in what He has already shown you?

October 15
RADICAL ADJUSTMENTS

"Show me, O LORD, my life's end and the number of my days; let me know how fleeting is my life. You have made my days a mere handbreadth; the span of my years is as nothing before you. Each man's life is but a breath." Psalm 39:4-5 (NIV)

When you compare your life to that of a breath, it makes life seem to be so insignificant. Yet, the psalmist is not measuring the value of life. God has already established the value of life. The psalmist is asking God to give him a glimpse of how fragile life is and how temporal life is.

How would you respond if God let you know that you only had thirty days to live? What would change about your current lifestyle? What adjustments would you make in order to live like you were dying in thirty days? If your remaining time on earth became a specific number of days that was clearly communicated to you, perhaps you would rearrange your current priorities. Maybe the way you allocate your time and energy would demonstrate radical adjustments once you found out that you only had thirty days to live. The number of your remaining days would directly impact how you would spend each moment.

Our tendency is to take life for granted. We so often feel invincible and act as though we are guaranteed several decades of life on earth. God has a way of reminding us how fleeting life is. Are you ready to die? Are you ready to live? Have you made reservations for eternity in Heaven?

THE RHYTHM OF LIFE

"Elijah was afraid and ran for his life. When he came to Beersheba in Judah, he left his servant there, while he himself went a day's journey into the desert. He came to a broom tree, sat down under it and prayed that he might die. 'I have had enough, LORD,' he said. 'Take my life; I am no better than my ancestors.'"
1 Kings 19:3-4 (NIV)

What kind of life am I living?

As you assess your current reality, you will find that life has a rhythm. You will experience a season of highs and a season of lows and a season of in-betweens. Life will be marked by mountain top experiences, valley experiences, and uneventful plateaus. Life has a certain rhythm that requires our faith to be anchored to the Rock, Jesus Christ.

Elijah had a mountain top experience on Mount Carmel and the power of God fell in a mighty demonstration. This would be considered a major spiritual marker in Elijah's life as well as a major spiritual victory over the prophets of Baal and the prophets of Asherah. Yet, Elijah descends into major depression following this mountaintop experience to the point of wanting God to take his life. Now that's pretty low!

God came to Elijah's rescue and provided him with rest, refreshment, revelation, and relationship. That's the rhythm of life. Our life today is similar in that we will experience major spiritual victories as well as some personal defeats that knock the wind out of us. The question becomes: What kind of life am I living? In the midst of the realities of life on a broken planet in a fallen world, am I living the life God has for me?

October 17
LOVING AND BEING LOVED

"Be imitators of God, therefore, as dearly loved children and live a life of love, just as Christ loved us and gave himself up for us as a fragrant offering and sacrifice to God." Ephesians 5:1-2 (NIV)

Who do I love and who loves me? Love is a fruit of the Spirit and an indicator of a Christ-centered life. Loving God and loving others is the outflow of the Christian life. God wants us to live a life of love. Our model to follow is Jesus. He demonstrated His love for us by giving Himself up for us on the cross.

Who do you love? Who are the people in your life who are the consistent recipients of your love? God calls us to love one another. God is love and those who know God love others. It is true that some people are difficult to love. Remember, God is not asking us to do anything He has not already done. God is not asking us to extend any measure of love that He has not already extended to us.

Who loves you? Of course, God loves you and He has clearly affirmed His love for you by allowing His only Son, Jesus, to die on the cross for you. Who else loves you? Begin to name them one by one in a prayer of thanksgiving to God for them. Express your gratitude to God for the people He has placed in your life to allow you to experience love personally. God is so good.

LIVING SACRIFICE

"Therefore, I urge you, brothers, in view of God's mercy, to offer your bodies as living sacrifices, holy and pleasing to God--this is your spiritual act of worship."
Romans 12:1 (NIV)

How do we respond to God's mercy? The fact that God pursued us with His redeeming love and did not give us what we deserved engenders a response. Think of where we would be had God's mercy not been applied to our hopeless estate. We were separated from God as a result of our sin. We deserved punishment, alienation, and eternal damnation. In His mercy, God provided the atonement for our sin through the sinless sacrificial death of Jesus on the cross.

In response to His mercy, God is not asking us to die for Him. God wants us to respond to His mercy by living for Him. Instead of being a dead sacrifice, God wants us to be a living sacrifice. Our spiritual act of worship that moves the heart of God is that of being holy and pleasing to Him. To be holy is to work out in practical daily living the holiness of Christ imparted to us at the moment of our salvation. We received the imputed righteousness of Christ that instantly gave us a right standing before our holy God. That event is to be followed by the process of living a holy life that is pleasing to God.

Offer your body as a living sacrifice by loving what God loves and hating what God hates. Live in perpetual dependence upon the power of the Holy Spirit to stay clean while living in this dirty world. Practice His Presence throughout the day and be sensitive to His prompting. Confess sin immediately. Choose to stay close and clean.

October 19
MAKE A KINGDOM SPLASH

"But as for you, continue in what you have learned and have become convinced of, because you know those from whom you learned it, and how from infancy you have known the holy Scriptures, which are able to make you wise for salvation through faith in Christ Jesus." 2 Timothy 3:14-15 (NIV)

Life is full of lessons. If you had only one month to live, how would you apply what you have learned up to this point in your life? Think about your exposure to God's Word and the verses you have memorized. Think about how much you have fed on God's Word and sought to apply the principles from the Bible.

Paul encouraged Timothy to continue in what he had learned from infancy from constant exposure to the holy Scriptures. Feeding on God's Word is to be our continual practice and our consistent discipline. Yet, it is not enough to just read the Bible, we must apply God's Word in daily living.

- *"Blessed are those who have learned to acclaim you, who walk in the light of your presence, O LORD." Psalm 89:15 (NIV)*
- *"Whatever you have learned or received or heard from me, or seen in me--put it into practice. And the God of peace will be with you." Phil 4:9 (NIV)*

Maybe a good start for you would be to commit to read through the Bible in one year. If you will read four chapters each day, you will cross the finish line in 365 days. Daily intake and application of God's Word will enable your dash to make a kingdom splash.

PASSION IN ACTION

"Never be lacking in zeal, but keep your spiritual fervor, serving the Lord."
Romans 12:11 (NIV)

What are you passionate about? What are you giving your time, energy, and resources to? What gets the best of you? Your answer unveils your zeal.

God placed zeal in you. Your passion is an expression of your spiritual DNA. God gives you the ability to be passionate in this life. However, it is possible to misdirect the passion God gives you. Your passion can be diverted to areas that are unhealthy or unfruitful. You can channel your passion to outlets that dishonor God or even to good things that rob God's best for you.

God's Word teaches us to keep our spiritual fervor. Our passion in action should be vertical in nature. We are to be passionate for God. Our zeal for God and His kingdom should never experience a deficit. As we nurture our passion for God, we are to keep our passion channeled in the paths that God provides.

Are you passionate about the things of God? Does your life give evidence to the passion God desires from you? Take some time to assess your current reality. See if your passion is misdirected. Examine your life to the level of identifying the source of your passion and the expression of your passion in action.

October 21
FORTIFY YOUR PASSION

"Do not let your heart envy sinners, but always be zealous for the fear of the LORD." Proverbs 23:17 (NIV)

The current of our culture is counter Christian. As you seek to live out your faith in a fallen world, you will quickly discover that walking in reverence to God and in full devotion to Jesus will place you in the minority. You may forfeit popularity in this sin saturated culture, but you will not forfeit your position in Christ. You may not be affirmed by society for your faithfulness to God, but you will be rewarded by God who is all-knowing and who takes care of His own.

Don't allow the prosperity of the wicked to distract you in this life. Don't allow the visible affluence of the disobedient to diminish your passion for the things of God. Always be zealous for the Lord. Guard your heart and fortify your passion for God. Revere God as your Heavenly Father. Revere God as the One who created you, pursued you, rescued you, and empowers you for victorious living. Revere God for His holiness. Revere God for His nature and character. Demonstrate your devotion to God by your unwavering allegiance to His redemptive plan.

What if you had less than thirty days to live? How would your loyalty be adjusted? Would your allegiance to God's agenda expand? How differently would you channel your passion?

Let's live life for God with the intensity of our final days on the earth. God deserves our best! God deserves our reverence and our diligence!

"Brothers, my heart's desire and prayer to God for the Israelites is that they may be saved. For I can testify about them that they are zealous for God, but their zeal is not based on knowledge. Since they did not know the righteousness that comes from God and sought to establish their own, they did not submit to God's righteousness. Christ is the end of the law so that there may be righteousness for everyone who believes." Romans 10:1-4 (NIV)

Paul identifies the possibility of being zealous for God and yet not being saved. Paul examined the fruit of the Israelites in his day and detected their zeal for God. He noticed that their zeal was not based on knowledge. As a result, their pursuit of righteousness was faulty. They were unwilling to submit to God's righteousness and as a result they failed to recognize Christ.

Don't allow your zeal to blind you from truth. Before you put your passion in action, make sure you are grounded in the truth of God's revelation. God has made His salvation plan known. Make certain of your personal born again experience. Revisit your conversion and trace your zeal from that moment to now.

What if you had less than one month to live? How would you inform your passion in order to properly unleash your passion for the things of God? Stay in the know. Invest time in securing a daily intake of God's Word. If you want to know the heart of God, read His Word. If you want to know the blessings of God, obey His Word.

God honors obedience! If you want to put your passion in action, be zealous to know and obey God's Word!

October 23
CONTAGIOUS PASSION

"'Now fear the LORD and serve him with all faithfulness. Throw away the gods your forefathers worshiped beyond the River and in Egypt, and serve the LORD. But if serving the LORD seems undesirable to you, then choose for yourselves this day whom you will serve, whether the gods your forefathers served beyond the River, or the gods of the Amorites, in whose land you are living. But as for me and my household, we will serve the LORD." Joshua 24:14-15 (NIV)

Joshua's passion for God was contagious. He was willing to take responsibility for the spiritual condition of his home. Joshua made a bold proclamation that as for he and his household, they would serve the Lord. He did not apologize for his passion to obey God. His loyalty to God was expressed through his passion for God. Joshua's passion to lead his family spiritually impacted the nation.

- *"'Now then,' said Joshua, 'throw away the foreign gods that are among you and yield your hearts to the LORD, the God of Israel.'"* Josh 24:23 (NIV)
- *"And the people said to Joshua, 'We will serve the LORD our God and obey him.'"* Josh 24:24 (NIV)

It is interesting that Joshua did not ask the people to do anything he had not already done. Joshua put his passion in action by leading his family to revere and serve the Lord. Now the people could respond to his example and to his exhortation.

Are you putting your passion in action in such as way as to impact your family and those in your sphere of influence? Is your passion for God contagious or difficult to detect?

PASSIONATE INTERCESSION

"I thank my God every time I remember you. In all my prayers for all of you, I always pray with joy because of your partnership in the gospel from the first day until now, being confident of this, that he who began a good work in you will carry it on to completion until the day of Christ Jesus." Philippians 1:3-6 (NIV)

The Apostle Paul demonstrated his love for the church at Philippi by his passionate intercession for them. He prayed with joy because of their partnership in the gospel. He prayed with confidence knowing that God began a good work in them and would bring it to completion. Paul's prayer life was energized by his love for the believers at Philippi. Paul was not alone. The Holy Spirit joined in the divine communication by interceding for the saints in Philippi. Jesus interceded for them from the right hand of God in Heaven.

- *"In the same way, the Spirit helps us in our weakness. We do not know what we ought to pray for, but the Spirit himself intercedes for us with groans that words cannot express. And he who searches our hearts knows the mind of the Spirit, because the Spirit intercedes for the saints in accordance with God's will." Rom 8:26-27 (NIV)*
- *"Who is he that condemns? Christ Jesus, who died--more than that, who was raised to life--is at the right hand of God and is also interceding for us." Rom 8:34 (NIV)*

When you pray for others, you have the divine privilege of joining the Holy Spirit and Jesus in the ministry of intercession. Put your passion in action by embracing the ministry of intercessory prayer. Who will you begin to pray for today?

October 25
PASSION FOR THE BIBLE

"Do you not know that in a race all the runners run, but only one gets the prize? Run in such a way as to get the prize." 1 Corinthians 9:24 (NIV)

Life is not a sprint, but a marathon.

The Greeks had two athletic festivals: the Olympic games and the Isthmian games. Paul's audience would immediately connect this running imagery with the Isthmian games in their city of Corinth. Instead of receiving a gold, silver, or bronze medal like in our current day Olympics, only one prize was awarded in the Isthmian games. The winning runner would receive a wreath. Nothing was awarded to the runner who came in second or third. Only one person got the prize!

Paul is encouraging us as believers to run in such a way as to get that prize. We are to live the Christian life with passion. God desires our best and God deserves our best. So, how are you running the Christian race? Are you running with passion? Too often, we divert our passion to other venues. We rob God and we give our best to that which has no eternal value.

How you live is just as important as how much time you have left on this earth. The quality of your life is just as vital as the quantity of your remaining days. How will you live your life? If you had less than one month to live, would your passion in the race of life be vertical? Would your passion for God and His agenda be evident?

GIVE JESUS THE REINS

"I have been crucified with Christ and I no longer live, but Christ lives in me. The life I live in the body, I live by faith in the Son of God, who loved me and gave himself for me." Galatians 2:20 (NIV)

Are you dying to live? You can spend your entire life trying to figure out how to really live. Your constant pursuit can be saturated with seeking to discover life. Meanwhile, life happens while you are trying to get a grasp on life.

Paul gives tremendous insight into the life God has for you. In order to live, you must die. The life God has for you is really not your life. As a follower of Jesus Christ, you have been crucified with Christ. You have already died to yourself so that Christ can live in you. Don't miss the parallel. You died so that Christ can live in you and through you. Yet, the life you now live in the body is lived by faith in Jesus, who loved you and gave Himself for you. You are dying to live.

- *"Then he said to them all: 'If anyone would come after me, he must deny himself and take up his cross daily and follow me. For whoever wants to save his life will lose it, but whoever loses his life for me will save it.'" Luke 9:23-24 (NIV)*
- *"And if the Spirit of him who raised Jesus from the dead is living in you, he who raised Christ from the dead will also give life to your mortal bodies through his Spirit, who lives in you." Rom 8:11 (NIV)*

Put your passion in action by allowing Jesus to live His life in and through you. Give Jesus the reins to your life and let Him have His way in you. Surrender to His Lordship and submit to His prompting. Your passion will be evidenced by your obedience.

October 27
SLIPPERY SLOPE

"When the woman saw that the fruit of the tree was good for food and pleasing to the eye, and also desirable for gaining wisdom, she took some and ate it. She also gave some to her husband, who was with her, and he ate it. Then the eyes of both of them were opened, and they realized they were naked; so they sewed fig leaves together and made coverings for themselves." Genesis 3:6-7 (NIV)

Have you ever inherited anything? You may have inherited some furniture, jewelry, or money from a loved one who passed away. Perhaps you have not ever been in an official capacity to inherit earthly goods as of yet. There is one thing we have in common with every human being who has ever lived, who is currently alive, or who will be born. That one common thread is inheriting the sin nature from our relatives, Adam and Eve. That's right! You can trace your family tree all the way back to Adam and Eve. We have inherited their sin nature.

Adam and Eve were both selfish and selfless. Eve selfishly put her way above God's way by doubting God's Word and succumbing to the serpent's temptation. Eve was selfless in that she gave some of the forbidden fruit to her husband, Adam. Adam was selfish in that he also disobeyed God's instruction and placed his own personal desire above God's instruction. In their fallen state, they did exhibit selflessness in sowing fig leaves together and making coverings for themselves. Actually, they were trying to cover up their sin.

Why do we do the things we do? Why do we willfully walk through doors we should not enter and cross bridges we should not cross? Why do we operate in the cycle of selfishness? It all goes back to the Garden of Eden. We are simply feeding the sin nature that we inherited.

Hope is on the way!

GOD'S SACRIFICIAL LOVE

"Then the man and his wife heard the sound of the LORD God as he was walking in the garden in the cool of the day, and they hid from the LORD God among the trees of the garden. But the LORD God called to the man, 'Where are you?'"
Genesis 3:8-9 (NIV)

God demonstrated His selfless and sacrificial love in the Garden of Eden. As Adam and Eve were trying to hide from God due to their willful disobedience, God asked Adam a question that revealed the heart of God and the sinfulness of man. God called to Adam, "Where are you?"

The truth is that God knew exactly where Adam was both physically and spiritually. God did not need Adam to identify his location. God wanted Adam to consider and contemplate his own personal spiritual state. God wanted Adam to recognize his disobedience and rebellion. God demonstrated sacrificial love as He killed an animal that He created in order to provide covering and cleansing for Adam and Eve.

God's provision taught Adam and Eve that the shedding of blood was necessary for the removal of sin. The demonstration of selfless and sacrificial love also taught Adam and Eve that sin comes at a high cost. Adam and Eve received God's forgiveness but had to suffer the consequences of their sin. They were banished from the Garden of Eden. God's selfless and sacrificial love includes tough love.

Think of ways in which God has demonstrated His selfless and sacrificial love in your life. You may want to revisit the spiritual markers in your life and assess them based on God's selfless and sacrificial love.

October 29
WASHING FEET

"It was just before the Passover Feast. Jesus knew that the time had come for him to leave this world and go to the Father. Having loved his own who were in the world, he now showed them the full extent of his love." John 13:1 (NIV)

Jesus gave so freely to others. His compassion is without comparison. He caused the lame to walk, the mute to speak, the deaf to hear, and the blind to see. Children were drawn to Him and His love for them was unmatched. Jesus simply loved people.

The public ministry of Jesus was visible, tangible, and contagious. He was an irresistible influence. His love for people also had a private dimension. We are invited into an intimate setting where the evening meal is being served and Jesus is surrounded by His disciples. Jesus captured this moment to show them the full extent of His love.

Jesus poured water into a basin and began to wash his disciples' feet. Think about that for a moment. The master chose to serve. Jesus embraced an act of kindness that demonstrated His security and His selfless love. The Son of God chose to serve sinful man. The removal of dirt from their feet was a selfless portrait of love that was a preview of the sacrificial love Jesus would demonstrate upon the cross.

Are you willing to show the full extent of your love for others? Are you willing to express the selfless and sacrificial love of Jesus to others? Maybe God will bring someone in your path today that needs to know that kind of love. Be ready to release God's love!

Love that Initiates

"But now a righteousness from God, apart from law, has been made known, to which the Law and the Prophets testify. This righteousness from God comes through faith in Jesus Christ to all who believe. There is no difference, for all have sinned and fall short of the glory of God, and are justified freely by his grace through the redemption that came by Christ Jesus." Romans 3:21-24 (NIV)

God took the initiative to come to your rescue.

Have you ever questioned your own value and worth? That's a normal part of life. Everyone wants to feel valued and valuable. God established your value by taking the initiative to rescue you from your sin and to robe you in His righteousness.

God has made His righteousness known through His Word and the Word made flesh (John 1:14). When you place your faith in the completed work of Jesus on the cross, you receive the righteousness of Christ. The truth is that we have all sinned and fall short of God's glory. We have missed the mark of His perfection and His holiness. Yet, God chose to justify us freely by His grace through the redemption that came through Jesus.

God took the initiative to demonstrate His selfless and sacrificial love. Before you decided what you would do with God, God decided what to do with you. Before you turned to God, God turned to you! Your value is measured by the price He paid to remove your sin and to robe you in His righteousness. You are valued and you are valuable to God. His love for you is the certification of your value.

What will you do with the love God has shown you? How will you treat others now that you have experienced God's love firsthand?

October 31
LOVING GOD AND OTHERS

"If anyone says, 'I love God,' yet hates his brother, he is a liar. For anyone who does not love his brother, whom he has seen, cannot love God, whom he has not seen." 1 John 4:20 (NIV)

Is it possible to love God and hate your brother? Can you have the love of God residing in you and at the same time have hatred toward others festering in your spirit? The duplicity seems to be incongruent to the life of love that God calls us to and that Jesus exemplified on the earth.

Turn inward for a moment and examine your own current reality. Is there anyone you are fertilizing hatred toward? Do you have someone in your life to whom your love has extinguished and your hatred has ignited? Doing life in a fallen world is inundated with landmines of hatred. You will not lack opportunities to be wounded by hurtful words and by harmful people. People will let you down.

You cannot love God and hate others at the same time without your relationship with God being affected. God's love in you demands expression. When you choose to hate the people God created and the people Jesus died for, you restrict God's love within you. God wants you to hate what He hates and love what He loves. God passionately hates sin, but passionately loves the sinner.

Who is your brother? Who is your sister? How would God define your level of love? You will notice daily tests that reveal the authenticity of your love for others. Do you love God? Do you love others?

Loving God and loving people is the entirety of the Bible for present day expression.

LOVING DIFFICULT PEOPLE

"You have heard that it was said, 'Love your neighbor and hate your enemy.' But I tell you: Love your enemies and pray for those who persecute you, that you may be sons of your Father in heaven. He causes his sun to rise on the evil and the good, and sends rain on the righteous and the unrighteous." Matthew 5:43-45 (NIV)

Loving the lovable is not much of a challenge. But, to love those who are difficult to love requires a new perspective and a new enabling. God not only wants us to love our neighbor as ourselves, but to also love our enemies. Some people are hard to love.

Jesus brings a new dimension to the concept of love in His Sermon on the Mount. Not only are we to love our enemies, but we are to pray for those who persecute us. Showing love to those who have wounded us is only possible by the enabling of the Lord Jesus.

- *"When they hurled their insults at him, he did not retaliate; when he suffered, he made no threats. Instead, he entrusted himself to him who judges justly." 1 Pet 2:23 (NIV)*
- *"That is why I am suffering as I am. Yet I am not ashamed, because I know whom I have believed, and am convinced that he is able to guard what I have entrusted to him for that day." 2 Tim 1:12 (NIV)*

Jesus is our pattern for loving our enemies.

November 2
DEVOTION IN MOTION

"Large crowds were traveling with Jesus, and turning to them he said: 'If anyone comes to me and does not hate his father and mother, his wife and children, his brothers and sisters--yes, even his own life--he cannot be my disciple.'" Luke 14:25-26 (NIV)

Idolatry is a word we seldom use. Whenever you allow someone or something to take the place of God in your life, you commit the sin of idolatry. The first and second of the Ten Commandments speak to this concept directly (Ex 20:3-4). Whatever or whomever becomes the object of your worship becomes your idol.

Jesus infuses this earthly tendency of ours into His teaching on becoming a disciple. To become a follower of Jesus Christ, you must be willing to remove the idols in your life. Your loyalty to Christ is to be unmatched and undivided. Jesus becomes your focus and the object of your worship, devotion, and loyalty.

The fifth commandment of the Ten Commandments refers to the honoring of our parents (Ex 20:12). Jesus is not contradicting the fifth commandment. He does not want you to dishonor your parents. Jesus is saying that your love for Him should be such a priority, that in comparison, your love for your family would look like hate.

Your love, loyalty, and devotion to Jesus is to be your top priority and the expressed passion of your life. Don't allow anything or anyone to compete for that place in your life. Don't allow anything or anyone to rob your allegiance to the One who gave His life for you. Jesus has already demonstrated His selfless and sacrificial love. Now, it's your turn to demonstrate your selfless and sacrificial love for Jesus.

CLASSROOM OF PREPARATION

"Jesus answered him, 'I tell you the truth, today you will be with me in paradise.'"
Luke 23:43 (NIV)

The thief on the cross received the greatest gift of all, the gift of eternal life. In our vernacular, we would say that he was in the ninth inning with two outs and a full count. His next decision would determine his future. When the thief made the decision to turn to Christ, his forever was radically changed. Instead of going to hell, the thief, now as a newly converted child of God, went to Heaven.

We rejoice in the immense mercy and grace Jesus demonstrated upon the cross for this thief. However, this thief had no time to grow spiritually and to develop his spiritual muscles. Was he authentically saved? Yes! Did he have time to develop into a mature follower of Christ? No!

Fortunately, you have the privilege of knowing Christ personally and growing in your love relationship with Him. The challenge for you is not the matter of salvation, but the matter of sanctification. Are you growing? Are you becoming who Christ made you to be? You have both the privilege and responsibility to maximize the time you have in order to grow spiritually.

What have you learned so far in your spiritual journey? Life on earth is a classroom of preparation for the life to come. How are you utilizing what God has given you with the time you have? Are you intentional about your spiritual maturation? Are you growing in your love relationship with Jesus?

November 4
TEACHABILITY

"It was he who gave some to be apostles, some to be prophets, some to be evangelists, and some to be pastors and teachers, to prepare God's people for works of service, so that the body of Christ may be built up until we all reach unity in the faith and in the knowledge of the Son of God and become mature, attaining to the whole measure of the fullness of Christ." Ephesians 4:11-13 (NIV)

Where do you fit in this picture? God has placed equippers in your life to help you develop into a fully devoted follower of Jesus Christ. God has placed a systematic process within the local church to promote spiritual maturity. Are you an intentional part of the process?

Take a close look at your level of participation in the life of the local church family. Are you being built up? Are you reaching unity in the faith and in the knowledge of Jesus and becoming mature? Are you attaining to the whole measure of the fullness of Christ? What is your level of teachability? Your spiritual maturity will be proportionate to your teachability. Are you teachable as you listen to your pastor's message? Are you teachable as you sit under the teaching of a godly small group leader? Are you teachable as you spend time alone with God in prayer and Bible reading?

Make the most of the opportunities God has given you to grow spiritually. Maximize the moments you sit under anointed teaching from God's Word. Move from hearing and reading God's Word to applying God's Word in daily living. Live out what God is depositing in you.

"Then we will no longer be infants, tossed back and forth by the waves, and blown here and there by every wind of teaching and by the cunning and craftiness of men in their deceitful scheming. Instead, speaking the truth in love, we will in all things grow up into him who is the Head, that is, Christ." Ephesians 4:14-15 (NIV)

Your stability is linked to your teachability.

Are you grounded in God's Word? The anchor holds! In this life on planet earth, your faith will be challenged. Your beliefs will undergo scrutiny. The values you hold dear will be resisted. The world's system and the anti-Christian culture will seek to dominate the landscape of your faith.

Are you able to grow spiritually in a hostile environment? You must make a decision to conform to the culture or to confront the culture. As you grow spiritually, your roots will go deeper and your stability will become more evident.

Notice that in all things you will grow up into him who is the Head, that is, Christ. In all types of situations and scenarios, you can grow. Regardless of your current reality, you can and should grow. Maybe you are facing a challenging situation or a difficult relationship and wonder how you will grow in the midst. The good news is that God can cause you to grow through whatever you are facing. God does not waste the difficulties we face. God will bring you through at a deeper level than you entered the circumstances.

Remain teachable. Allow God to form you and fashion you through the challenges of life. Let God strengthen your resolve to remain faithful at all costs. Finish strong!

November 6
CONFORMITY TO CHRIST

"For those God foreknew he also predestined to be conformed to the likeness of his Son, that he might be the firstborn among many brothers." Romans 8:29 (NIV)

We take comfort in knowing that in all things God works for the good of those who love Him and are called according to His purpose (Rom 8:28). Our comfort is found in the sovereignty of God, knowing that He is on His throne and has the final say. Yet, there is more to the purpose of God than our comfort. God also treasures our conformity to Christ.

The ultimate goal for the believer is to be conformed to the image of Christ. To become like Christ requires our participation. God provides the environments and opportunities for our transformation. We get to join God in His redemptive activity. Our teachability determines the level of our conformity. Are we responsive to God's corrective measures? Are we sensitive to God's prompting?

> • *"For he chose us in him before the creation of the world to be holy and blameless in his sight. In love he predestined us to be adopted as his sons through Jesus Christ, in accordance with his pleasure and will--to the praise of his glorious grace, which he has freely given us in the One he loves." Eph 1:4-6 (NIV)*

God's desire for us is that we operate as holy and blameless in His sight. We are clean before Him because we have received the imputed righteousness of Christ. However, there is a practical daily response to God's work to conform us into the image of Christ.

When you stand before God one day to give an account for your life, how many adjustments will be needed in order for you to be completely like Christ?

MOVE FROM MILK TO MEAT

"We have much to say about this, but it is hard to explain because you are slow to learn. In fact, though by this time you ought to be teachers, you need someone to teach you the elementary truths of God's word all over again. You need milk, not solid food!" Hebrews 5:11-12 (NIV)

How long have you been a child of God? When did you have your conversion experience? Recount the moment you turned from your sin and confessed Jesus as Lord of your life. Now take a look at your life now compared to then. How much have you grown spiritually since the day of your salvation? What has changed over the years related to your spiritual maturity?

As you grow spiritually, you develop an appetite for the meat of God's Word. You move from the elementary truths of God's Word to the deeper things of God. There is a clear process of movement from milk to meat. If you have been a follower of Christ for several years, then your appetite ought to give evidence to the level of your spiritual maturity.

If you are slow to learn, then it is time to examine your level of teachability. When you are teachable, you receive, believe, and apply God's Word. Your teachability enables you to experience progress in your spiritual journey. Feeding on God's Word becomes a delight instead of a duty.

What is your level of spiritual maturity? What is keeping you from reaching your God-given potential? God has designed you for physical and spiritual growth.

November 8
MATURE AND COMPLETE

"Perseverance must finish its work so that you may be mature and complete, not lacking anything." James 1:4 (NIV)

Where do you lack? That's a personal question to say the least, but an important one to consider. God's desire is for you to be complete, not lacking anything. One of the tools God uses is the conduit of perseverance. Why would you need to embrace perseverance? Living the Christian life in the laboratory of our fallen world demands a response. As a follower of Jesus Christ, you get to choose your response. You can persevere or you can buckle. You can breakthrough or you can break down.

Perseverance is a mark of a maturing Christian. As you mature spiritually, you learn how to respond to adversity. Your response to adversity reveals your level of spiritual maturity and develops your spiritual maturity. The process includes your teachability. What will you learn from the chisel of adversity? Will you become bitter or will you become better?

God values your maturity. God wants you to be complete. Rely on God's power to persevere in this life. Your perseverance informs your spiritual maturity and impacts your eternity. God is building you. You are still in process! You are still on the assembly line! Be patient, God is working!

ADD TO YOUR FAITH

"For this very reason, make every effort to add to your faith goodness; and to goodness, knowledge; and to knowledge, self-control; and to self-control, perseverance; and to perseverance, godliness; and to godliness, brotherly kindness; and to brotherly kindness, love." 2 Peter 1:5-7 (NIV)

Warm memories flood my mind as I think about our annual tradition of adding lights to the outside of my house growing up. Each Christmas, my brother and I would go up into the attic to retrieve the Christmas lights. We would spend hours untangling them and threading them throughout the shrubbery. Each bush would be covered in lights. We would also get up on the roof to strategically place lights along the edge of the roofline. Each year, we would add to our collection of lights. It was a blast!

Your body is the temple of the Holy Spirit. You house the Spirit of God. Your daily privilege is adding to what God has begun in your life. The faith that you were given by God to become His child and to be adopted into His family is the faith that God wants you to add to. Adorn your faith with goodness, knowledge, self-control, perseverance, godliness, brotherly kindness, and love. Add these to your life as you would add Christmas lights to your house. These qualities are to be added to your faith by a conscious decision.

You get to participate with God in your development. Be teachable. Allow God to show you areas of your life that need improvement. Cooperate with God in building you into the man or woman of God that He created you to be.

What are you adding to the temple of the Holy Spirit? You are the walking tabernacle of God's Presence. You may be the only Jesus others see in their lifetime.

November 10
RAPTURE READY

"For the Lord himself will come down from heaven, with a loud command, with the voice of the archangel and with the trumpet call of God, and the dead in Christ will rise first. After that, we who are still alive and are left will be caught up together with them in the clouds to meet the Lord in the air. And so we will be with the Lord forever." 1 Thessalonians 4:16-17 (NIV)

If you are a child of God, then there is no need to fear death. You will either experience the Rapture or the resurrection. If you are still alive when Jesus comes for His Bride, you will be raptured. You will be snatched up from your earthly existence. However, if you die before the the Rapture occurs, you will not experience the sting of death (I Cor 15:55). To be absent from the body is to be present with the Lord (2 Cor 5:6-8). The moment you take your last breath on earth, you are ushered instantaneously into the Presence of the Lord.

Are you Rapture ready? Have you solidified your spiritual status? Do you have the assurance of salvation? The Bible is clear that you can know that you have eternal life.

- *"And this is the testimony: God has given us eternal life, and this life is in his Son. He who has the Son has life; he who does not have the Son of God does not have life." 1 John 5:11-12 (NIV)*
- *"I write these things to you who believe in the name of the Son of God so that you may know that you have eternal life." 1 John 5:13 (NIV)*

Revisit the day of your salvation. Spend some time tracing the spiritual markers in your life. Thank God for His assurance of your salvation. Now that you are Rapture ready, invest your life in making a kingdom impact for the glory of God. Make your life count for eternity!

STAY CONNECTED

"Remain in me, and I will remain in you. No branch can bear fruit by itself; it must remain in the vine. Neither can you bear fruit unless you remain in me." John 15:4 (NIV)

How will you live before you go? Your time on earth is limited. James compares life to a mist that appears and then vanishes (James 4:14). Compared to eternity, our time on earth is brief. Yet, how you choose to live your life on planet earth has eternal implications. Each moment matters for eternity.

Jesus identifies the abiding relationship made available to you. Without having an abiding relationship with Jesus, you cannot bear fruit. He is the vine. He is the source of real life. You are the branch. Your role in the relationship is to stay connected to the vine. You become the conduit through which Jesus bears His fruit. Your fruitfulness is proportionate to your abiding relationship with Jesus. To remain in Christ is to stay connected to Him through a growing relationship with Him.

Once you have established the connection through your faith in the completed work of Jesus on the cross, your eternal relationship with Christ is solidified. Now that you know Christ personally, you are to grow in your relationship with Christ progressively. Moment by moment you enjoy the abiding relationship whereby you experience His life flowing through you. As the life of Christ flows through you, His life is expressed through you to a watching world. Fruit is evidenced as a result of your abiding relationship with Christ.

November 12
TRUST GOD

"Trust in the LORD with all your heart and lean not on your own understanding; in all your ways acknowledge him, and he will make your paths straight."
Proverbs 3:5-6 (NIV)

Trust God with the remainder of your days. Your departure from planet earth has already been scheduled by God. He knows when you will take your final breath of earthly air. God is all-knowing and God is eternal. He sees the entirety of your life. He already knows every decision you will make and every path that you will take. In His foreknowledge, God already knows what the final chapter of your earthly existence looks like.

Are you willing to trust God with your life? Are you willing to place your life completely in His hands? Live your remaining days with the focus and tenacity of a passionate follower of Christ. Don't rely on your own understanding. In all your ways, acknowledge the sovereignty of God. Live with the awareness of God's purity, power, and perspective. God is for you. He demonstrated His love for you before you had a chance to weigh in on the transaction (Rom 5:8). God took the initiative to bring you into a love relationship with Himself.

Place God first in your life (Matt 6:33) and He will make your paths straight. Give Him the proper place of allegiance and loyalty. God deserves your devotion and your worship. Make no room for apathy or lethargy. With the time you have left on this earth, trust God with all of your heart. Allow your love relationship with Him to demonstrate who you are and whose you are!

THE REST OF YOUR LIFE

"Therefore, since Christ suffered in his body, arm yourselves also with the same attitude, because he who has suffered in his body is done with sin. As a result, he does not live the rest of his earthly life for evil human desires, but rather for the will of God." 1 Peter 4:1-2 (NIV)

What are you going to do with the rest of your life?

Jesus is our model to follow. He suffered in His body for our benefit. Jesus died on the cross to pay the penalty for our sin. He was willing to become the sinless sacrificial lamb that took away our sin. Jesus nailed our sin to the cross. He paid the debt we could not pay.

What will you do with what Jesus has done for you? Will you live your life for earthly human desires or for the will of God?

- *"The end of all things is near. Therefore be clear minded and self-controlled so that you can pray. Above all, love each other deeply, because love covers over a multitude of sins." 1 Pet 4:7-8 (NIV)*
- *"Each one should use whatever gift he has received to serve others, faithfully administering God's grace in its various forms." 1 Pet 4:10 (NIV)*

Live for the will of God. Allocate your time, your energy, and your resources to live for the will of God. Live in light of the eternity. Pray, love deeply, and serve faithfully. Don't waste your life! Live for the will of God!

November 14
SOLIDIFY YOUR WALK

"We must pay more careful attention, therefore, to what we have heard, so that we do not drift away." Hebrews 2:1 (NIV)

Departure readiness includes making sure that you are saved and being conscientious about how you live each day. Every moment matters in God's economy. As followers of Jesus Christ, we are to be attentive to how we think, how we speak, and how we act. Our thought-life, our conversation, and our conduct are vital to departure readiness.

- *"Therefore, holy brothers, who share in the heavenly calling, fix your thoughts on Jesus, the apostle and high priest whom we confess." Heb 3:1 (NIV)*
- *"See to it, brothers, that none of you has a sinful, unbelieving heart that turns away from the living God." Heb 3:12 (NIV)*

Fixing our thoughts on Jesus is an act of our will. We must consciously and persistently fix our thoughts on Jesus. Our beliefs determine our behavior. Guarding against a sinful, unbelieving heart is our moment by moment responsibility.

How attentive are you to what you already know from God's Word? Are you obeying what God has already revealed to you? Make no provision for drifting from God. Fortify your faith and solidify your daily walk with God.

Authenticating Discipleship

"This is to my Father's glory, that you bear much fruit, showing yourselves to be my disciples." John 15:8 (NIV)

Are you ready to leave?

Hit the pause button for just a moment and take a close look at your life. What have you done with the life God has given you? What have you done with the opportunities God placed in your path? Have you spent your life or invested your life? What remains?

You bring glory to God through the fruit you bear. The fruit validates and authenticates your discipleship. Your devotion as a follower of Jesus Christ is measured by the fruit that is born through your life. The focus is not on bearing fruit, but rather on abiding. Staying connected to Christ through an intimate love relationship will result in a fruit-bearing life.

- *"In the same way, let your light shine before men, that they may see your good deeds and praise your Father in heaven." Matt 5:16 (NIV)*
- *"'By this all men will know that you are my disciples, if you love one another.'" John 13:35 (NIV)*

The fruit of kindness will be expressed through your life as you abide in Christ. Your compassion for the lost and your commitment to sharing the gospel will be in direct proportion to the level of your abiding relationship with Christ. The fruit of love will be evidenced by your life in relation to your connectivity to Christ as the ultimate source of love. The life of Christ will flow through you to impact the lives of others.

Are you bringing glory to God? If so, then you are living in light of eternity. You are departure ready!

November 16
PRUNING FOR PRODUCTIVITY

"He cuts off every branch in me that bears no fruit, while every branch that does bear fruit he prunes so that it will be even more fruitful." John 15:2 (NIV)

Without pruning, there is no productivity.

God wants us to be fruitful. In order for us to bear fruit that remains, God initiates the process of pruning. As the gardener, God removes those things in our lives that prevent the life of Christ from flowing through us. He allows us to go through seasons of adversity to address those fruit-restricting areas of our lives.

> • *"Our fathers disciplined us for a little while as they thought best; but God disciplines us for our good, that we may share in his holiness. No discipline seems pleasant at the time, but painful. Later on, however, it produces a harvest of righteousness and peace for those who have been trained by it." Heb 12:10-11 (NIV)*

The loving hand of our attentive Heavenly Father brings correction when we drift from His best. Without pain, there is no change. God allows pain to come into our lives to bring us to the place of full surrender. When we reach the level of acknowleging our sin and recognizing God's desire, the pruning begins to enable the flow of Christ to nourish the areas of our life that bring glory to God.

Will there be a major change when you stand before God? Will you be responsive to God's pruning in your life now so that when you stand before God very little will be needed to make you like Christ? Allow God to conform you into the image of Christ.

It's Your Move

"But the chief priests stirred up the crowd to have Pilate release Barabbas instead." Mark 15:11 (NIV)

Have you ever encountered injustice? Have you ever been treated unfairly? I think we have all been there. It hurts! The scars serve as a constant reminder. In our verse today, we find a word that compels us to contemplate. It is the soothing word, instead. Let me take this punishment instead of you. Allow me to receive this penalty instead of you. Jesus will be flogged and crucified instead of Barabbas. The innocent man dies in his place. The guilty man goes free. Jesus receives what he doesn't deserve while Barabbas receives what he doesn't deserve. Jesus receives death! Barabbas receives life! Is that justice? Should the guilty go free?

It depends who takes the initiative. "But God demonstrates his own love for us in this: While we were still sinners, Christ died for us" (Rom 5:8 NIV). Christ died instead of us! Yes, while we were still sinners! How can you demonstrate that kind of love? Who in your sphere of influence needs to know what instead looks like?

Forgive instead of holding a grudge. Show acceptance instead of forging a gap. Offer help instead of ignoring the need. Appreciate Jesus instead of taking Him for granted. It's your move!

November 18
COMPELLING LOVE

"If anyone has material possessions and sees his brother in need but has no pity on him, how can the love of God be in him?" 1 John 3:17 (NIV)

When you pull up to a traffic signal and notice a man holding a cardboard sign saying, "Need food! Please help!", what kind of thoughts race through your mind? Do you wrestle with the notion to roll down your window and extend a dollar bill or maybe even a five dollar bill? Then again, you may start pondering what he might spend the money on. In your mind, you are thinking that he may take the money and go buy alcohol, cigarettes, or a lottery ticket. You question whether he will really use the money to buy food as his sign advertised.

Does God expect us to use good judgment? Yes! But, God also expects us to help meet needs. Remember this concept: God does not bless you based on how that person spends the money you give. God blesses you based on your heart in giving to meet needs.

John takes the concept of meeting needs into the arena of the family of God. We are to help fellow believers. In fact, if we are unwilling to use the resources God has blessed us with to help a brother in need, then how can the love of God be in us? In other words, God's love is evidenced as we meet needs.

God's love compels us to be generous. Generosity will not flow naturally. It is a supernatural experience. God has blessed us to be a blessing. Ask God to show you some needs this week that He wants you to meet for His glory!

UNFAILING LOVE

"Have mercy on me, O God, according to your unfailing love; according to your great compassion blot out my transgressions." Psalm 51:1 (NIV)

David came to the point of desperation after committing the sins of adultery and murder. God used the prophet Nathan to confront David. Nathan used a parable to personalize David's sin and then injected the piercing accusatory statement, "You are the man!"

Have you heard these lyrics before? "It's me! It's me O Lord, standing in the need of prayer!" Both David and the prodigal son would have embraced this song. It is common throughout our earthly existence to go through seasons of personalization. In fact, if you want to become Christ-like and reach your God-given potential then you must be willing to acknowledge your sin personally.

Personalization is looking into the mirror and confronting the reality of your own sin before you start judging others. The next step is to personalize God's mercy, unfailing love, and compassion.

Now let's get personal. What specific area of your life is in desperate need of God's touch? Identify the sin that entangles you and trace Satan's strategy. How does the enemy attack you? When are you most susceptible to sin? Where are you when you are most vulnerable to the enemy's flaming arrows? Is it when you travel? Is it when you are home alone? Is it when you are at work?

Personalize Psalm 51:1 and pray it to God right now. Go ahead and pray this Scripture and see how God reveals his mercy, unfailing love, and compassion.

November 20
FACING TRANSITION

"God is our refuge and strength, an ever-present help in trouble. Therefore we will not fear, though the earth give way and the mountains fall into the heart of the sea, though its waters roar and foam and the mountains quake with their surging." Psalm 46:1-3 (NIV)

Are you currently facing any of life's transitions? Maybe you are preparing for graduation and anticipating the future. Perhaps you are considering retirement and wonder if this is the right time. As a primary caregiver, you may be seeking God concerning transitioning a loved one into an assisted living center. It could be that you have purchased a new home and are trying to get settled and find order amidst the chaos. Regardless of your particular season of transition, God is more than sufficient to see you through.

God is our refuge! We can go to Him. In fact, our first response to life's transitions should be to go to Him. He already knows what we are facing and what challenges we will face. Remember, He is all knowing!

God is our strength! We will run out of fuel at some point. The fumes are not sufficient, but God is. Allow Him to be your source of strength today. Allow God to have access to your life and your transitions.

God is an ever-present help in trouble. There's no where you can go to get away from God's Presence. He is omnipresent! He is your help to face life's transitions. Rest in Him. Give Him your worry. Give Him your confusion.

SELECTIVE MEMORY

"For I know my transgressions, and my sin is always before me." Psalm 51:3 (NIV)

How's your memory? Can you remember your favorite vacation from your childhood? Can you remember learning how to swim or braving the high diving board for the first time? Do you remember the day you got your driver's license? There's power in memory.

Memory can paralyze us with fear or mobilize us to persevere. Memory can blockade us like a brick wall or project us forward like a smooth water slide. It depends on how you utilize your memory.

Satan uses memory to ridicule and demean us. He uses our memory to stifle our growth and to discredit our progress. Satan will bring to our minds the darkness of our past in order to cripple us.

Yet, where Satan seeks to bring death and destruction, God can bring life and victory! God uses memory to remind us where we would be without His abundant grace and abiding peace. God allows us to remember our sin so that we will know where He brought us from.

David acknowledged his sin. David affirmed the reality of sin always being before him in his memory. The question is not: Why do I remember my sin? The question is: What will I do in response to my ability to remember my sin?

God wants us to remember that He rescued us from our sin so that we can live the abundant life. So, when Satan reminds you of your past just remind him of God's provision of cleansing through the shed blood of His Son and our Savior, the Lord Jesus! Yes! Now that's using memory in victory!

November 22
LIVING AS CLAY

"But the pot he was shaping from the clay was marred in his hands..."
Jeremiah 18:4 (NIV)

Whenever you purchase an item that has an "as is" tag on it, you accept the fact that it may be flawed. In other words, the item may not be perfect. The beauty of salvation is that God accepted us "as is" and brought us into a vibrant love relationship with Himself to move us from "as is" to "what could be" in His hands. Yes! We were marred in His hands. But, He lovingly and patiently removes the imperfections of our attitude, behavior, and speech.

Being on the Potter's wheel can be painful at times. As God allows us to go through suffering and sorrow in this life, the areas of our life that do not reflect Christ-likeness will be dealt with. God will grow us through the pain. He will mold us and shape us through adversity.

Bathsheba endured some difficult seasons in her life. She experienced loneliness, grief, delays, disappointment, and shattered dreams. Yet, God redeemed all of those seasons in her life to bring her into a deeper relationship with Himself. She would have never become a Proverbs 31 woman without the adversity that God allowed her to face. She was marred in His hands. As a result of the loving touch of the Potter's hands, she became a masterpiece!

Are you on the Potter's wheel? Be patient. Allow God to mold you. He took you "as is" and He is shaping you for eternal significance.

God Works

"And we know that in all things God works for the good of those who love him, who have been called according to his purpose." Romans 8:28 (NIV)

While you were sleeping, God was working. He does not sleep. God is always at work. His work is continuous and consistent. Whatever you are facing today, God is working. Whatever you are dreading today, God is working. Whatever you are fearing today, God is working.

In all things, God works! He takes the initiative. Regardless of how confusing your current circumstance may seem to you, God is at work. He takes the initiative to work for your good and His glory. In all things God works for the good of those who love Him.

Do you love Him? Have you been called according to His purpose? Then you can walk in assurance today knowing that in all the things you face, in all the things you are wrestling with, in all the things that seem impossible, God works for your good. He will do what is best for you. He formed you and fashioned you and He will orchestrate all of the circumstances that surround you in order to work for your good.

Now that is the favor of God! You are favored by God. You are His treasure. Trust Him.

November 24
MULTIPLY YOUR BLESSING

"Another of his disciples, Andrew, Simon Peter's brother, spoke up, 'Here is a boy with five small barley loaves and two small fish, but how far will they go among so many?'" John 6:8-9 (NIV).

The situation looked bleak as the disciples tried to figure out a way to feed the five thousand men. When you add in the women and children, the need to feed triples in number. Philip quickly responded to Jesus that it would take more than eight months' wages to provide each person with a bite. Then Andrew brings a little boy with a sack lunch to Jesus.

We do not know the boy's name, but we know something about his heart. This little boy was willing to serve to benefit others. He was willing to give up his lunch so that others could eat. Jesus maximized this little boy's generosity and multiplied the blessing to meet all the needs. Not only did the little boy get to eat, but the multitudes ate as much as they wanted. Miraculously, the leftovers filled twelve baskets (John 6:13).

What if we chose to serve to benefit others? How would Jesus use us to spread His love if we consistently put the needs of others before our own?

BENEFIT OTHERS

"For even the Son of Man did not come to be served, but to serve, and to give his life as a ransom for many." Mark 10:45 (NIV)

Consumerism dominates our cultural landscape. We easily slide into a what have you done for me lately mindset. In the natural, being served by others has instant appeal. We crave being served. Scratch my back and then I will let you scratch my back again.

In God's kingdom economy, the focus shifts from selfishness to selflessness. As God's kingdom citizens, we are to move away from a "me-first" mentality in order to embrace the "others-first" lifestyle.

Jesus consistently lived the "others-first" lifestyle. As the Son of God, He had every right to be served, yet He chose to serve to benefit others. Jesus is our model to follow. Jesus is the ultimate example for us to emulate. We will never find a more accurate portrait of servitude than the One who gave His life for us.

Who will benefit from your life today? Ask God to elevate your sensitivity to each opportunity to serve to benefit others.

November 26
SERVE OTHERS

"Joseph, a Levite from Cyprus, whom the apostles called Barnabas (which means Son of Encouragement), sold a field he owned and brought the money and put it at the apostles' feet." Acts 4:36-37 (NIV)

We are introduced to Barnabas in the flow of the movement of God known as the Jerusalem church. There were no needy people among the flock because the church family willingly sold some of their houses and land and brought the proceeds to the apostles for distribution. Barnabas embraced the "others-first" lifestyle. He sold a field he owned and brought the money to the apostles.

His real name was Joseph, but the apostles called him Barnabas. The name Barnabas means Son of Encouragement. Barnabas lived in such a way as to add value to the lives of others. He was the kind of believer who would draw out the best in others.

> • *"The purposes of a man's heart are deep waters, but a man of understanding draws them out." Prov 20:5 (NIV)*

Are you serving to benefit others? What if you sought to draw out the best in others? Think about the people God has placed in your sphere of influence. Think about your family, your friends, and your frequent acquaintances. What if you chose to serve to benefit them?

Live in such a way as to add value to others. It's your serve!

"When he came to Jerusalem, he tried to join the disciples, but they were all afraid of him, not believing that he really was a disciple. But Barnabas took him and brought him to the apostles. He told them how Saul on his journey had seen the Lord and that the Lord had spoken to him, and how in Damascus he had preached fearlessly in the name of Jesus. So Saul stayed with them and moved about freely in Jerusalem, speaking boldly in the name of the Lord."
Acts 9:26-28 (NIV)

Imagine the New Testament without Barnabas. What if Barnabas was unwilling to step up and stand in the gap for Saul (Paul)? What if Paul would not have been accepted by the apostles in the church at Jerusalem? Barnabas chose to serve Paul by befriending him and establishing him within the church at Jerusalem. As a result, Paul went on three missionary journeys and gave birth to many churches. Because Barnabas was willing to serve to benefit others, Paul was able to write what is now half of our New Testament. Remove Barnabas and we lose Paul. If we lose Paul, we lose half of the New Testament. Do you think that Barnabas made an eternal impact by serving to benefit others?

What a wonderful example of serving! Barnabas is such a great example of what God can do with a person who is willing to serve to benefit others. Live to be a blessing! Choose to serve to benefit others!

November 28
DO WHAT JESUS DID

"I have set you an example that you should do as I have done for you."
John 13:15 (NIV)

God has called you to serve. You were rescued by God and reconciled to God in order to serve God by serving to benefit others. Your life purpose on the earth is to be Jesus beginning in your Jerusalem. Jesus has demonstrated what a life yielded to God's purpose looks like. Jesus, though He was the master, chose to become the servant and wash His disciples' feet. The lowly task of touching and washing dirty feet was the portrait of servitude exhibited by Jesus.

As a follower of Jesus Christ, you are not asked to do anything Jesus has not already done. To learn how to love God and how to love people, simply examine the life of Christ. To learn how to serve God and how to serve people, fasten your focus on Jesus.

- *"Let us fix our eyes on Jesus, the author and perfecter of our faith, who for the joy set before him endured the cross, scorning its shame, and sat down at the right hand of the throne of God." Heb 12:2 (NIV)*
- *"To this you were called, because Christ suffered for you, leaving you an example, that you should follow in his steps." 1 Pet 2:21 (NIV)*

Do as Jesus has done for you. Serve others as Jesus has served you by giving His life for you. Benefit others as Jesus has benefited you by bringing you into a right relationship with God.

SERVE LIKE OUR SHEPHERD

"He himself bore our sins in his body on the tree, so that we might die to sins and live for righteousness; by his wounds you have been healed. For you were like sheep going astray, but now you have returned to the Shepherd and Overseer of your souls." 1 Peter 2:24-25 (NIV)

What motivates you to serve God? What motivates you to serve to benefit others? It's not our natural proclivity to serve. Serving is the result of an abiding relationship with Jesus. Selfishness flows like a river in the human race. Selflessness flows from the life of Christ through a believer fully yielded to Christ.

- *"But now, by dying to what once bound us, we have been released from the law so that we serve in the new way of the Spirit, and not in the old way of the written code." Rom 7:6 (NIV)*
- *"How much more, then, will the blood of Christ, who through the eternal Spirit offered himself unblemished to God, cleanse our consciences from acts that lead to death, so that we may serve the living God!" Heb 9:14 (NIV)*

Jesus took the initiative to pay the penalty for our sins so that we could die to sin and live for righteousness. As sheep, we follow our Shepherd's lead. Jesus was willing to serve to benefit us immediately and eternally. We have been released from the law that once bound us in order to serve in the way of the Spirit. We have been empowered to live the Christ-centered life by the Indwelling Holy Spirit. Jesus has provided the way for us to serve the living God!

What is keeping you from serving God with full surrender and absolute devotion? What is keeping you from serving to benefit others in power of the Holy Spirit?

November 30
SERVE IN LOVE

"You, my brothers, were called to be free. But do not use your freedom to indulge the sinful nature; rather, serve one another in love." Galatians 5:13 (NIV)

You are free! You have the freedom to serve and the freedom to choose not to serve. The freedom is yours to turn inward and become self-focused and self-absorbed. However, the freedom is yours also to turn outward and become other-focused. You can embrace the freedom you have in Christ and unleash that freedom to serve God and to serve to benefit others.

Freedom can be abused. You can embrace your freedom to feed your flesh. As you feed the cravings of your sinful nature, your fleshly appetite will increase. Indulgence is a natural byproduct of our fallen nature. It is possible to drift into selfishness and self worship. Idolatry is simply the perversion of freedom.

What if you captured your freedom in Christ like a sail capturing the wind in order to serve one another? Your mobility and your maneuverability for the Lord would be catalytic. Operating in the freedom that you have in Christ removes the curtain of darkness over the horizon. You have been set free by the shed blood of Jesus to pursue God and to participate in His kingdom agenda. Serve one another in love. Impart to others the same unconditional love you have graciously received from God in Christ.

"Now about spiritual gifts, brothers, I do not want you to be ignorant."
1 Corinthians 12:1 (NIV)

What's in your toolbox? You need tools to do life and to meet needs. Repairs around the house require certain tools. Whenever you are in need of a pair of pliers, it seems that a screwdriver just won't do. Specific tools help us in various facets of life in the physical realm.

Within the body of Christ, God has equipped us for service. The tools God gives us are spiritual gifts. We receive these gifts at the moment of our conversion experience. When we turned from our sin and to Christ alone for salvation, we instantaneously received the Person of the Holy Spirit. When He came to indwell us, the Holy Spirit brought spiritual gifts to impart to us in our new life in Christ.

You cannot serve God and fulfill His mission apart from His enabling. God equips us for service with specific spiritual gifts for us to employ. God is the giver of the spiritual gifts. It is our job to discover the spiritual gifts God has given us and to utilize them in service to Him.

December 2
GIFTED TO SERVE

"There are different kinds of gifts, but the same Spirit. There are different kinds of service, but the same Lord. There are different kinds of working, but the same God works all of them in all men." 1 Corinthians 12:4-6 (NIV)

The Trinity is working for your productivity within the body. You will notice that there are different kinds of gifts, different kinds of service, and different kinds of working. That's a reality of the diversity within the body of Christ. Then you will notice that the same Spirit, the same Lord, and the same God works all of these in all of the members of the body of Christ. That's a reality of the unity within the body. Your productivity within the body is determined by the activity of the Trinity through your life.

Are you willing to allow God to accomplish His plan in you and through you? God does not want you to operate in isolation from the body of Christ. You are a vital part of the body and every part is necessary to accomplish God's kingdom agenda. What is the level of your receptivity to God's activity?

You are not expected to produce for God. God wants to produce through you. You are not expected to work for God. God wants to work through you. So, it's not about you. It's all about God and His activity through your life fully yielded and fully devoted to His activity.

What adjustments do you need to make in your life right now in order for God to have His way? What is inhibiting the activity of the Trinity in and through your life?

COMMON GOOD

"Now to each one the manifestation of the Spirit is given for the common good."
1 Corinthians 12:7 (NIV)

God gifts you to serve others. The spiritual gifts you receive at salvation give evidence to the reality of the Holy Spirit dwelling in you. Your body is the temple of the Holy Spirit (1 Cor 6:19). The Holy Spirit expresses Himself to the Body of Christ through spiritual gifts. The manifestation of the Holy Spirit is to benefit the Body of Christ.

God values unity. This unity is displayed relationally within the Trinity. God desires that you display the same unity within the Body of Christ as you serve to benefit others by employing the spiritual gifts you have received. Why does God manifest the Holy Spirit through the spiritual gifts? God does this for the common good of the Body of Christ.

You have been given spiritual gifts for the common good of those within the family of God. The local expression of the Body of Christ, God's family, is the local church. God desires that you serve to benefit others by exercising your spiritual gifts through the life of your local church.

December 4
EMPLOY SPIRITUAL GIFTS

"Just as each of us has one body with many members, and these members do not all have the same function, so in Christ we who are many form one body, and each member belongs to all the others." Romans 12:4-5 (NIV)

You are unique. God has formed you and fashioned you for His glory. You were created by God to fulfill His purposes in your generation. Part of His plan for your life includes you becoming part of the Body of Christ through a saving relationship with Jesus Christ. Your expression of that relationship takes place in a local church setting with fellow believers. You become a vital member of the Body of Christ with the privilege and responsibility of serving in and through the local church.

You complete the Body of Christ in that local church by fulfilling the function God has gifted you for. Each member of that local body of believers adds value to the redemptive purposes of God through faithfully employing the spiritual gifts given by God. Though diverse by design, the local expression of the Body of Christ is unified as each one fulfills his or her function within the body.

The beauty of the local church is that you belong to all the other members. You are linked to other believers within that local expression of the Body of Christ. You are valuable and you are vital to the effective functioning of the church. God has gifted you to serve alongside other members of the body. You belong because you believe in the finished work of Jesus on the cross. You matter to God and you matter to the local church. Are you currently serving faithfully in the ministry of your local church? Are you using the spiritual gifts God has given you in service to Him and to others? If not, why not? If so, how so?

"It was he who gave some to be apostles, some to be prophets, some to be evangelists, and some to be pastors and teachers, to prepare God's people for works of service, so that the body of Christ may be built up until we all reach unity in the faith and in the knowledge of the Son of God and become mature, attaining to the whole measure of the fullness of Christ." Ephesians 4:11-13 (NIV)

You are in the process of becoming. God is building you, growing you, developing you, and equipping you. God is placing people in your path to help you in the maturation process. Have you positioned yourself in an environment where you consistently sit under the preaching and teaching of a godly pastor-teacher?

Are you currently being equipped for service? It is important that you shadow a godly man or woman who faithfully exercises his or her spiritual gifts. Observe their lifestyle and take note of how they walk with God and how they serve to benefit others. You may want to consider taking a spiritual gift inventory in order to discover the spiritual gifts God has given you. A vital component to being equipped is that of participating in ministry opportunities that enable you to develop the spiritual gifts you have discovered.

God's desire is for you to be built up within the Body of Christ and to reach unity in the faith and in the knowledge of the Son of God. Are you becoming mature? Are you attaining to the whole measure of the fullness of Christ?

December 6
WEIGH THE BENEFIT

"What benefit did you reap at that time from the things you are now ashamed of? Those things result in death!" Romans 6:21 (NIV)

Sin never delivers what it promises. Sin promises pleasure, but produces pain. Sin promises escape, but produces entrapment. Sin promises freedom, but produces bondage. When you look into the rear view mirror of your life, you will quickly discern the reality of sin's consequences. Think of the shame that clutters the landscape of your past as a result of poor choices.

Weigh the benefit of the things you are now ashamed of. I'm sure that if you could go back into your past, there are choices you would love to retrieve and mistakes you would love to remove. In Christ, you are forgiven. The penalty of your sin has been paid in full by the atoning work of Jesus on the cross. Yet, it is a healthy exercise to think through the benefit you reaped as a result of your poor choices. The reality that poor choices produced death brings you to the place of walking in the fear of the Lord. You recognize that God is all-knowing and all-seeing.

- *"Make level paths for your feet and take only ways that are firm."* Prov 4:26 (NIV)
- *"In the paths of the wicked lie thorns and snares, but he who guards his soul stays far from them." Prov 22:5 (NIV)*

What does victory look like in a fallen world? The portrait of victory is a child of God thinking through the consequences of sin before stepping through a door that is dishonoring to God. Victory comes in the form of a wise decision to weigh the benefit of walking in the way of the Lord.

"Be self-controlled and alert. Your enemy the devil prowls around like a roaring lion looking for someone to devour." 1 Peter 5:8 (NIV)

In his book, *Finishing Strong*, Steve Farrar reminds us, "You've got an enemy who hates your guts and will do anything to keep you from finishing strong." The enemy we combat is the devil. Peter depicts the enemy as a roaring lion on a mission to devour. Your identity in Christ has positioned you in opposition to the devil and his agenda. You are on the devil's radar.

God has empowered you to walk in victory. God has equipped you with spiritual armor to combat the enemy. You are not powerless. You are not without hope and without help.

- *"Finally, be strong in the Lord and in his mighty power. Put on the full armor of God so that you can take your stand against the devil's schemes." Eph 6:10-11 (NIV)*
- *"Therefore put on the full armor of God, so that when the day of evil comes, you may be able to stand your ground, and after you have done everything, to stand." Eph 6:13 (NIV)*

God wants you to finish strong. God wants you to cross the finish line of life with integrity. You cannot run this race without God's provision. Your flesh is too weak. Your flesh craves impurity, compromise, and sin. The only way to finish strong is through daily surrender to the Lordship of Christ and through daily detection of the real enemy. Be self-controlled and alert! Put on the full armor of God! Stand!

December 8
BLESSED TO BE A BLESSING

"He who has been stealing must steal no longer, but must work, doing something useful with his own hands, that he may have something to share with those in need." Ephesians 4:28 (NIV)

You may have disengaged from this verse since you immediately recognized that you are not a thief. You are not stealing. You, in fact, have a strong work ethic and would never dream of stealing. So what is God trying to say to you through this verse?

God wants you to embrace a strong work ethic so that you can be a blessing to others. His desire is for you to work diligently so that you can share with those in need. You ought to get all the education you can so that you can excel and be the best at what God called you to do. Why? Because God deserves your best!

However, it is not about you! It is about positioning yourself in alignment with God's priorities so that you can be a blessing to others. God does not bless you so that you can funnel the blessings into your self-centered pursuits. God blesses you in order to expand your capacity to bless others. Do you have anything left to share with those in need? Statistics show that the average American lives on 120% of his or her income. That means we spend more than we make. Maybe it's time to re-think the American dream.

The life God blesses is the life given to being a blessing to those in need. You are blessed to be a blessing.

"And you also were included in Christ when you heard the word of truth, the gospel of your salvation. Having believed, you were marked in him with a seal, the promised Holy Spirit, who is a deposit guaranteeing our inheritance until the redemption of those who are God's possession--to the praise of his glory."
Ephesians 1:13-14 (NIV)

If you believe, you will receive. At the moment of conversion, you receive the baptism of the Holy Spirit. It is an instantaneous experience, not a subsequent event. The indwelling Presence of Christ, the Holy Spirit, comes to live inside of you. Having believed on the gospel of Jesus Christ, you were marked in Christ with the seal of the Holy Spirit.

The seal speaks of authenticity. The seal speaks of identification. You belong to God. You are His creation. You became His child and were adopted into His family when you placed your faith in Jesus alone for salvation. You were marked with a seal. That seal is the Person of the Holy Spirit.

Did you notice the Trinity in these two verses? God the Father, God the Son, and God the Holy Spirit are expressed in verses thirteen and fourteen. Look closely and you will see "Christ" and then "Holy Spirit" and then "God" which form the Trinity which means three in one.

God created you. Jesus redeemed you. The Holy Spirit inhabits you. Your conversion is the real deal which has been sealed.

December 10
REAP WHAT YOU SOW

"Do not be deceived: God cannot be mocked. A man reaps what he sows."
Galatians 6:7 (NIV)

The law of the harvest originates with God. As Creator of the universe, God has established the system upon which life exists and operates. You reap what you sow. God has made that a reality. There's no need to be deceived and there's no need to seek to mock God.

- *"Sow for yourselves righteousness, reap the fruit of unfailing love, and break up your unplowed ground; for it is time to seek the LORD, until he comes and showers righteousness on you."* Hosea 10:12 (NIV)
- *"Peacemakers who sow in peace raise a harvest of righteousness."* James 3:18 (NIV)

Let's connect the law of the harvest with how you live your life. Think about the way you invest your time, energy, and resources. How are you sowing your life in service to God? How are you currently investing in the kingdom of God? You will reap what you sow.

You can be absolutely sure that God's Word is absolutely true. The law of the harvest is an absolute formulated by God. God knows what you have sown. God knows the motive behind what you have sown. God even knows what you will reap and when you will reap as a result of what you have sown and how you have sown. Your activity in God's economy matters for eternity.

"For we are God's workmanship, created in Christ Jesus to do good works, which God prepared in advance for us to do." Ephesians 2:10 (NIV)

Salvation is a gift, not a reward. You cannot perform enough good works to earn salvation. You receive the gift of eternal life by the grace of God through faith in the completed work of Jesus on the cross. If salvation is a gift, how do good works add value?

God graciously gave His best, Jesus, to pay the sin debt you owed. It is a gift. If you try to pay for the gift one has given, then you cheapen the gift. What can you add to the finished work of Jesus on the cross? His atoning work is complete.

You were uniquely designed by God and for God. You are His masterpiece, His treasure, and the apple of His eye. You are His workmanship. He formed you and fashioned you for His glory. You are not an accident! You are here on purpose!

You cannot add to the salvation that God provided to you by His grace through faith. However, as His workmanship, you are created to do good works and to serve. You don't serve for salvation; you serve as a result of the salvation gift you have received. Good works are a result of a grateful heart. Gratitude for what God has initiated and our faith has activated results in good works.

Are you willing to display God's splendor today? You are His workmanship created in Christ Jesus to do good works! Who will benefit from your life of service today?

December 12
DEVELOP SPIRITUAL MUSCLES

"From him the whole body, joined and held together by every supporting ligament, grows and builds itself up in love, as each part does its work." Ephesians 4:16 (NIV)

God rewards your service both here and in the hereafter. There are immediate rewards for serving God and there are eternal rewards for serving God. In the here and now, your faith grows as you serve. As you exercise the spiritual gifts God has given you, God multiplies the impact and expands your faith. The body of Christ benefits from your faithful service and your personal faith deepens.

Serving develops your spiritual muscles just as working out with weights develops your physical muscles. The motion of you joining God in His activity generates the need for God's provision of strength, courage, and faith. Your love relationship with the Lord deepens as you live out your faith through daily serving to meet needs and to benefit others.

Is your faith growing? Are you placing your "yes" on the altar each day and making yourself available for God's use? Have you intentionally sought to exercise the spiritual gifts God has given you in order to benefit others?

"Here is a trustworthy saying that deserves full acceptance: Christ Jesus came into the world to save sinners--of whom I am the worst. But for that very reason I was shown mercy so that in me, the worst of sinners, Christ Jesus might display his unlimited patience as an example for those who would believe on him and receive eternal life." 1 Timothy 1:15-16 (NIV)

During my sophomore year in high school, I worked in a large grocery store. After spending a week outside fetching grocery baskets, I was promoted to mopping floors on the inside. A few weeks later I catapulted to the next level, that of being a display clerk. My job was to build captivating displays at the end of each aisle. Customers who came in just for milk and bread would often be drawn to one of the displays and end up purchasing one of the featured items.

God specializes in displaying His grace by featuring His children. One of God's featured converts was Saul who became Paul. God intersected Saul's path on the road to Damascus and transformed his life. Saul became Paul and was transformed from being a persecutor of the church to a preacher of the gospel. He was transformed from a murderer to a minister.

Later in Paul's life, he writes to one of his young sons in the ministry, Timothy, to describe how God specializes in placing His children on the display of His transforming grace.

God will display what He transforms. God will show off those who have experienced His grace expressed in His kindness to them in Christ. Will you allow His grace and kindness expressed to you to be put on display this week?

December 14
THE JESUS JERSEY

"You were taught, with regard to your former way of life, to put off your old self, which is being corrupted by its deceitful desires; to be made new in the attitude of your minds; and to put on the new self, created to be like God in true righteousness and holiness." Ephesians 4:22-24 (NIV)

Live up to the jersey you wear.

Our culture is saturated with a passion for sports. From the stands to the playing field, excitement and anticipation flow like a white water rafting river. The current is swift as fans and players hyper-focus on the game at hand.

It's all about the jersey you wear. There is a team you are pulling for. You sacrifice for that team. You cheer on and promote that team. Your loyalty is lavished on that team. You are an authentic fan.

When you become a child of God, you receive a new jersey. Once you are adopted into God's family, you are fitted with the Jesus jersey. Now you are playing to please Jesus. You are representing Jesus on this broken planet. You are robed in His righteousness and blessed with a new identity.

Are you living up to the jersey you wear? Do those closest to you know what team you are on? Is it evident to your neighbors, schoolmates, and co-workers that your loyalty is to Jesus and His game plan?

"While they were there, the time came for the baby to be born, and she gave birth to her firstborn, a son. She wrapped him in cloths and placed him in a manger, because there was no room for them in the inn." Luke 2:6-7 (NIV)

Make room for Jesus. He is the hope of the world. There is no other option for men, women, boys, and girls to be saved from eternal damnation. There is no other option for anyone to be delivered from the clutches of the enemy. Jesus is God's response to the fall of man. Jesus is the ultimate expression of God's love.

- *"For God so loved the world that he gave his one and only Son, that whoever believes in him shall not perish but have eternal life." John 3:16 (NIV)*
- *"But God demonstrates his own love for us in this: While we were still sinners, Christ died for us." Rom 5:8 (NIV)*

Will you make room for Jesus? Will you give Him first place in your life? Your heart can be His manger. Jesus came so that you would know Him personally and to enable you to invest the rest of your life to making Him known.

Seize the opportunities that God gives you this week to make Jesus known. World missions begins right where you are.

December 16
GOD'S AGENDA

"Suddenly a great company of the heavenly host appeared with the angel, praising God and saying, 'Glory to God in the highest, and on earth peace to men on whom his favor rests.'" Luke 2:13-14 (NIV)

God's agenda is global.

You are here to bring glory to God. You have been created by God to fulfill His agenda. God's agenda is global and your purpose is to live for His global glory. Don't waste your life. You are too valuable to God. Don't wade in the pool of apathy. Time is to too short.

> • *"Why, you do not even know what will happen tomorrow. What is your life? You are a mist that appears for a little while and then vanishes." James 4:14 (NIV)*

The brevity of life and certainty of death are realities that should motivate us to passionately bring God glory every moment of each day. What are you doing for the global glory of God? It is impossible to be self-consumed and live for the global glory of God. It is impossible to be self-centered and live for the global glory of God.

The angels got it. They demonstrated at Jesus' birth that their focus was to bring glory to God. God alone is worthy of our adoration. God alone is worthy of a life focused on bringing Him glory. Are you willing to reorient your life around living for the global glory of God?

SHARE HIS PROMISE

"He told them, 'This is what is written: The Christ will suffer and rise from the dead on the third day, and repentance and forgiveness of sins will be preached in his name to all nations, beginning at Jerusalem. You are witnesses of these things. I am going to send you what my Father has promised; but stay in the city until you have been clothed with power from on high." Luke 24:46-49 (NIV)

God is a promise keeper.

Jesus developed His disciples by investing time with them. He modeled what He wanted to multiply in them and through them. Jesus commissioned His followers to preach in His name to all nations. Then Jesus affirmed that He would send them what His Father had promised. He instructed them to stay in Jerusalem until they received the impartation of the promise.

God is the promise giver and He is a promise keeper. The promise He gave to the followers of Christ was the Person of the Holy Spirit. The promise He gives to every person who receives the gift of eternal life is the Holy Spirit.

> • *"We know that we live in him and he in us, because he has given us of his Spirit."* 1 John 4:13 (NIV)

Are you a child of the promise? Have you been born into God's family? God's glory lives in you in the Person of the Holy Spirit. Will you live for the global glory of God by sharing His promise with all nations beginning with your neighbors?

December 18
UNIFIED PRAYER

"They all joined together constantly in prayer, along with the women and Mary the mother of Jesus, and with his brothers." Acts 1:14 (NIV)

Anticipating Christmas generates major excitement and energy. You can feel it in the air as people saturate their flower beds, yards, and homes with decorative lights. The traffic heightens as shoppers strategically complete their Christmas lists. Travelers prepare to make their rounds among the family traditions. Anticipation of celebrating the birth of Christ brings out the best in us.

Following the ascension of Christ, a hundred and twenty believers were gathered in the upper room anticipating the arrival of the Holy Spirit. They were anticipating the fulfillment of the Father's promise. They all joined together. They continued with one accord in prayer. The Greek word is "homothumadon" which means with one mind, one accord, and one passion. In the language of the New Testament, it means to have the same mind and to rush along in unison.

God honored their unity as demonstrated in their continual praying together. God allowed them to express their unity through a ten day prayer meeting of anticipation. Unified prayer was their preparation for the impartation of the Holy Spirit on the Day of Pentecost.

Do you pray in anticipation of God's answer? Have you experienced unified prayer with other believers? What if you brought unified prayer into your Christmas experience?

"When the day of Pentecost came, they were all together in one place. Suddenly a sound like the blowing of a violent wind came from heaven and filled the whole house where they were sitting. They saw what seemed to be tongues of fire that separated and came to rest on each of them. All of them were filled with the Holy Spirit and began to speak in other tongues as the Spirit enabled them." Acts 2:1-4 (NIV)

God speaks your love language.

The joy of Christmas is celebrating the birth of Jesus and giving meaningful gifts to those we love. Jesus came to give us the ultimate gift, eternal life. As we exchange gifts this Christmas, it is an expression of valuing others. As you shop for that perfect gift to bless someone dear to you, you thoughtfully consider what they need and what they like. You consider their tastes, interests, and desires. You focus your gift on their uniqueness.

God speaks your love language in that He meets you at your greatest point of need. Salvation has come in the miracle of the manger, Jesus, born to bring life everlasting. On the Day of Pentecost, God demonstrated that the gospel is for everyone. He broke through the ethnic and language barriers by allowing those present in Jerusalem to hear the gospel in their own language. As the people groups represented in Jerusalem on the Day of Pentecost returned to their homeland, the gospel spread.

- *"Those who accepted his message were baptized, and about three thousand were added to their number that day."* Acts 2:41 (NIV)

God's love language is universal. The miracle of Christmas is that in Christ, God's glory may be revealed to all nations. Are you available for God's use?

December 20
THE ULTIMATE GIFT

"For God so loved the world that he gave his one and only Son, that whoever believes in him shall not perish but have eternal life." John 3:16 (NIV)

According to the Registry of Peoples and Languages, there are 6,809 distinct languages. There are more than twelve thousand ethnic identities or people groups. With over 6.7 billion people on the planet, the world's population is massive. What kind of hope is available to such a mass number of diverse people?

The hope of the world is found in John 3:16. If you had to condense the entire Bible into a single verse, it would be John 3:16. God's love for all people groups is captured by this one verse. The wonderful news is that God took the initiative to provide us with the gift of eternal life through His one and only Son, Jesus. God chose to robe Himself in flesh and become like us so that we could become like Him.

Whoever believes receives God's gracious salvation gift. There is no greater love. There is no greater gift. Bundle all the gifts from every Christmas you have experienced and you will not come close to the ultimate love gift God has provided in Jesus.

Now that you have received God's gift of eternal life, be willing to make His gift known to others. You can present the saving news of Jesus to any lost person anywhere and radically change their forever! You can share the ultimate gift with a world in need of our Savior.

HAVE YOU HEARD?

"The shepherds returned, glorifying and praising God for all the things they had heard and seen, which were just as they had been told." Luke 2:20 (NIV)

The Christmas story is rooted in God's nature and character.

God's story is the story of redemption. In His grace and mercy, God has come to us in order to rescue us from our sin and our eternal damnation. God's redemptive activity is an outflow of His holiness and compassion. God became like us so that we could become like Him.

The shepherds responded to God's invitation by going into Bethlehem to see Jesus lying in a manger. They shared their angelic experience with Joseph and Mary to affirm their belief in Jesus as the savior of the world. The shepherds returned with an attitude of praise and adoration for all that God had done in their midst. They identified that their personal experienced lined up with God's revelation.

God keeps His word. When God speaks, you will know that His activity is just as He said. The shepherds anchored their faith in the certainty of God's revelation. You can trust God to do what He says He will do. There isn't a fraction of error. God speaks so that we can know Him, serve Him, and make Him known throughout the earth.

December 22
WORTH TREASURING

"But Mary treasured up all these things and pondered them in her heart."
Luke 2:19 (NIV)

Think back to a Christmas experience you had in which you were deeply moved. Do you remember the specifics of the event that made it so touching? With our modern day affinity for technology, you probably captured the experience with a camera or a video recorder. Special moments are worth capturing and worth sharing.

Mary's experience was beyond words. Though cameras were nonexistent at that time, God gave Mary the wonderful capacity to treasure up all the things that the shepherds had shared with her concerning Jesus. She pondered them in her heart. Mary gathered all the information coming her way about Jesus and she embraced God's activity. Can you imagine how she felt? Mary was chosen by God to bring the Savior into our world.

Have you recognized the value God places on you? For Christmas, retrace the spiritual markers in your life. Spend time reflecting on each one. Treasure each one and ponder them in your heart. Consider how God is at work in you, around you, and through you to bring His light and His love into our world of desperation.

"And there were shepherds living out in the fields nearby, keeping watch over their flocks at night. An angel of the Lord appeared to them, and the glory of the Lord shone around them, and they were terrified. But the angel said to them, 'Do not be afraid. I bring you good news of great joy that will be for all the people. Today in the town of David a Savior has been born to you; he is Christ the Lord. This will be a sign to you: You will find a baby wrapped in cloths and lying in a manger.'" Luke 2:8-12 (NIV)

God's activity is perpetual.

God is always at work. He never sleeps and never takes a power nap. God's activity is redemptive. In His redemptive activity, God chose to announce His good news of great joy to shepherds. Shepherds were considered unclean in their day. They were not honored for their vocational choice. Though despised by people, they were loved by God. God allowed the shepherds to participate in His redemptive activity.

Is there anyone you have been praying for lately who is in need of salvation? Have you had moments of doubt? Maybe you have wondered if it is even possible for God to convince them of their need for salvation. You may have felt that they are beyond God's reach. The good news of great joy is that there is not a person on planet earth beyond God's reach. For Christmas, be reminded of God's activity. Ask God to heighten your awareness of His activity. Make yourself available for the redemptive activity of God in the one you have been praying for. God is working!

December 24
OUR RESPONSE

"When the angels had left them and gone into heaven, the shepherds said to one another, 'Let's go to Bethlehem and see this thing that has happened, which the Lord has told us about.' So they hurried off and found Mary and Joseph, and the baby, who was lying in the manger. When they had seen him, they spread the word concerning what had been told them about this child, and all who heard it were amazed at what the shepherds said to them." Luke 2:15-18 (NIV)

God's revelation demands a response.

God speaks. God reveals Himself so that we may know Him and serve Him. God invites us to join Him in His redemptive activity. He includes us in the redemptive process. Yes! God could accomplish His mission without us. He doesn't need us. God chooses to use us in communicating His love to a lost and drifting world.

The shepherds responded to God's invitation through instant obedience. They hurried off to find Jesus! There wasn't a delay to calculate the cost of obedience. They passionately sought the Lord and responded to God's offer instantly. The shepherds are examples of how God's revelation demands a response. They could have responded in apathy or in resolve.

What has God revealed to you? Have you responded to God's revelation by obeying instantly? What is keeping you from walking in the light God has given you? Imagine responding to God with a resolute, "Yes, Lord!" For Christmas, consider what God has been speaking into your life. Make a decision to trust God and His perfect timing. Decide to obey Him instantly. Leave the results up to God!

"All this took place to fulfill what the Lord had said through the prophet: 'The virgin will be with child and will give birth to a son, and they will call him Immanuel' --which means, 'God with us.'" Matthew 1:22-23 (NIV)

Merry Christmas to you and your family!

The day we have been anticipating all year is finally here. We have the wonderful privilege of celebrating the birth that changed our past, present, and future. Jesus is born!

God is with us. God is for us. God is in us. This day of celebration goes far beyond simply a day of exchanging gifts and seeing our loved ones. This day marks the day when God became like us so that we could become like Him. Have you received the ultimate gift made available to you by God? Have you received God's gift of eternal life? If so, then say so!

- *"The shepherds returned, glorifying and praising God for all the things they had heard and seen, which were just as they had been told." Luke 2:20 (NIV)*
- *"I pray that you may be active in sharing your faith, so that you will have a full understanding of every good thing we have in Christ." Philem 1:6 (NIV)*

Are you willing to share the ultimate gift that you have received with others? Jesus came to earth, lived, died, rose from the dead, and ascended back to Heaven so that we could have eternal life and share it with others. Now that's what Christmas is all about!

December 26
VERTICAL EXPRESSION

"Worship the LORD with gladness; come before him with joyful songs."
Psalm 100:2 (NIV)

What are you passionate about? Perhaps you get excited about engaging in life-giving activities such as playing golf, fishing, shopping, scrap-booking, or painting. Maybe your passion is decorating your home or working in the yard.

God wants you to bring your passion to public worship. Whenever you assemble with other believers in a corporate setting to worship God, you can choose to engage or to totally disengage. God gives you the freedom to passionately pursue Him in public worship. God desires your passionate worship and God deserves your passionate worship.

It is so easy to direct our passion toward so many other things in life and then bring God the leftovers when we come to a worship service with other believers. We can enter a beautiful worship center filled with fellow believers and drift into a dormant posture for worship. Instead of giving God our best, we can so easily be distracted by the tugs of this life. It is possible to worship our work and fail to work at our worship designed to express our love to God.

Do you worship the Lord with gladness? Is there passion in your expression of worship? Come into His Presence with joyful songs. If you have been delivered from the flames of hell and placed on the road that leads to life, then you have a song to sing. Passionately express your worship to the One who gave you eternal life!

"'For I know the plans I have for you,' declares the LORD, 'plans to prosper you and not to harm you, plans to give you hope and a future.'" Jeremiah 29:11 (NIV)

God has plans for your life. Where are you currently in relation to God's plans? Have you had some bumps along the way? Have you experienced any delays or detours? God factored in your response to His plans before you were ever born. God knew how you would navigate the path He has for you. Remember, nothing catches God by surprise. God sees the totality of your life from beginning to end. He knew when you would be born and where you would live and even the personality you would express. God's plans always prevail.

- *"But the plans of the LORD stand firm forever, the purposes of his heart through all generations." Psalm 33:11 (NIV)*
- *"Many are the plans in a man's heart, but it is the LORD's purpose that prevails." Prov 19:21 (NIV)*

You can anchor your life in God's plans. His plans are to prosper you, to give you hope and a future. Your future goes beyond this present life. Your future includes eternity. God's plans stand firm forever. Where Satan puts a period, God puts a comma. God's purpose prevails.

You may not know what tomorrow holds, but you know who holds tomorrow!

December 28
YOUR PRIVILEGE

"You will seek me and find me when you seek me with all your heart."
Jeremiah 29:13 (NIV)

God is worth the pursuit.

One of the highest privileges of life is that of seeking God. When you contemplate the vast canyon between God's bigness and our smallness, God's holiness and our sinfulness, humility becomes our reality. The fact that God, the Creator of the entire universe, would even desire that we seek Him is beyond comprehension. Yet, God chose to create us so that we may know Him personally and intimately.

When you read the Bible from cover to cover, you will discover the story of God reconciling us to Himself so that we could have the capacity to seek Him and find Him. God does not force us to seek Him. God enables us to respond to His love. God gives us the freedom to choose Him or to reject Him.

- *"O God, you are my God, earnestly I seek you; my soul thirsts for you, my body longs for you, in a dry and weary land where there is no water." Psalm 63:1 (NIV)*
- *"Seek the LORD while he may be found; call on him while he is near." Isaiah 55:6 (NIV)*

What are you doing with the highest privilege you have been given? Are you neglecting your love relationship with God? Have you drifted from your first love? Renew your commitment to seek the Lord. Renew your passion to seek the Lord with all your heart. Earnestly seek the Lord while He may be found. He is worth the pursuit!

"We must pay more careful attention, therefore, to what we have heard, so that we do not drift away." Hebrews 2:1 (NIV)

Carelessness and neglect will produce a lifestyle of drifting. Our natural proclivity in this fallen world is to drift from God's best. God reminds us in His Word to be attentive to what we have heard from Him so that we will not drift away.

- *"Keep my commands and you will live; guard my teachings as the apple of your eye." Prov 7:2 (NIV)*
- *"But the seed on good soil stands for those with a noble and good heart, who hear the word, retain it, and by persevering produce a crop." Luke 8:15 (NIV)*

The condition of your heart determines the level of your receptivity to God's Word. When your heart is cold and indifferent to the things of God, then His Word will not take root in your life. As your heart softens and becomes open to God's Word, the fruit will become evident.

What have you heard from God recently? Are you walking in obedience to what God has revealed to you? Are you being attentive to your love relationship with God?

RENEW SPIRITUAL MARKERS

"So I gave you a land on which you did not toil and cities you did not build; and you live in them and eat from vineyards and olive groves that you did not plant."
Josh 24:13 (NIV)

The children of Israel drifted from God's best and slipped into immorality. Joshua called them back into alignment with God's will and God's way. Joshua reviewed the spiritual markers that God had established for them. God gave Abraham many descendants and later raised up Moses and Aaron to deliver them from Egyptian bondage. God enabled them to cross the Red Sea on dry ground and to defeat the Amorites. God turned Balaam's curse into a blessing and delivered them out of his hand. God enabled them to miraculously cross the Jordan.

Joshua reminded the children of Israel of the faithfulness of God. The spiritual markers served as reminders of God's provision. The blessings of God were clearly evident in each of the spiritual markers.

Review your spiritual markers. Identify the times in your life when God made Himself known to you in a special way. You may have a spiritual marker that was formed in the midst of adversity where God reminded you of His protection over you. You may have a spiritual marker that was established as a result of God revealing His unconditional love to you through your saving relationship with Jesus.

Spiritual markers are vital for the Christian life. As you review your spiritual markers, you will gain a sense of stability. Your faith is strengthened as you review the activity of God in your life.

PREPARE FOR THE NEW YEAR

"'Now then,' said Joshua, 'throw away the foreign gods that are among you and yield your hearts to the LORD, the God of Israel.'" Josh 24:23 (NIV)

After reviewing the spiritual markers God established for the children of Israel, Joshua called them to a moment of decision. Though they had come out of Egypt, it was now time to get Egypt out of them. Instead of influencing the cultures they conquered, the idolatry of the cultures infiltrated their lifestyles. Joshua exhorted the children of Israel to throw away the foreign gods that were among them.

As you prepare for the New Year, consider the value of removing your idols. What is an idol? An idol is anything that hinders your love relationship with God. In prayer, ask the Lord to search your heart and to reveal unconfessed sin in your life.

Whatever you cover, God will uncover. Whatever you uncover, God will cover. You may want to spend some time looking back over every year of your life and writing down specific sins that you committed. This is a very personal and private process. After you write down the specific sins the Holy Spirit brings to your mind, confess them one-by-one and claim God's forgiveness over each one. Destroy the sheet of paper that you use to write on or hit the "delete" button on your computer if you choose to type your list.

Now walk in the freedom and forgiveness that God provides. Step into the New Year with the clarity of having removed your idols and confessed your sin.

NOTES

NOTES

NOTES

INDEX